Photograph of Charles Darwin is reproduced by kind permission of The Charles Darwin Museum, Down House.

Darwinism and Divinity

Essays on Evolution and Religious Belief

Edited by
John Durant

Basil Blackwell

Introduction, compilation and editorial matter
©John Durant, 1985

First published 1985

Basil Blackwell Ltd
108 Cowley Road, Oxford OX4 1JF, UK

Basil Blackwell Inc.
432 Park Avenue South, Suite 1505,
New York, NY 10016, USA

British Library Cataloguing in Publication Data
Darwinism and divinity: essays on evolution
   and religious belief.
   1. Darwin, Charles — Influence   2. Theology,
   Doctrinal — History   3. Religion and science
   — History
   I. Durant, John
   230   BT78
   ISBN 0-631-14188-X

Library of Congress Cataloging in Publication Data
Durant, John.
   Darwinism and divinity.
   Includes index.
   1. Evolution--Religious aspects.   I. Title.
BL263.D84   1985   231.7'65   84-28362
ISBN 0-631-14188-X

Typeset by Dentset, Oxford
Printed in Great Britain by Page Bros Ltd, Norwich

Darwinists are not necessarily hoofed and horned monsters, but are occasionally of pacific habits, and may even be detected in the act of going to church

Leslie Stephen, 'Darwinism and Divinity' in *Essays on Freethinking and Plainspeaking*, 1873

Contents

Contributors

Eileen Barker is Dean of Undergraduate Studies, London School of Economics and Political Science. She is particularly interested in the relationship between science and religion in contemporary society and in new religious movements, and she is the author of *The Making of a Moonie: Brainwashing or Choice?* (Blackwell, 1984).

John Hedley Brooke is a Senior Lecturer in history of science at the University of Lancaster, where until recently he was Principal of Bowland College. His research interests include the history of chemistry and the historical relations between scientific and religious beliefs, and he is currently completing a volume on the latter subject for Cambridge University Press.

John Durant is Staff Tutor in Biological Sciences in the Department for External Studies, University of Oxford. His research interests include the history of evolutionary and behavioural biology and the social relations of modern science, and he is the author of numerous articles on these and related topics.

Mary Midgley is a writer and a moral philosopher with an interest in evolution. Her latest book is *Wickedness: A Philosophical Essay* (Routledge & Kegan Paul, 1984).

Jim Moore teaches history of science and technology at the Open University. He has worked on radio and television documentaries with the BBC and he serves as an editorial consultant to the Collected Letters of Charles Darwin. His first book was entitled, *The Post-Darwinian Controversies: A Study of the Protestant Struggle to Come to Terms with Darwin in Great Britain and America, 1870–1900* (Cambridge University Press, 1979).

Arthur Peacocke is Director of the Ian Ramsey Centre, St. Cross College, Oxford. A physical biochemist and a theologian, he has a long-standing interest in the relationship between Christianity and natural science, and he is the author of *Intimations of Reality: Critical Realism in Science and Religion* (University of Notre Dame Press, 1984).

Vernon Reynolds is Lecturer in Physical Anthropology, University of Oxford. His research interests are in primatology and the relationship between cultural processes and natural selection. He is the author of *The Biology of Human Action* (Freeman, 1976; 2nd edition, 1980), and co-author with Ralph Tanner of *The Biology of Religion* (Longman, 1983).

Ralph Tanner was formerly a lecturer in comparative sociology at Heathrop College, University of London. He is particularly interested in comparative religion, and he is the co-author with Vernon Reynolds of *The Biology of Religion* (Longman, 1983).

Introduction

John Durant

On 20 November 1980 there appeared in the correspondence columns of Britain's leading scientific periodical *Nature* a letter criticizing two new exhibits at the British Museum (Natural History) in London. According to the palaeontologist Beverly Halstead these exhibits, *Dinosaurs and their Relatives* (1979), and *Man's Place in Evolution* (1980), were simply 'vehicles for the promotion of a system of working out relationships known as cladistics'. (Cladistics is a method of classifying organisms based exclusively on evolutionary branching relationships, and in recent years it has been the subject of a great deal of scientific controversy.) Halstead suggested that the Museum had fallen victim to its own Public Services Department's 'fanatical' commitment to cladistics, and he attributed this commitment to a Marxist bias against the Darwinian idea of gradual change in nature and society (Halstead, 1980).

This extraordinary accusation provoked a considerable correspondence in *Nature* which continued into the summer of 1981. By this time, the argument had taken in a third exhibit, *Origin of Species*, which had opened in the spring to mark the forthcoming Darwin centenary; and out of an original concern with cladistics, it had come to centre on two much larger issues: the scientific status of evolutionary theory; and the implications of this theory for religious belief. These exchanges overlapped with another on the moral and political implications of evolutionary social theory (see Rose, 1981; and subsequent replies); and shortly after they finished, the prospect of a major legal battle over evolution at Little

Rock, Arkansas served to restart discussion (see Darnbrough *et. al.*, 1981; and subsequent editorials and correspondence). Thus, throughout the whole of 1981 and much of 1982, *Nature's* readers were witness to an extended discussion of the scientific, philosophical, religious and political implications of the Darwinian theory of evolution by natural selection.

Clearly, there is something rather special about Darwinism. More than a century after the death of its founder, it continues both to divide biologists and to arouse the active opposition of large numbers of lay people. During the past decade, the pros and cons of Darwinism have been debated with an intensity that has few parallels elsewhere in modern science. Amongst biologists, there have been at least four areas of disagreement: on the question of the place of evolutionary theory in science, a group of so-called 'transformed cladists' has rejected the use of evolutionary assumptions in palaeontology; on the question of the pace and pattern of evolution, the proponents of 'punctuated equilibrium' have challenged the more orthodox 'gradualism' of most Darwinians; on the question of the mechanism of evolution, there has been much argument about the relative importance of natural selection and 'genetic drift', as well as sporadic interest in old ideas such as the inheritance of acquired characteristics and new ones such as 'molecular drive'; and on the question of the relationship between animal and human evolution, the proponents of sociobiology have revived a century-old conflict about the social and political implications of natural selection (see Caplan (ed.) 1979; Cherfas (ed.) 1982; Maynard Smith (ed.) 1982; and Ridley, forthcoming). As if things were not already complicated enough, many of these debates have been seized upon by self-styled 'scientific creationists' as indications that all is far from well with evolution. Starting from relatively small beginnings in the 1960s, the scientific creationists have mounted an increasingly powerful assault on evolution, particularly in the United States. With their claim that Darwinism is not only atheistic and immoral but also speculative and unscientific they have had considerable influence on local communities, local school boards and state legislatures. Thus far, in fact, it is only in the federal courts of the United States that they have met with no success (see Nelkin, 1982; and Barker, this volume).

As Halstead's letter to *Nature* reveals, it is not only the scientific creationists who are concerned about the ideological dimension of debates about origins. On the contrary, there is a characteristic tone of moral concern detectable in the writings of almost everyone who is interested in Darwinism at anything beyond the level of the narrowest technicalities. This is so familiar a feature of the literature that we are apt to take it for granted; and yet it is difficult to think of another commensurable area of scientific theorizing (except, perhaps, the so-called 'nature/nurture' debate) where discussions take place in anything like the same way. In the case of Darwinism, of course, the moral concern was there from the very beginning. Take, for instance, the first reactions to the *Origin of Species* of two eminent Victorian scientists. On Christmas Eve 1859, Darwin's old friend and teacher the geologist Adam Sedgwick wrote to tell his former pupil that he had read the *Origin* 'with more pain than pleasure' (Darwin, 1887, vol. 2, p.248); while just a month before, the young blood Thomas Huxley had written to tell Darwin that in writing the *Origin* he had 'earned the lasting gratitude of all thoughtful men' (Darwin, 1887 vol. 2, p.232). Now Sedgwick believed that Darwin had made a great mistake, while Huxley was convinced that he had achieved a great advance; but this is not all that either man was saying. To Sedgwick, Darwinism threatened to degrade the human race by disrupting the intimate connections between science and theology. To Huxley, also, Darwin's work marked a break between science and theology; but so far from regarding this as a tragedy, Huxley saw it as a triumph for the free spirit of rational and scientific inquiry by which alone humankind might save itself from enslavement to a cruel and indifferent universe. Although they agreed on very little else, therefore, Sedgwick and Huxley were at least united in their conviction that far more was at stake in the *Origin* than its title appeared to suggest.

Of course, they were absolutely right. It is only by the most narrow-minded effort of will that one can read Darwin's most famous work and confine one's thoughts to the question of how new species arise in nature. Admittedly, this is the only question with which the book deals explicitly; but we know that this is simply because Darwin disciplined himself strictly to avoid all of the larger issues that were raised by his views. Evidently, he hoped in this way to encourage a dispassionate consideration of the argument;

yet in the event most people saw straight through the pretence (which in any case Darwin was unable quite to keep up until the end), and they proceeded to discuss the larger issues as if he had confronted them head-on. From 1859 up until the present, thoughtful people have responded to the *Origin* by pondering a series of fundamental questions. Is the theory of evolution by natural selection essentially correct? If so, what are its implications for traditional views about God and the universe? And above all, what new light does it throw on the human condition, past, present and future? These questions are dramatic, but they are not melodramatic. For Darwinism really does address some of the most profound issues that human beings confront. This point was made rather well by the evolutionary biologist Richard Dawkins in his book *The Selfish Gene* (1976). Starting his account with a chapter entitled simply 'Why are People?', Dawkins wrote:

> Darwin made it possible for us to give a sensible answer to the curious child whose question heads this chapter. We no longer have to resort to superstition when faced with the deep problems: Is there a meaning to life? What are we for? What is man? After posing the last of these questions, the eminent zoologist G. G. Simpson put it thus: 'The point I want to make now is that all attempts to answer that question before 1859 are worthless and we will be better off if we ignore them completely'.

Small wonder, then, that Darwinism continues to be a matter of such general concern.

This book has its origins in a conference organized by the British Society for the History of Science in 1982 to mark the centenary of Darwin's death.[1] The aim of the conference was to explore the vast and vexed question of the relationship between evolutionary theory and religious belief. This is a daunting question, for it arises naturally in many different fields of inquiry and is the sole prerogative of none. If natural scientists claim to possess particular expertise, so also do theologians; and if philosophers see a role for their talents, so too do historians and social scientists. Very often in the past, conflict over evolution and religious belief has arisen not out of genuine disagreements over matters of fact or philosophy but rather out of people's inability or unwillingness to assimilate what those working in other fields have been saying. Partly in order to overcome such academic parochialism, the conference offered a series of contrasting views from scholars working in a variety of relevant disciplines. *Darwinism and Divinity* consists of these original papers and a number of additional, specially commissioned contributions. By bringing together analyses from within biological anthropology, history, philosophy, sociology and theology it is hoped that the book provides a broader and deeper perspective on its subject than is obtainable from any single point of view.

Following my own attempt to set the scene in chapter 1, the historian of science John Hedley Brooke looks closely at what Darwin himself thought about the religious implications of his work. He identifies the particular ways in which Darwin's science was indebted to theology, tracing the complex interaction between Darwin's growing confidence in his evolutionary theory and his increasing doubts about religious belief in the second half of his life. In chapter 3 the historian Jim Moore analyses a quite remarkable episode in the long struggle of Christian theologians to come to terms with evolutionary theory. Focusing on late nineteenth century America, he shows how readily liberal Protestants reinterpreted their faith in terms of the evolutionary philosophy of Herbert Spencer. That it was Spencer rather than Darwin who proved attractive to so many theologians before 1900 was to cause some difficulty later on, when Spencer's reputation plummeted and Darwin's soared. But in chapter 4 the physical chemist and theologican Arthur Peacocke demonstrates that liberal theology has responded to this development with some spirit. Today, he suggests, the materials are available for a genuine synthesis of Christian theology and Neo-Darwinian biology, a synthesis in which the processes of genetic variation and natural selection are seen as modes of divine creation and incarnation.

True to the spirit of the book, chapter 5 neatly inverts this image by asking the question, What contribution do religious beliefs about, for example, creation, life and death make to the operation of Darwinian processes in humankind? Applying evolutionary principles to religious beliefs regarding procreation, the anthropologist Vernon Reynolds and the sociologist Ralph Tanner argue that, in many contexts, such beliefs may be adaptive in the

Darwinian sense of contributing to the relative reproductive success of those who hold them. Of course, that religious beliefs may have biologically useful consequences tells us nothing in itself about whether or in what sense they may be valid. In chapter 6, the philosopher Mary Midgley assesses the validity of a cluster of rather extravagant religious beliefs held by – of all people – atheistic or agnostic evolutionists! Arguing that evolution has become the 'creation-myth of our age', she takes to task those whose zeal for Darwinism leads them to project it as a cure for souls. Finally, we conclude with what is surely the most extraordinary and perplexing aspect of contemporary debates about Darwinism and divinity, namely the resurgence in the United States over the past two decades of fundamentalist anti-evolutionism. In chapter 7, the sociologist Eileen Barker traces the rise of so-called 'scientific creationism', finding in a unique combination of conservative ideology and rampant scientism a clue to its very considerable influence today. Her analysis makes sobering reading for anyone who advocates a more active involvement of 'lay' people in science and technology decision-making.

Darwinism and Divinity makes no pretence to being the last word on the subject of evolution and religious belief (it is doubtful if such a thing is even possible). The book is best regarded not as a series of definitive statements, but rather as a number of contrasting views from within different disciplines. In a sense, each chapter re-shakes the kaleidoscope of knowledge and values and discovers a new pattern of issues and ideas. Hopefully, readers will notice significant relationships between the patterns on display and will be led to shake the kaleidoscope once more on their own behalf. If this happens, the book will have more than served its purpose.

John Durant
Oxford 1985

NOTE

1 The conference took place in the rooms of the Linnean Society of London on 12 November 1982. The editor is grateful both to the Council of the British Society for the History of Science and to the Officers of the Linnean Society of London for their assistance in the organization of this meeting.

REFERENCES

Caplan, A. L. (ed.) (1978) *The Sociobiology Debate. Readings on Ethical and Scientific Issues,* New York and London, Harper and Row.

Cherfas, J. (ed.) (1982) *Darwin up to Date,* London, IPC Magazines.

Darnbrough, C. et al. (1981) 'American Creationism', *Nature* **292** 2 July 1981, pp.95–6.

Darwin, F. (ed.) (1887) *The Life and Letters of Charles Darwin,* 3 vols, London, John Murray.

Dawkins, R. (1976) *The Selfish Gene,* Oxford, Oxford University Press.

Halstead, L. B. (1980) 'Museum of Errors', *Nature* **288** 20 November 1980, p.208.

Maynard Smith, J. (1982) *Evolution Now: A Century After Darwin,* London, Macmillan.

Nelkin, D. (1982) *The Creation Controversy. Science or Scripture in the Schools,* New York and London, W. W. Norton.

Ridley, M. (forthcoming) *The Problems of Evolution,* Oxford, Oxford University Press.

Rose, S. (1981) 'Genes and Race', *Nature* **288** 20 November 1980, p.208.

1

Darwinism and Divinity:
A Century of Debate

John Durant

INTRODUCTION

Sigmund Freud once argued that what he termed 'the universal narcissism of men, their self-love' had suffered 'three severe blows from the researches of science'. These blows had been administered by Copernicus, who had revealed that the earth is not the centre of the universe; by Darwin, who had demonstrated that 'man is not a being different from animals or superior to them'; and of course by Freud himself, who had shown *'that the ego is not master in its own house'* (Freud, 1953–74, 17, pp.140–3). Obviously, Freud's argument is profoundly self-serving, but it is based on a more general view of the psychological significance of science that has long been influential in our culture. According to this view, science has de-mythologized our world; that is, it has replaced a traditional picture of the universe in which everything revolves around the drama of human life and death with a more accurate but far bleaker picture of a universe utterly devoid of centre, direction or human purpose. First in cosmology, then in biology, and finally (at least according to Freud) in psychology, we have been confronted and affronted with the knowledge that we are mere fragments in a world that appears to be neither about us nor for us.

Ever since the Enlightenment, the idea of scientific cosmology as the dispeller of the comfortable illusions of pre-scientific or traditional world-views has been commonplace amongst historians, philosophers and scientists; and ever since 1859, Charles Darwin's *Origin of Species* has figured prominently in virtually all accounts of this idea. It is not hard to see why. The path from Copernicus to Darwin is not only the path from one major scientific 'revolution' to another (see Kuhn, 1959; Ruse, 1979) but also the path from space to time, from our position in the sky above our heads to our origin in the earth beneath our feet. Darwin himself was well aware of the historic parallel, and he concluded the *Origin* by marvelling that, 'whilst this planet has gone cycling on according to the fixed law of gravity, from so simple a beginning endless forms most beautiful and most wonderful have been, and are being, evolved' (Darwin, 1959, p.759). Whether or not this was the cue for the many subsequent comparisons between Darwin and Newton (see, for example, Glass, 1959, pp.267–8; and Chapman and Duval, (eds) 1982, p.1), it has always been widely assumed that Darwinism helped to complete the task of de-mythologizing the universe that began with the work of the scientific revolutionaries in the seventeenth century.

This assumption is closely linked to the view that there is a fundamental conflict between scientific knowledge and religious belief. Once again, this view pre-dates the Darwinian debates of the nineteenth century. Indeed, it received what is arguably its most successful instantiation in the work of the Enlightenment philosopher August Comte, who suggested that human thought tends to progress through three distinct stages: the *theological,* in which natural phenomena are seen as the products of supernatural agencies; the *metaphysical,* in which such agencies are replaced by abstract forces; and the *positive,* in which the search for hidden causes is abandoned altogether in favour of pure description of observable phenomena. Clearly, this so-called law of the three stages of human thought sets theology and metaphysics in opposition to science by making them its primitive antecedents. To the positivists and their sympathizers, the growth of science entails the decline of metaphysics and theology, as the task of explaining the world is handed over to those who know best how the job is to be done; and since it is only to be expected that those being made redundant in this fashion should offer some resistance on behalf of thier profession, the history of science is expected to consist of a series of confrontations between the advancing armies of science and the retreating forces of metaphysics and theology. As Thomas

Huxley once put it, 'Extinguished theologians lie about the cradle of every science as the strangled snakes beside that of Hercules' (Huxley 1893–4, 2, 52).

Huxley made this colourful remark in a review of the *Origin of Species*, and of course he went on to play a major part as Darwin's 'bulldog' in a debate that was widely seen as a straightforward battle between progressive scientific truth and reactionary theological dogma. Huxley's legendary encounter with the Bishop of Oxford in 1860 *is* legendary precisely because it exemplifies such a battle. In their satirical *1066 and All That*, Sellar and Yeatman provide a delightful *reductio ad absurdum* of the legend's significance: 'In the year 1860 occurred the other memorable date in the history of evolution-and-religion, viz. "Huxley versus Wilberforce, Eighteen Sixty". This is also called "The Battle Royal at Oxford", and was when T.H. Huxley conquered Bishop Wilberforce in the great Darwinian Revolution. The Darwinian Revolution was a Good Thing as from this time onwards Science stopped being stifled by Religion and thus was able to reveal the Truth' (quoted in Moore, 1982, p.167; for a very different interpretation of what happened in Oxford, see Lucas, 1979). In fact, this is only barely a caricature of what the episode came to mean to at least some Victorians. For example, one man who was present and spoke at the Oxford meeting was the American chemist-turned-historian J.W. Draper. Some years later he wrote a popular *History of the Conflict Between Religion and Science*, whose organizing principle was that 'the history of science is not a mere record of isolated discoveries; it is a narrative of the conflict of two contending powers, the expansive force of the human intellect on one side, and the compression arising from traditionary (sic) faith and human interests on the other' (Draper 1875, p.vi). Draper's view was soon massively endorsed by A.D. White (1896), and it came to dominate debates about science and belief for almost a century (for reviews see Russell, Hooykaas & Goodman, 1974; and Moore, 1979, Part 1).

In recent years there has been increasing dissatisfaction amongst historians with Draper's 'conflict thesis'. Indeed, there has grown up a school of thought which takes exactly the opposite point of view, namely that, far from having been held back by religious belief, modern science was in fact actively promoted by it.

According to Hooykaas (1972), Jaki (1978), Torrance (1981) and others, it was a distinctively Christian view of nature as created, contingent and orderly, which fostered empirical research in the sixteenth and seventeenth centuries; and this, they suggest, is why the scientific revolution occurred when and where it did (rather than, for example, in classical Greece). Their argument gains support from the work of the sociologist Robert Merton and his followers, who have documented the existence of a close relationship between Puritanism and the institutionalization of science before 1800 (Merton, 1970); and it has led to the re-examination of nineteenth-century science to see whether even here, in the debates that did so much to foster the conflict thesis, there may be evidence to justify a different interpretation. Ever since W.F. Cannon (1961) initiated the 'revaluation' of Darwin's achievement, the trend amongst historians of evolution-and-religion has been away from the ideas of conflict and warfare and towards those of mutual influence and even harmony. Thus, in his comprehensive survey of Protestant responses to Darwinism in the late nineteenth century, Jim Moore argues that Darwin's theory bore close affinities to certain forms of Protestant belief, and that it was most easily accepted by those whose theology was 'orthodox' (Moore, 1979). So much, it would seem, for Huxley's 'extinguished theologians'.

Faced with so many different opinions about the historic relationship between science and religious belief, cautious readers may suspect that rather more is at stake than a mere point of intellectual history. They will be right to do so. Undoubtedly, supporters of the conflict thesis have tended to be anti-clerical and/or anti-religious, and many of them have used history of science for anti-Christian purposes. Similarly, supporters of what has been termed the 'revisionist' position have tended to be sympathetic towards religious belief, and many of them have used history of science to defend the claims of Christianity. Neither argument, of course, is particularly satisfactory. On the one hand, it is perfectly possible to accept the conflict thesis *and* any particular set of religious beliefs – for it may be held that theologians of the past simply misunderstood the situation and saw conflict where none actually existed; and on the other, it is equally possible to accept the revisionist view that Christianity produced science while still rejecting any particular set of religious beliefs – for it may be supposed that, in sowing the seeds of science, Christianity unwittingly sowed the seeds of its own destruction (Gruner, 1975). The point here is that the relationship between Christianity and science cannot be resolved exclusively in the domain of history. However, history is certainly *relevant* to the question; and this relevance can only be enhanced by a critical awareness of its potentialities as a source of rationalizations for particular positions in the debate.

The aim of this chapter is to provide an overview of debates about the religious significance of the idea of evolution, both immediately prior to and since the publication of the *Origin of Species*. Obviously, it is not possible to do justice to so large a theme in so small a space; but it is hoped that, by touching on most of the topics discussed in more detail in later chapters, this overview will serve not merely as a guide to the rest of the book but also as a framework within which to interpret the many different views that have been taken of the relationship between Darwinism and Divinity. For the sake of clarity, the discussion is organized partly historically and partly thematically. This has the obvious advantage that it permits division of the subject in the most convenient way, but it has the equally obvious disadvantage that it may be mistaken for 'objective' history. I hope it is now clear that in this of all fields there is no such thing as objective history; but lest any doubt remain, let it be said that what follows is an interpretation of issues as they have arisen over the past 150 years rather than an attempt at a 'neutral' narrative of events and ideas.

THE ORIGIN OF DARWINISM

In his important book *Genesis and Geology*, C.C. Gillispie wrote that, in the decades prior to the publication of Darwin's *Origin of Species*, 'the difficulty as reflected in scientific literature appears to be one of religion (in a crude sense) *in* science rather than one of religion *versus* science' (1951, p.ix). This is the essential starting-point for any assessment of the relationship between Darwinism and religious belief. Throughout the first half of the nineteenth century, natural history was part of a larger debate about the interrelationships between God, nature, human nature and society. Natural theology, the study of the existence and attributes of God as manifested in the works of nature, had been central to the work of the English naturalists since the seventeenth century; and despite (or rather because of) the Enlightenment, it was powerfully reaffirmed around 1800 in the writings of the Anglican clergymen Thomas Malthus (1798) and William Paley (1802). According to Malthus, nature and human nature were governed by providential laws which set limits to what might be achieved by social engineering, at the same time that they rewarded Christian virtue with worldly success;, while according to Paley, nature and human nature were a congeries of happy contrivances demonstrating the wisdom, justice and benevolence of the Creator to his fortunate people.

Malthus and Paley set the terms of inquiry for English natural history over the next fifty years. Of course, there were many different interpretations on offer during this period. For example, while some naturalists followed the Malthusian line of seeing the handiwork of God in the laws of nature, others took up Paley's preoccupation with the argument from design. Moreover, amongst those interested in design, some adopted a utilitarian version of the argument in which functional contrivance was the primary object of interest, while others preferred an idealist approach which gave greater weight to the perfection of organic form as revealed in embryonic development and the history of life (Bowler, 1977; Ospovat, 1981). Natural theology embraced many different scientific and theological interests, and one of the major reasons for its continuing importance throughout the first half of the nineteenth century was that it served to unite naturalists from diverse religious traditions (Brooke, 1979). Above all, however, the most striking characteristic of natural theology was its ability to integrate knowledge and values within a coherent world-view. Consider by way of illustration the extraordinary performance of the Reverend Adam Sedgwick on Tynemouth beach during the summer meeting of the British Association for the Advancement of Science in 1838. On the Friday afternoon of the meeting, Cambridge University's Woodwardian Professor of Geology led an excursion to the mouth of the river Tyne. According to Sir John Herschel, Sedgwick 'stood upon the point of a rock a little raised' in order to address 'some 3000 or 4000 colliers and rabble (mixed with a sprinkling of their employers)'. There he led his audience 'from the scene around them to the wonders of the coal-country below them, thence to the economy of a coal-field, then to their relations to the coal-owners and capitalists, then to the great principles of morality and happiness, and last to their relation to God, and their own future prospects'. The talk, said Herschel, produced a 'sensation such as is not likely to die away for years' (Clark and Hughes, 1890, vol.1, pp.515–16).

On Tynemouth beach Sedgwick spoke for a tradition in which pebbles, piety and politics were intimately intertwined. A few years later, he spoke for it once again, this time to defend it against what he saw as the outrageous views contained in an anonymous book entitled *Vestiges of the Natural History of Creation* (1844). *Vestiges* argued the case for a natural law of development governing the history of life, and it extended this law to embrace the physical, mental and moral qualities of humankind. In a venomous 85-page critique in the *Edinburgh Review*, Sedgwick lashed the unknown author of the work for sins that were at once scientific and spiritual (Sedgwick, 1845). If the book were true, he told his colleague Charles Lyell, 'the labours of sober induction are in vain; religion is a lie; human law is a mass of folly, and a base injustice; morality is moonshine; our labours for the black people of Africa were works of madmen; and man and woman are only better beasts!' (Clark and Hughes, 1890, vol. 2, pp.83–4). Here indeed was a world-view on the point of collapse.

The publication of *Vestiges* marks a critical point in Victorian debates about science and belief. On the one hand, the book outraged many natural theologians; but on the other (and rather ironically), it was written very largely from a natural theological perspective. Its author (who was, in fact, the Edinburgh publisher Robert Chambers) pointed out in reply to his critics that his aim had been simply to show that 'the whole revelation of the works of God presented to our senses and reason is a system based on . . . LAW; by which, however, is not meant a system independent or exclusive of the Deity, but one which only proposes a certain mode

of his working' (Chambers, 1845, p.3). Here Chambers touched a
raw nerve. For many natural theologians had left conveniently
vague the meaning of crucial terms such as 'creation', 'providence'
and 'law', preferring to give little more than the comfortable
impression that the path from nature up to nature's god was broad
and straight. To many of Chambers' readers, however, a 'natural
law' of animal and human development was not so much a
stepping-stone as a massive obstacle in this path; and the fact that
the obstacle should have been set up in the name of true religion
served merely to make it the more offensive. As John Brooke has
put it, by appealing to Providence 'in the context of a ...
hypothesis that smacked of both materialism and determinism, the
author of *Vestiges* had sold the pass' (Brooke, 1979, p.50). Fifteen
years later, Darwin was to make a similar move on behalf of his
own very different and (in the long run) very much more successful
theory of organic origins.

The *Origin of Species* is the last great work of Victorian natural
theology. At first sight this may seem an absurd proposition, and
certainly it should be qualified with the statement that it is also the
greatest (if not actually the first) work of Victorian evolutionary
naturalism. Nevertheless, it is important to recognize that Darwin
was trained in the tradition of English natural theology, that the
problems with which he dealt were those of English natural
theology, and that the audience at which he aimed the *Origin*
consisted overwhelmingly of English (or at any rate English-
speaking) natural theologians (Cannon, 1961; Young, 1970;
Ospovat, 1981; Brooke, this volume). For consider this: Darwin
received virtually the whole of his formal instruction in natural
history whilst preparing for the Anglican ministry at Christ's
College, Cambridge; theory was provided by Paley, whose work
made a lasting impression, and practical classes were conducted by
the Reverend John Stevens Henslow (botany) and the Reverend
Adam Sedgwick (geology). It would require quite extraordinary
powers of inattention to survive such an education without
acquiring a thorough acquaintance with the principles of natural
theology, and we know that Darwin was very far from being an
inattentive student. Furthermore, the marks of this early education
are clearly visible in his later work. Very briefly, both Darwin's

life-long conviction that 'the whole universe is full of adaptations', and his life-long confidence that these were to be understood as 'direct consequences of still higher laws' (Gruber and Barrett, 1974, pp.416–20) followed from a Paleyan view of the world coupled with the belief, widespread amongst English natural theologians in the 1820s and 1830s, that 'with regard to the material world . . . we can perceive that events are brought about not by insulated interpositions of Divine power, exerted in each particular case, but by the establishment of general laws' (Whewell, 1834, p.356).

This last quotation is taken from the Reverend William Whewell's Bridgewater Treatise on *Astronomy and General Physics Considered with Reference to Natural Theology*.[1] What makes it especially significant is that Darwin placed it in the frontispiece of the *Origin* alongside a famous passage by Francis Bacon on the 'two books of divine revelation'. Together, these passages gave notice that the book fell squarely within the conventions of natural theology; and Darwin further underlined this point in his final chapter, where he stated that, 'to my mind it accords better with what we know of the laws impressed on matter by the Creator, that the production and extinction of the past and present inhabitants of the world should have been due to secondary causes, like those determining the birth and death of the individual' (Darwin, 1959, pp.757–8). The secondary causes that Darwin invoked are well known: variation; over-reproduction and the struggle for existence; and natural selection, or the differential survival and reproduction of favourable over unfavourable variations. What is not so well-known, however, is that Darwin explicitly invited his readers to see these causes as the means adopted by the creator to populate the earth.

The claim that Darwinism was developed within the tradition of English natural theology raises a host of difficult questions, not least concerning the nature of Darwin's personal views on religion, and these are taken up by John Brooke in chapter 2 of this volume. For present purposes, however, the important point is simply that the *Origin* represents a secularizing trend in mid-Victorian natural theology; a trend in which the revelation of God in the works of nature came to be seen as having been written exclusively in the language of law. To many of Darwin's generation the uniformity of nature was 'the veil behind which, in these latter days, God is hidden from us' (Hutton, 1885, p.196). The image of the veil captures both the manifest secularity and the latent religiosity of much Victorian scientific writing, in which 'Nature' and 'Law' (often capitalized as a mark of respect) replaced God as the ultimate ground of being and value. Relevant here, perhaps, are William Darwin's reminiscences at about the time that the Darwin family was assembling materials for the *Life and Letters of Charles Darwin* (1887). 'As regards his respect for the laws of Nature', William wrote of his father, 'it might be called reverence if not a religious feeling. No man could feel more intensely the vastness and the inviolability of the laws of nature, and especially the helplessness of mankind except so far as the laws were obeyed' (Darwin, 1883). It was to the moral, religious and political implications of humankind's subordination to the law of evolution by natural selection that the Darwinian debates of the late nineteenth-century were principally directed.

THE RECEPTION OF DARWINISM

The first and most obvious fact about the initial theological response to the *Origin* is that it was extremely mixed. Some writers rejected Darwin's arguments outright, some accepted them with little or no apparent difficulty, and some were unsure which way to jump. Predictably enough, Adam Sedgwick fell into the first of these categories. For him, the *Origin* was simply 'the system of the author of the *Vestiges* stripped of his ignorant absurdities' (Clark and Hughes, 1890, vol. 2, pp.359–60). Writing to acknowledge receipt of the *Origin* on Christmas Eve 1859, Sedgwick told Darwin that he had read parts of the book 'with absolute sorrow, because I think them utterly false and grievously mischievious' (Darwin, 1887, vol. 2, pp.248). This response may be contrasted with that of another Anglican clergyman–naturalist who received a complimentary copy of Darwin's work. In his letter of thanks, Charles Kingsley admitted that the *Origin* would oblige him to rethink much that hitherto he had taken for granted. He went on, 'I have gradually learnt to see that it is just as noble a conception of Deity, to believe that He created primal forms capable of self-development into all forms needful *pro tempore* and *pro loco*, as to believe that He required a fresh act of intervention to supply the *lacunas* which he himself had made. I question whether the former be not the loftier thought' (Darwin, 1887, vol. 2, pp.287–8).[2]

If Sedgwick's response was the more common amongst Anglican clergymen in 1859, Kingsley's was the more prescient. For after the initial heat had gone out of the debate in the early 1860s, assimilation of the idea of evolution within the church of England proceeded quite rapidly. Major landmarks in this process were: the publication of *Essays and Reviews* (Jowett et al., 1861), a collective work of biblical criticism that created an even greater stir than the *Origin* itself; Darwin's burial in Westminster Abbey (1882); the publication of *Lux Mundi* (Gore (ed). 1889), a collective work by English Anglo-Catholics amongst whom there were three thorough-going evolutionists; and the consecration of Frederick Temple, one of the original contributors to *Essays and Reviews*, as Archbishop of Canterbury (1896). Throughout this process of assimilation, three issues dominated Anglican (and most other Christian) discussions: the interpretation of scripture; the relationship between God and nature, as expressed in the doctrines of creation, providence and incarnation; and the moral and spiritual status of humankind. The way in which these issues were faced may be illustrated by a brief examination of the work of Frederick Temple.

Temple's contribution to *Essays and Reviews* was entitled 'The Education of the World', and it had as its theme the steady progress of Christendom towards a manly tolerance and respect for truth. In common with the other authors of the volume, Temple urged his readers to confront the latest products of historical and natural science with a steady and untroubled gaze. 'If geology proves to us that we must not interpret the first chapters of Genesis literally', he wrote, '. . . the results should still be welcome' (Temple, 1861, p.47). Here, then, the first issue was decided by the abandonment of biblical literalism. Temple did not deal fully with the second and third issues until 1884, when he gave the Bampton Lectures in the University of Oxford on *The Relations between Religion and Science*. Here, he argued in some detail that natural theology was strengthened by the Darwinian theory of evolution. While followers of Paley had once imagined that the creator had exercised his creative effort in the production of each and every species, Temple suggested that followers of Darwin might suppose him to have done so once and for all time, in the production of primordial life-forms endowed with the capacity to evolve into all the rest in the course of time. Such a view added force to the argument from design for the existence of God: 'He did not make the things, we may say; no, but He made them make themselves' (Temple, 1884. p.115). Having thus secured the doctrine of creation, Temple went on to underline the uniqueness of human nature. Not only did 'the enormous gap' separating human from animal nature indicate 'an exceedingly early difference of origin', but also it was quite possible that the 'spiritual faculty' had been implanted by 'a direct creative act' (Temple, 1884, pp.176, 186).

It is interesting to observe how Temple's reconciliation of Paley and Darwin was accomplished. First, Paley's conception of God as craftsman was saved, with the scope for divine craftsmanship being confined to the first production of life and (possibly) the creation of the human spirit. Second, Paley's teleology (that is, his view of the purposiveness of organic existence) was preserved in the idea that life had been created 'with a view to' the progressive unfolding of higher forms up to and including humankind. Third and last, Paley's theodicy (that is, his explanation of the existence of evil in the world) was not only retained but greatly reinforced by the hope of better things yet to come. Where Paley had been hard pressed to salvage the idea that, as he put it, ours was 'a happy world after all', Temple was able to argue that the manifest imperfections of the world were like 'the imperfections of a half-completed picture not yet ready to be seen', or 'the bud which will presently be a beautiful flower'. The 'doctrine of Evolution', he assured his readers, meant a 'perpetual progress' in which pain was gradually diminished and pleasure enhanced through 'the survival of the fittest' (Temple, 1884, pp.117–118).

Temple's views should not be taken as representative of all Anglican (let alone all Christian) thinking about evolution in the late nineteenth century. But they were typical of a large body of liberal Protestant scholarship that found in the 'doctrine of Evolution' (note the capital letter) the basis for a new natural theology of providential progress. What is most notable about this

natural theology is that it owed far more to the writings of Herbert
Spencer than it did to those of Charles Darwin. For although, in a
very general sense, Darwin shared the optimistic mid-Victorian
view that humankind had progressed and would continue to
progress from barbarity to civility (Greene, 1981, pp.95–127), he
was adamant that the law of natural selection contained no
cast-iron guarantees. 'There is nothing in my theory necessitating
in each case progression of organization', he told one critic, 'though
Natural Selection tends in this line, and has generally thus acted'
(Darwin, 1903, vol. 1, p.164). Spencer, on the other hand, was
quite convinced that progress was 'not an accident, not a thing
within human control, but a beneficient necessity' (Spencer, 1890,
vol. 1, p.60). His grandiose philosophy was based on the idea that
the entire universe – nature, human nature and society – was
ascending towards ultimate perfection through the operation of
inexorable natural laws. As James Moore shows in chapter 3 of this
volume, such a vision was particularly attractive to liberals who
wished to unite Christianity and natural science within a philosophy of orderly moral, social and spiritual improvement.

The fact that the assimilation of Darwin by late-Victoran
theologians turns out as often as not to have been the assimilation
of Spencer instead, is not particularly surprising. For where
Darwin offered a theory of organic change, Spencer offered a
metaphysic based on change; where Darwin's universe was at the
mercy of time and chance, Spencer's had a clear and comforting
direction; and perhaps above all, where Darwin detected only the
amoral processes of reproduction, competition and selection,
Spencer discerned in nature the foundations of right conduct –
evolution was, to use his term, the 'survival of the *fittest*'. Such a
world-view lent itself very readily to re-interpretation in theological
terms. Thus, the Scottish Free-Churchman Henry Drummond
enjoyed great success with his books *Natural Law in the Spiritual
World* (1883) and *The Ascent of Man* (1884; 6th ed. 1897), which
provided a Spencerian view of human moral, social and spiritual
development. Noting that 'Nature, as a moral teacher, thanks to
the Darwinian interpretation, was never more discredited than at
this hour', he suggested a more 'balanced' interpretation, involving
not only Darwin's 'struggle for life' but also a 'struggle for the life of

others' that the great naturalist had all but ignored. As the one principle produced selfish competition and dominated the life of the lower organisms, the other produced altruistic co-operation, and governed the development of humankind. In this way, Drummond suggested, 'That Christian development, social, moral, and spiritual, which is going on around us, is as real an evolutionary movement as any that preceded it. A system founded on Self-Sacrifice . . . is not a foreign thing to the Evolutionist' (Drummond, 1897, p.443). In such ways did Spencer's cosmology provide a new mythic base for Christian theology.

It would be a mistake to think that Darwin's distinctive view of evolution was completely rejected in the late nineteenth century. Although it did not meet with the general approval of *either* the scientific *or* the theological communities (Bowler, 1983), there were Christians who saw it as providing a far more acceptable view of God's relationship with nature and humankind than Spencer's metaphysics of universal progress (Moore, 1979, pp.252–98). The Oxford Anglo-Catholic Aubrey Moore, for example, urged the essential orthodoxy of the *Origin*. Unable to accept Temple's view of God 'making all things make themselves' – which he regarded as closer to deism than to Christian theism – Moore pointed out what many natural theologians had apparently forgotten, namely that a theory of God's occasional intervention in nature entailed the idea of his 'ordinary absence' (Moore, 1889, pp.184–5). By reasserting the immanence of God in nature, Moore was able to welcome every new discovery about origins as at once a fact of nature and an act of God; and, as Arthur Peacocke's contribution to this volume makes clear, his work prefigured many subsequent attempts to incorporate Darwinism into a Christian view of creation and incarnation.

Looking back on the late nineteenth century as a whole, it is striking how similar were the preoccupations of those naturalists, philosophers, social theorists and theologians who debated the larger implications of evolutionary theory. Overwhelmingly, their common concern was with the consequences for traditional beliefs about human nature, morality and society of a biological account of origins. The extent to which they came to terms with the idea of evolution at all was a measure of how far they were able to integrate this idea with their own more immediate and vital interests in the past state, present condition and future prospects of the human race. In general, it was only as natural theologians saw their way to a new, optimistic creed rooted in the philosophy of evolutionary naturalism that they welcomed Spencer and Darwin as the allies of true religion. William Paley, one feels sure, would have been proud of them.

THE REJECTION OF DARWINISM

Between 1921 and 1929 anti-evolution bills were brought before no less than 37 American state legislatures. These bills sought to outlaw the teaching of all but the biblical doctrine of creation in public schools and colleges, and they were passed into law in Tennessee (1925), Mississipi (1926), Arkansas (1928) and Texas (1929). The American Civil Liberties Union reacted to this legislation by persuading John Thomas Scopes, a high school teacher in Dayton, Tennessee, to put its so-called 'monkey law' to the test. What followed may or may not have been *The World's Most Famous Court Trial* (1925), but it certainly focused national and international attention on popular anti-evolutionary sentiment in the American South. The trial brought together two of America's foremost attorneys – Clarence Darrow for the defence, and William Jennings Bryan for the prosecution – and at times it bordered on pure farce. Darrow objected (unsuccessfully) to the opening of the court proceedings each day with prayer; and Bryan objected (successfully) to every one of Darrow's expert witnesses. Finally, Darrow invited Bryan himself to be sole witness for the defence; and in an extraordinary cross-examination he grilled him publicly on his personal beliefs about origins. Technically, this was completely irrelevant: Bryan's testimony was eventually struck from the record; and Scopes was duly convicted (he later got off on a technicality). But the spectacle of a major public figure struggling over such hoary riddles as whether Joshua had really made the sun stand still, and where Cain had managed to find a wife, made a laughing-stock of Bryan, of Dayton and of anti-evolutionism. After the Scopes trial, and with the loss of its leader (Bryan died a few days later), the American anti-evolutionary movement went into a gradual decline from which it was not to recover until the late 1960s.

Few episodes in the history of modern thought appear to confirm quite so well the idea of inevitable conflict between science and belief as the clash between evolutionary biologists and 'fundamentalist' Protestants in the American South during the twentieth century. Like the encounter between Huxley and Wilberforce, that between Darrow and Bryan is easily portrayed as a straightforward contest between progressive scientific truth and reactionary religious dogma. However, this is a patently inadequate interpretation of the dispute. For as we have seen there were resources within both Darwinism and divinity that made reconciliation perfectly possible. What was it, then, about Bryan and the people he represented that led them to reject this option? Let us consider Bryan first, since he was the driving force behind organized opposition to evolution in the key period between 1920 and 1925.

Formerly Secretary of State under Woodrow Wilson, and three times Democratic Presidential candidate himself, William Jennings Bryan was known as 'The Great Commoner', a title that reflected his consistent support for the common people on issues such as women's suffrage and workers' rights. According to his biographer, Bryan saw politics as 'applied Christianity' (Levine, 1965, p.250). Central to his life-work was a clear moral vision of the link between healthy religious faith and a healthy society. 'Belief in God is almost universal', he wrote, 'and the effect of this belief is so vast that one is appalled at the thought of what social conditions would be if reverence for God were erased from every heart' (Bryan, 1922, p.26). In religion as in politics Bryan was a democrat, and he opposed a biblical criticism which would make theological truth the exclusive property of intellectuals on exactly the same grounds that he opposed a monopoly capitalism which would make economic wealth the exclusive property of industrialist 'robber barons'. Truth, like wealth, he believed, should be equally accessible to all.

Bryan's opposition to Darwinism arose out of this religious and political ideology. 'The objection to evolution', he wrote, 'is not, primarily, that it is not true. The principal objection . . . is that it is

highly harmful to those that accept it' (Bryan, 1924, p.144). Of
course the harm that Bryan had in mind was fundamentally moral.
As early as 1904 he had publicly doubted the Darwinian
interpretation of human origins; and a year later, after reading
Darwin's *Descent of Man,* he warned that 'such a conception of
man's origin would weaken the cause of democracy and strengthen
class pride and the power of wealth' (quoted in Levine, 1965,
pp.261–2). Bryan's wariness of social Darwinism grew during the
First World War, when he read works by the evolutionists Vernon
Kellogg (1917) and Benjamin Kidd (1920) which claimed to find a
direct connection between Darwinism and the growth of German
militarism. Convinced that his worst fears were being confirmed in
the trenches of Europe, Bryan announced that Darwinism was 'the
most paralyzing influence with which civilization has had to
contend during the last century' (quoted in Levine, 1965, p.263).
Henceforth, he campaigned tirelessly on behalf of 'a greater
majority on my side than in any previous controversy'; and against
the baseless and debasing 'presumptions, probabilities and inferences' of Darwinian biology (Bryan, 1922, p.91). Thus it was that a
man who had been 'a radical all his life' ended his days in
Tennessee 'an ultra-conservative' (Levine, 1965, p.vii).

It is important to establish what Bryan's opposition to Darwinism was not. First, it was not a simple-minded defence of biblical
literalism; for during the Scopes trial Bryan admitted that it did not
bother him particularly how long the creation described in Genesis
had actually taken, and that for all he knew 'It might have
continued for millions of years' (*The World's Most Famous Court Trial,*
1925, p.303). Secondly, it was not a blanket rejection of modern
science; for Bryan had a great respect for the high standards of
scientific knowledge, with which he believed Darwinism compared
very badly (Bryan, 1922, p.94). Thirdly and last, it was not a
straightforward rejection of evolution, for Bryan explicitly left open
the possibility of a natural origin for plants and animals (Bryan,
1922, p.104). The simple fact is that Bryan's wrath was directed
only at the hypothesis of human evolution by natural selection, and
it was directed at this hypothesis only because Bryan regarded it as
profoundly subversive of Christian morality and American civilization. The hypothesis, he wrote,

does incalculable harm. It teaches that Christianity impairs the race physically. That was the first conclusion at which I revolted. It led me to review the doctrine and reject it entirely. If hatred is the law of man's development; that is, if man has reached his present perfection by a cruel law under which the strong kill the weak – then, if there is any logic that can bind the human mind, we must turn backward toward the brute if we dare to substitute the law of love for the law of hate. (Bryan, 1922, pp.107–8)

It is now possible to see how Bryan's concerns took him to the head of the 'fundamentalist' movement in the 1920s. Fundamentalism was a particular brand of militantly anti-modernist Protestant evangelicalism that took its inspiration from a series of tracts published between 1910 and 1915 under the general title *The Fundamentals* (Marsden, 1981, p.4; see also Furniss, 1954, and Gatewood, 1969). A populist creed that united religious with political conservatism, fundamentalism emerged as a powerful force in the wake of a post-war cultural crisis that led many Americans to see sinister links between the external threats of German militarism and Russian Bolshevism and the internal growth of religious and political liberalism. In this context, Darwinism came to be seen as the most identifiable corrupting influence on American society. Prominent fundamentalist preachers linked the name of Darwin with a whole catalogue of social ills, from international conflict to the collapse of family life. 'The day is not distant', railed the revivalist Mordecai Ham in one of his most famous sermons, 'when you will be in the grip of the Red Terror and your children will be taught free love by the damnable theory of evolution' (quoted in Gatewood, 1966, p.44). Bryan, of course, was no mere rabble-rouser. Indeed in many ways he was unsuited to leadership of the fundamentalist cause – for example, his religion was too temperate, and his politics were far too progressive. However, on the issue of evolution and morality he found himself in sympathy with a genuinely populist movement; and by becoming its spokesman he gave it a focus and a national significance that it would never otherwise have achieved.

It should not be supposed that Bryan and the fundamentalists were alone in seeing important connections between evolutionary theory and larger moral, social and political issues. On the contrary, such connections were widely celebrated by many of the leading advocates of evolution in North America, who looked to Darwin's theory as a new basis for secular and liberal values. Consider, for example, Maynard Shipley's 'Science League of America', an organization set up explicitly to counteract the propaganda of the fundamentalists. Speaking at a meeting of the League in San Francisco in 1925, Luther Burbank claimed that science and science alone was the key to America's national salvation; and he went on to advocate eugenics as the first step towards 'the building of a better humanity' (Shipley, 1927, pp.387–91). Burbank was followed by David Starr Jordan, Chancellor of Stanford University and Chairman of the Eugenics Committee of the American Breeders Association, who argued that from science 'we learn what is right and wrong'; and then by W.E. Ritter, President of the Science Service in Washington, who asserted that, in the light of evolution, 'man's destiny is in his own hands in a sense we had not suspected before', and who concluded with an appeal for the establishment of a new secular religion based upon the findings of biology (Shipley, 1927, pp.189–99). If Bryan believed that it was the message of Darwinism that, as he put it, 'Christianity impairs the race physically', it was primarily because he lived in an era of rampant social Darwinism. Moreover, his claim that this was the first conclusion at which he had revolted – that it was this that had led him 'to review the doctrine and reject it entirely' – suggests that such social Darwinism played a significant part in the rise of anti-evolutionary sentiment in the post-war period. The evolutionary debates of the 1920s appear to have been the product of conflict, not between belief and science, but rather between opposing beliefs, each of which appealed to nature for ideological support, albeit in very different ways.

THE LEGACY OF DARWINISM

Fundamentalism is not representative of Christian responses to Darwinism in the twentieth century. Rather, it is best understood as a reaction against the continuing trend amongst liberal theologians towards closer and closer conformity with the idea of evolution.

After 1900, so-called 'Modernism' constituted a powerful movement within theology, and its hallmark was the attempt to make
Christianity scientific. In general, modernists adopted the kind of
optimistic cosmology that had been so popular in the late
nineteenth century, in which the theological concepts of creation
and providence were re-interpreted in evolutionary terms. By
emphasizing both the immanence of God in nature and the gradual
ascent of nature and humankind towards divinity, they sustained a
powerful synthesis of science, religion and the politics of 'progressive' social reform. 'Evolution', wrote the Baptist modernist
Walter Rauschenbusch, 'has prepared us for understanding the
idea of the reign of God toward which all creation is moving'
(quoted in Moore, 1981, p.27). This was the ideology that came
under attack in the early 1920s. In the aftermath of a world war
that shattered so many liberal illusions, not only fundamentalism
but also the 'neo-orthodoxy' of the Swiss theologian Karl Barth and
his followers represented the rejection of a complacent natural
theology that identified God too closely with the grand march of
natural and human history.

Despite these reactions, the liberal tradition of accommodation
to evolution continued to thrive. Within the Anglican communion,
for example, it may be traced from the writings of Frederick
Temple and F.R. Tennant (1909) at the turn of the century,
through those of William Temple (1934), L.S. Thornton (1928)
Charles Raven (1953) in the middle of the century, to the more
recent work of Arther Peacocke (1979; 1981; and this volume).
Typical in many respects of this tradition was the Cambridge
theologian and historian of science Charles Raven. Raven was a
Christian socialist who had found time to study Mendelian genetics
under William Bateson whilst reading for an undergraduate degree
in divinity. He saw the nineteenth century, the 'century of conflict,
Genesis and geology, the origin of species, the problem of miracles,
the higher criticism', as having bequeathed to Christendom a
tragically divided world-view (Raven, 1953, p.12). He set himself
the task of overcoming this divide by developing a unified
philosophy that did justic to both science and belief. The elements
of this philosophy are by now rather familiar. Raven argued that
cosmic, biological and human history were parts of a single,

divinely inspired evolutionary process. Projecting into this process both his Christian faith and his socialist vision of progress towards the kingdom of God on earth, he defended a holistic conception of organic and social development in which spiritual purpose informed the struggle of nature towards greater and greater perfection. Admittedly, this was scarcely a Darwinian view of evolution; but for Raven Darwinism was an overly deterministic and mechanistic system. Far more promising, he believed, were the efforts of men like Conwy Lloyd Morgan and Alfred North Whitehead to construct an evolutionary philosophy of nature in which life, mind and spirit were regarded as parts of the basic furniture of universe (Raven, 1953, pp.186–203).

One of the most striking features of liberal, 'reconciling' theology in the twentieth century has been its steady convergence with religious evolutionary humanism of a non- or even anti-Christian character. Nowhere is this convergence more apparent than in the reception accorded to the work of the remarkable French Jesuit and palaeontologist Pierre Teilhard de Chardin (1881–1955). Teilhard's philosophical writings were suppressed during his lifetime, but their posthumous publication created a considerable stir (see, for example, Hanson (ed). 1970). Briefly, Teilhard attempted the complete recasting of Christian theology in evolutionary terms. Each element within the Christian world–view – matter, life, mind and spirit; the birth of the cosmos, the person and work of Christ and the ultimate redemption of humankind – was treated alike as a moment in the evolutionary ascent of the cosmos towards the 'omega point' of ultimate unity with God. Teilhard's philosophy was heady stuff, and it met with predictably mixed reactions within the scientific community. But amongst those who were generally approving of it, by far the most interesting were a number of prominent evolutionary biologists already engaged in the attempt to find within Darwinism the seeds of a new, secular and humanistic religion. Indeed, the English edition of Teilhard's *The Phenomenon of Man* appeared with an introduction by Julian Huxley which praised the work as 'a remarkable success' that 'opened up vast territories of thought to further exploration and detailed mapping' (Teilhard de Chardin, 1970, p.22). A few years later the eminent evolutionary geneticist Theodosius Dobzhansky organized his personal inquiry into *The Biology of Ultimate Concern* around what he termed 'The Teilhardian Synthesis' (Dobzhansky, 1971, p.108).

What was it about the writings of a Jesuit Priest that so caught the imaginations of Huxley and Dobzhansky? In his autobiography, Huxley recalled his meetings with Teilhard after 1946. The two men, he stated, had been 'in almost general agreement over the essential facts of cultural and organic evolution', though Teilhard had never given full credit to Darwin's theory of natural selection; and their 'ineradicable divergence of approach' in theology had been tolerable only because of this 'scientific agreement' (Huxley 1972, vol. 2, p.24). Now baldly stated, Huxley and Teilhard's scientific agreement amounted to little more than a general consensus on what had happened in the prehistoric past. (On the deeper questions of how and why it had happened, for example, they were poles apart.) This seems barely sufficient to account for their mutual admiration, and it must be set alongside the fact that in addition they were united in their belief that what had happened in the prehistoric past was of overwhelming moral, social and religious significance. Ever since the 1920s, Huxley had been convinced that, 'in the fact of evolutionary progress . . . the forces of nature conspire together to produce results which have value in our eyes' (Huxley, 1923, pp.40–1). Quoting Matthew Arnold's famous definition of God as 'a power, not ourselves, that makes for righteousness', he had virtually deified the evolutionary process as the basis in science for a new 'religion without revelation' (Huxley, 1923, pp.262–3; and 1927). In the global metaphysics of Teilhard, Huxley discovered that such deification could be accomplished as well on the basis of Catholic theology as on that of humanistic science. In each case, all that was required was the steady conviction, beloved by liberals, that progress is the fundamental law of history.

In recent years, the convergence of theology and science upon a form of religous evolutionary humanism has reached its apotheosis in the writings of some sociobiologists. In his major work *Sociobiology: The New Synthesis* (1975), Harvard entomologist Edward O. Wilson makes strong claims for the ability of evolutionary biology to account not only for human social behaviour but also for religious beliefs and practices. 'It is a reasonable hypothesis', he writes 'that magic and totemism constituted direct adaptations to the environment and preceded formal religion in social evolution' (Wilson, 1975, p.560). Of course, there is nothing particularly new about this functionalist view of religion. Indeed, it was clearly formulated almost a century ago by the social philosopher Benjamin Kidd (1894), who argued that religion had been a crucially important non-rational sanction for ethical conduct during human evolution. But sociobiology has provided a newly refined theoretical framework within which to interpret behaviour; and as Vernon Reynolds and Ralph Tanner demonstrate in chapter 5 of this volume, it raises for the first time the serious prospect of biological investigation of the adaptive value of religion. At the same time, however, it presents us with a curious dilemma. For to explain religion in non-cognitive terms might be thought to undermine its credibility; and if this is so, then sociobiology may well threaten the very phenomenon whose biological utility it sets out to establish. Wilson himself is aware of this problem, for in his more recent book *On Human Nature* he sets his account of the sociobiology of religion alongside an impassioned plea for the re-investment of 'the mythopoeic requirements of the mind' in 'the evolutionary epic . . . [which] . . . is probably the best myth we will ever have' (Wilson, 1978, pp.200-1).

This brings us back once again to the deification of the evolutionary process. Mary Midgley explores this theme in more detail in chapter 6 of this volume; but in the present context it is worth noting how very similar are the creation myths of Christian theism and religious evolutionary humanism. Each provides an account of the natural order and of the place of humankind within it; each casts its account in the form of a narrative epic centred upon the origin and destiny of humankind; and each derives from its account practical lessons for the ordering of human affairs, together with the comforting reassurance that the universe is on the side of our noblest aspirations. As the philosopher John Passmore once observed, 'it is astonishing just how often 'god-smashing' evolutionists have substituted for the ancient gods a new god–man as he is to be, with powers of a kind which had ordinarily been ascribed only to the divine' (Passmore, 1970, p.240). This, surely, is Wilson's position. Reasoning, as he puts it, 'in direct line from the humanism of the Huxleys, Waddington, Monod, Pauli, Dobzhansky, Cattell, and others', he concludes *On Human Nature* by looking forward to the construction of 'the mythology of scientific materialism . . . kept strong by the blind hopes that the journey on which we are now embarked will be farther and better than the one just completed' (Wilson, 1978, pp.206, 209).

It might be supposed that all theologians would view with a certain amount of alarm this takeover bid for faith on the part of religious evolutionary humanism. But such is not the case. Indeed, Wilson's analysis of religion is heavily indebted to the work of the American theologian R.W. Burhoe, who has for many years been developing what he terms a 'scientific theology' (Wilson, 1978, p.248; Burhoe, 1981). Burhoe has pushed the evolutionary analysis of belief to its logical conclusion. Regarding religion as the 'missing link' between animal selfishness and human altruism, he argues for its continuing importance to humanity on purely biological grounds. God-language, Burhoe suggests, is a pre-scientific representation of the fact of human dependence upon a sovereign cosmic order. To say that we are always and utterly dependent on the will of God is, for him, quite literally the same thing as saying that we are dependent upon natural selection, 'the ultimate and awful judge whose laws man must find and obey if he is to continue thus to flourish' (Burhoe, 1981, p.74). At this point, where the role of priest collapses into that of genetic counsellor, it is impossible to distinguish in any meaningful sense between Darwinism and divinity; for the one has been transformed into the other.

CONCLUSION

I began this chapter with the conventional image of Darwinism as a potent force for the de-mythologization of world-view, but I have ended up with the unconventional image of it as a major ingredient within the mythic world-view of religious evolutionary humanism. I believe that each of these images captures something of the truth. On the one hand, there can be no doubt that Darwinism *was* a secularizing force in the nineteenth century. It contributed very materially to a separation of spheres in which increasingly distinct professional communities of scientists and theologians were able to get on with their work without having to pay much attention to one another (Turner, 1974; Young, 1980). On the other hand, however, it is equally the case that evolutionary theory in general and Darwinism in particular have always tended to blur the simple distinction between knowledge and values. For all thoughtful Darwinians, including Darwin himself, have recognized that there are strong links between questions such as, Where have we come from? What sort of creatures are we? And what could we or should we do with our lives? To try to draw neat lines around each of these questions, labelling some 'scientific' and others 'religious' or 'moral', is counterproductive, since it is in the connections between them that all the crucial issues are located.

I have argued that there are resources within evolutionary theory that make it attractive to certain kinds of theology. Darwin opened the door to a particular form of alliance by presenting natural selection as a 'secondary law' instituted by the creator to populate the earth. Overwhelmingly, however, it has been the idea of evolution as a law of progressive historical development culminating in humankind that has proved most attractive to biologically-minded theologians and theologically-minded biologists. This is an area of interaction that deserves closer study. For the Darwinian theory of evolution by natural selection contains no 'law of progress'; and whether and in what way it applies to human culture, where such a law is most urgently sought, are still matters of intense debate within the human sciences. In the past, attempts to derive optimistic lessons from biology concerning the future of humankind have owed far more to prior religious or political convictions than they have to any independent insights derived from science; and, as the example of Julian Huxley illustrates, this has been the case even where those involved have been major authorities on Darwinism. There is nothing in a scientific training, it would seem, that immunizes a person against their own prejudices.

One of the most ironic aspects of the deification of Darwinism in the twentieth century has been the encouragement that such idolatry has afforded to the forces of religious anti-evolutionism. I

have argued that in the 1920s the association between evolutionism, on the one hand, and secularism and liberalism, on the other,
helped to fan the flamês of popular anti-evolutionary sentiment.
Significantly, the same association appears to be playing its part in
the current battle between evolutionists and so-called 'scientific
creationists' in the United States. The resurgence of anti-
evolutionism over the past few years is dealt with in some detail by
Eileen Barker in the final chapter of this volume. All that needs to
be said here is that this phenomenon is as deeply ideological today
as it was 60 years ago. In the foreword to the best-known textbook
of scientific creationism, for example, the authors declare that, 'in
the name of modern science . . . a nontheistic religion of secular
evolutionary humanism has become, for all practical purposes, the
official state religion promoted in the public schools' (Morris, ed.,
1974, p.iii). To learn more about this religion we have only to read
on, for at various stages in the book it is linked with atheism,
materialism, mechanism and liberalism, as well as with behaviour-
ism, libertinism, racism and communism (Morris, ed., 1974,
pp.196–201, 252). Obviously, none of these labels is intended as a
compliment, but it would be wrong to dismiss them as nothing
more than a cheap exercise in mud-slinging. For much of the
energy of the creationist movement arises from a sense of moral
outrage at the advance of an evolution-centred world-view that has
the audacity to parade its secular, liberal values as if they were the
objective findings of science. Here at least, if not in matters of
biological fact and theory, creationism has a point of which the
scientific community might do well to take heed.

   The most obvious conclusion that emerges from this rapid survey
of more than a century of debates is that Darwinism continues to be
caught up in as wide a range of moral, religious and political issues
as ever. In itself, this fact is both unavoidable and unexceptionable,
for the day we cease to discuss Darwinism in this broad context will
be the day we cease to take it seriously. What is to be regretted,
however, is that so often the attempt to bring Darwinism to bear on
fundamental questions leads to its mythologization. If there is any
truth in the theory of evolution by natural selection (and a century
of research suggests that there is), it must surely constitute one of
the most vital clues we possess to our origin, nature and ultimate

destiny. But we shall stand little chance of learning anything very new or very enlightening from this theory if we treat it merely as a mirror, holding it up to reveal only those things about past, present and future we wish most to see. We have a long way still to go in our understanding of the relationship between Darwinism and divinity.

NOTES

1 In 1825 the Earl of Bridgewater left £8000 in his will for the commissioning of a series of works 'On the Power, Wisdom, and Goodness of God, as manifested in the Creation'.
2 Significantly, Darwin was so impressed by this response that he obtained Kingsley's permission to incorporate it in the second edition of the *Origin* (Darwin, 1959, pp.167–8).

REFERENCES

Bowler, P.J. (1977) 'Darwinism and the Argument from Design: Suggestions for a Re-evaluation', *Journal of the History of Biology* **10**, pp.29–43.
Bowler, P.J. (1983) *The Eclipse of Darwinism: Anti-Darwinian Evolution Theories around 1900*, Baltimore, Johns Hopkins University Press.
Brooke, J.H. (1979) 'The Natural Theology of the Geologists: Some Theological Strata', in L.J. Jordanova and R.S. Porter (eds) *Images of the Earth, Essays in the History of the Environmental Sciences*, Chalfont St Giles, British Society for the History of Science, pp.39–64.
Bryan, W.J. (1924) *Seven Questions in Dispute*, New York, Fleming H. Revell & Co.
Bryan, W.J. (1922, reprinted 1971) *In His Image*, New York, Books for Libraries Press.
Burhoe, R.W. (1981) *Toward a Scientific Theology*, Belfast, Christian Journals Ltd.
Cannon, W.F. (1961) 'The Bases of Darwin's Achievement: A revaluation', *Victorian Studies* **5**, pp.109–32.
Chambers, R. (1844) *Vestiges of the Natural History of Creation* London, John Churchill; reprinted with an introduction by Sir Gavin De Beer, Leicester, Leicester University Press (1969).
Chambers, R. (1845) *Explantations: A Sequel to the Vestiges of the Natural History of Creation*, London, John Churchill.

Chapman, R.C. and Duval, C.T. (eds) (1982) *Charles Darwin: A Centennial Commemorative*, Wellington, New Zealand, Nova Pacifica.

Clark, J.W. and Hughes, T. (1890) *The Life and Letters of the Reverend Adam Sedgwick* 2 vols, Cambridge.

Darwin, C.R. (1959) *The Origin of Species . . . A Variorum Text*, Morse Peckham (ed.), Philadelphia, University of Pennsylvania Press.

Darwin, F. (ed.) (1887) *The Life and Letters of Charles Darwin*, 3 vols, London, John Murray.

Darwin, F. (ed.) (1903) *More Letters of Charles Darwin*, 2 vols, London, John Murray.

Darwin, W.G. (1883) 'A Reminiscence of Charles Darwin', 4 June 1883, Darwin Papers, box 112, folios 19–22, Cambridge University Library.

Dobzhansky, T. (1971) *The Biology of Ultimate Concern*, London, Collins.

Draper, J.W. (1875) *History of the Conflict between Religion and Science*, London, Henry King and Co.

Drummond, H. (1883) *Natural Law in the Spiritual World*, London, Hodder and Stoughton.

Drummond, H (1894) *The Ascent of Man*, (6th ed. 1897) London, Hodder and Stoughton.

Freud, S. (1959–74) *The Standard Edition of the Complete Psychological Works of Sigmund Freud*, James Strachey (ed.), 24 vols, London, Hogarth Press.

Furniss, N.F. (1954) *The Fundamentalist Controversy, 1918–1931*, New Haven (Conn.), Yale University Press.

Gatewood, W.B. (1966) *Preachers, Pedagogues and Politicians: The Evolution Controversy in North Carolina 1920–1927*, Chapel Hill (N. Car), University of North Carolina Press.

Gatewood, W.B. (1969) *Controversy in the Twenties: Fundamentalism, Modernism, and Evolution*, Nashville (Tenn.), Vanderbilt University Press.

Gillispie, C.C. (1951) *Genesis and Geology: A Study in the Relations of Scientific Thought, Natural Theology and Social Opinions in Great Britain, 1790–1850*, Cambridge (Mass.), Harvard University Press.

Glass, B. *et al.* (eds) (1959) *Forerunners of Darwin, 1745–1859*, Baltimore, Johns Hopkins University Press.

Gore, C. (ed.) (1889) *Lux Mundi: A Series of Studies in the Religion of the Incarnation*, London, John Murray.

Greene, J.C. (1981) *Science, Ideology, and World View. Essays in the History of Evolutionary Ideas*, Berkeley, University of California Press.

Gruber, H.E. and Barrett, P.H. (eds) (1974) *Darwin on Man: A Psychological Study of Scientific Creativity . . . together with Darwin's Early and Unpublished Notebooks*, London, Wildwood House.

Gruner, R. (1975) 'Science, Nature and Christianity', *Journal of Theological Studies*, **26**, pp.55–81.

Hanson, A. (ed.) (1970) *Teilhard Reassessed: A Symposium of Critical Studies in the Thought of Pierre Teilhard de Chardin*, London, Darton, Longmann & Todd.

Hooykaas, R. (1972) *Religion and The Rise of Modern Science*, Edinburgh, Scottish Academic Press.

Hutton, R.H. (1885) 'The Metaphysical Society: A Reminiscence', *Nineteenth Century* **18**, pp.177–96.

Huxley, J.S. (1923) *Essays of a Biologist*, London, Chatto & Windus.

Huxley, J.S. (1927) *Religion without Revelation*, London, Ernest Benn.

Huxley, J.S. (1972) *Memories*, 2 vols, Harmondsworth, Penguin Books.

Huxley, T.H. (1893–4) *Collected Essays*, 9 vols, London, Macmillan.

Jaki, S. (1978) *The Road of Science and the Ways of God*, Edinburgh, Scottish Academic Press.

Jowett, B. *et al.* (1861) *Essays and Reviews*, 5th ed., London, Longman, Green, Longman & Roberts.

Kellogg, V.L. (1917) *Headquarters Nights*, Boston, The Atlantic Monthly Press.

Kidd, B. (1894) *Social Evolution*, London, Macmillan.

Kidd, B. (1920) *The Science of Power*, London, Methuen.

Kuhn, T.S. (1959) *The Structure of Scientific Revolutions*, Chicago, University of Chicago Press.

Levine, L.W. (1965) *Defender of the Faith: William Jennings Bryan: The Last Decade, 1915–1925*, New York, Oxford University Press.

Lucas, J.R. (1979) 'Wilberforce and Huxley: A Legendary Encounter', *Historical Journal*, **22**, pp.313–30.

Malthus, T.R. (1798) *Essay on the Principle of Population*, London, J. Johnson.

Marsden, G.M. (1981) *Fundamentalism and American Culture: The Shaping of Twentieth Century Evangelicalism, 1870–1925*, Oxford, Oxford University Press.

Merton, R.K. (1970) *Science, Technology and Society in Seventeenth Century England*, New York, Harper Torchbooks.

Moore, A.L. (1889) *Science and the Faith: Essays on Apologetic Subjects*, London, Kegan, Paul, Trench, Trubner & Co.

Moore, J.R. (1979) *The Post-Darwinian Controversies. A Study of the Protestant Struggle to come to terms with Darwin in Great Britain and America 1870–1900*, Cambridge, Cambridge University Press.

Moore, J.R. (1981) *The Future of Science and Belief: Theological Views in the Twentieth Century*, Milton Keynes, Open University Press.

Moore, J.R. (1982) '1859 and all that: Remaking the Story of Evolution-and-Religion' in Chapman and Duval (eds) (1982) *Charles Darwin: A Centennial Commemorative*, pp.167–94.

Morris, H.M. (ed.) (1974) *Scientific Creationism*, San Diego, California, Creation-Life Publishers.

Ospovat, D. (1981) *The Development of Darwin's Theory: Natural History, Natural Theology, and Natural Selection, 1838–59*, Cambridge, Cambridge University Press.

Paley, W. (1802) *Natural Theology: or, Evidences of the Existence and Attributes of the Deity Collected from the Appearances of Nature*, London, R. Faulder.

Passmore, J. (1970) *The Perfectibility of Man*, London, Duckworth.

Peacocke, A.R. (1979) *Creation and the World of Science*, Oxford, Clarendon Press.

Peacocke, A.R. (ed.) (1981) *The Sciences and Theology in the Twentieth Century*, London, Oriel Press.

Raven, C.E. (1953) *Natural Religion and Christian Theology: Science and Religion*, Cambridge, Cambridge University Press.

Ruse, M. (1979) *The Darwinian Revolution: Science Red in Tooth and Claw*, Chicago, University of Chicago Press.

Russell, C., Hooykaas, R and Goodman, D. (1974) *'The "Conflict Thesis" and Cosmology'*, Milton Keynes, Open University Press.

Sedgwick, A. (1845) 'Vestiges of the Natural History of Creation', *Edinburgh Review* **82**, pp.1–85.

Shipley, M. (1927) *The War on Modern Science: A Short History of the Fundamentalist Attacks on Evolution and Modernism*, New York, A.A. Knopf.

Spencer, H. (1890) *Essays: Scientific, Political, and Speculative*, 3 vols., London, Williams and Norgate.

Teilhard De Chardin, P. (1970) *The Phenomenon of Man*, London, Fontana Books.

Temple, F. (1861) 'The Education of the World', in Jowett *et al.*, *Essays and Reviews*, pp.1–49.

Temple, F. (1884) *The Relations between Religion and Science*, London, Macmillan.

Temple, W. (1934) *Nature, Man and God*, London, Macmillan.

Tennant, F.R. (1909) 'The Influence of Darwinism upon Theology' *Quarterly Review* 211, pp.418–40.

Thornton, L.S. (1928) *The Incarnate Lord*, London and New York, Longmans, Green & Co.

Torrance, T.F. (1981) 'Divine and Contingent Order', in A.R. Peacocke (ed.) *The Sciences and Theology in the Twentieth Century*, pp.81–97.

Turner, F.M. (1974) *Between Science and Religion: The Reaction to Scientific*

Naturalism and Late-Victorian England, New Haven, Yale University Press.

Whewell, W. (1834) *Astronomy and General Physics Considered with Reference to Natural Theology,* London, William Pickering.

White, A.D. (1896) *A History of the Warfare of Science with Theology in Christendom,* 2 vols, London, Macmillan.

Wilson, E.O. (1975) *Sociobiology: The New Synthesis,* Cambridge (Mass.), Harvard University Press.

Wilson, E.O. (1978) *On Human Nature,* Cambridge (Mass.), Harvard University Press.

The World's Most Famous Court Trial (1925) Cincinatti, National Book Company.

Young, R. M. (1970) 'The Impact of Darwin on Conventional Thought', in A. Symondson (ed.) *The Victorian Crisis of Faith,* London, SPCK, pp.13–36.

Young, R.M. (1980) 'Natural Theology, Victorian Periodicals and the Fragmentation of a Common Context', in C. Chant and J. Fauvel (eds.) *Darwin to Einstein: Historical Studies on Science and Belief,* Harlow, Longman, pp.69–107.

2

The Relations Between Darwin's Science and his Religion

John Hedley Brooke

I was not able to annul the influence of my former belief, then almost universal, that each species had been purposely created; and this led to my tacit assumption that every detail of structure, excepting rudiments, was of some special, though unrecognized, service.

Charles Darwin

On the subject of religion, Charles Darwin once wrote, 'what my own views may be is a question of no consequence to any one but myself' (Darwin, 1887, vol. 1, p.304). The severity of that rebuke must have been felt by all who have sought to unravel the complex interrelations between his theology and his science. Nor is it the only deterrent. Of all private beliefs, those of a religious kind are often the most liable to fluctuation. And if they elude the man, by how much more must they elude his biographer. 'As you ask', Darwin replied to one correspondent, 'I may state that my judgment often fluctuates . . . I think that generally (and more and more as I grow older), but not always, . . . an Agnostic would be the more correct description of my state of mind' (p.304). But if Darwin's mind was unsettled by the question of how much he could believe, it was also unsettled by how much he could say. In a letter to his son George, written in October 1873, he confided that there was 'a fearfully difficult moral problem about the speaking out on religion'. The dilemma was clear enough: a subversive thesis had the better chance of success if it was not fired straight at the head of orthodoxies; and yet to conceal one's unorthodoxy was uncomfortable. 'I have never', he admitted to his son, 'been able to make up

my mind' (Darwin Papers, box 153). The dilemma was compounded by the additional issue: whether it was gentlemanly to
confess one's doubts if by so doing one risked hurting the feelings of
others (Darwin, 1887, vol. 1, p.305; Houghton, 1973, pp.400–1).
Consequently, there is no escaping the problem that Darwin's
public utterances on religious matters have to be interpreted with
such dilemmas in mind. When he wished to pretend that he had
not considered the mutual bearings of science and religion, he
would even adopt a meta-strategy. 'Many years ago', he told
Francis Ellingwood Abbot, 'I was strongly advised by a friend
never to introduce anything about religion in my works, if I wished
to advance science in England; and this led me not to consider the
mutual bearings of the two subjects' (Darwin Papers, box 139, folio
12; Darwin, 1887, vol. 1, p.306). It was certainly the view of his
cousin, Julia Wedgwood, that 'if he had ever said a word that was
either on the side of, or on the side against, what we mean by
Religion, he could not have taken the place he has' (Darwin
Papers, box 139, folio 12).

It should be clear from these introductory remarks that a
historian with a naive interest in the mutual bearings of science and
religion can suddenly find himself in a minefield. And if one were
looking for a further hazard one would surely find it in a long letter
that Julia Wedgwood wrote to Darwin's son Frank who declined to
incorporate it in the *Life and Letters*. 'Everyone', she had written,
'who feels Religion infinitely the most important subject of human
attention would be aware of a certain hostility towards it in [your
father's] attitude, so far as it was revealed in private life' (Darwin
Papers, box 139, folio 12). Evidently, any attempt to reconstruct a
Darwin sympathetic to conventional religious objectives, or a
Darwin for whom theology might have a positive bearing on
science, would have to be carefully circumscribed. In one sense it
was the bearing of religion on science that he had found
over-bearing. 'He felt', Julia continued, 'that he was confronting
some influence that *adulterated the evidence of fact*'.

Given these deterrents one might well abandon the question,
'What did Darwin think of his creator?'. Yet there are other
considerations which suggest that the enquiry might not be futile.
His later protestations notwithstanding, he clearly had thought

about the relations between science and religion, particularly
during that crucial period in the late 1830s when he tells us that he
thought much upon religion (de Beer, 1959, p.8). An entry in the
first of the transmutation notebooks shows that statements about
Galapagos data and questions about divine foreknowledge were
associated in his mind from the beginning: 'How does it come
wandering birds such [as] sandpipers not new at Galapagos – did
the creative force know these species could arrive – did it only
create those kinds not so likely to wander?' (de Beer, 1960,
pp.52–3). The fact that the notebook entries were private also
means that one *can* sometimes take them at face value. While some
of his theological remarks betray a concern to find formulations
that would give least offence, this is certainly not true of them all.
For example when he asks, 'has the creator since the Cambrian
formation gone on creating animals with the same general
structure?' and replies 'miserable limited view' (de Beer, 1960,
p.67), he can hardly be accused of truckling to popular opinion.
Despite the fluctuation of his religious beliefs, in both content and
strength, a fairly consistent position does emerge. 'In my most
extreme fluctuations', he wrote, 'I have never been an Atheist in the
sense of denying the existence of a God' (Darwin, 1887, vol. 1,
p.304). And on the positive side, he seems to have retained an 'inward conviction' that the universe as a whole could not be the product of chance. Certainly he became agnostic about the importance
that should be attached to such conviction (Darwin, 1887, vol. 1,
pp.306–7), but his standpoint made him a little unorthodox among
the agnostics. The *true* agnostic, Francis Darwin was reminded,
had no inward conviction on any such question (W. Graham to
F. Darwin, Darwin Papers, box 139 folio 12).

There are other reasons too why Darwin's dialogue with natural
theology still deserves attention. Ever since Cannon (1961)
identified certain structural parallels between the universe of
Darwin and the universe of the natural theologians, scholars have
had to recognize that there is a question over the extent to which
Darwin, while emancipating himself and his biology from the
strictures of Paley's thought, nonetheless continued to use its
structures. In recent years the question has acquired a new urgency
following the rapid expansion of the Darwin micro-industry. As the

manuscripts and notebooks for 1837 and 1838 have been combed, so contrary views have emerged concerning the precise point at which Darwin shed the concept of 'perfect adaption', an acknowledged legacy of the natural theology tradition (Ospovat, 1979).

Popular accounts of the Darwinian 'revolution' invariably suggest that Darwin self-consciously and successfully destroyed the argument from design, which had provided the backbone of natural theology from the time of Robert Boyle and John Ray in the late seventeenth century to Darwin's own day, where it was encountered in the well-known works of William Paley and diversified by the authors of the *Bridgewater Treatises*. The argument that living systems had been perfectly adapted to their environments by divine design was clearly vulnerable to Darwin's contention that adaptation was the result of a natural process. The antithesis between the two conceptions is well known. It was stated by Darwin himself in his *Autobiography:* 'the old argument from design in Nature, as given by Paley, which formerly seemed to me so conclusive, fails, now that the law of natural selection has been discovered' (Barlow, (ed.) 1958, p.87). There is evidence, too, that Darwin had recognized that failure concurrently with the emergence of what he called 'my theory'. In his *Essay on Theology and Natural Selection*, he commented adversely on the natural theology of John Macculloch:

> Macculloch . . . gives woodpecker as instance of beautiful adaptation – and then chamelion, which feeding on same food, differs in every respect, except in quick movement . . . In all these cases it should be remembered that animals could not exist without these adaptations – fossil forms show such losses. (Gruber and Barrett, 1974, p.418)

In this passage, there would seem to be an awareness that adaptation might be a *sine qua non* of survival without design having to be a *sine qua non* of adaptation. To some of Macculloch's more naive examples, Darwin was already responding, 'what trash'.

This conventional antithesis, between Paley's teleological argument and Darwin's ever more confident vision of adaptation as a process, is undeniable. It was probably in the autumn of 1838 that he inscribed those marginalia in his copy of Whewell's *History of the Inductive Sciences* to which Manier (1978) has drawn attention. Whewell's statement that 'the use of every organ has been discovered by starting from the assumption that it must have *some* use' was modified by Darwin to read, 'the relation of every organ has been discovered by starting from the assumption that it must have *some* relation'. With that modification he cut himself away from the teleological connotations which the world 'use' had for Whewell. Where the latter expounded Kant on the necessity of a regulative teleological principle in biology, Darwin calmly wrote, 'all this reasoning is vitiated, when we look at animals, on my view' (Manier, 1978, pp.51–5; Corsi, 1980a, p.355).

The conventional antithesis is undeniable. But is it all there is to say about the relations between natural selection and natural theology? The answer turns out to be emphatically not. Unfortunately the force of the antithesis, and the *gestalt* switch which often accompanies its appreciation, have encouraged certain reductionist tendencies in the reconstruction of the history, as when the author of a recent textbook insists that 'Darwin's whole life-work ultimately came to be a battle fought against the arguments put forward so ably by Paley' (Oldroyd, 1980, p.62). A more sophisticated example occurs in the work of Camille Limoges where the philosophical antithesis is made to perform historical work. The crucial period here lies between 1837, when Darwin first became a transformist, and the autumn of 1838 when he finally hit on natural selection as the key to the mechanism. According to Limoges (1970) the essential pre-requisite for Darwin to find the key was the rejection of the concept of perfect adaptation in favour of the recognition of imperfect adaptation, the latter making room for the crucial acknowledgement of *differential* adaptation. As David Kohn (1980, pp.103–6) has pointed out, that transition looks fine in logic but is not a copy of the route that Darwin actually took. On the basis of a fastidious reading of the notebooks, Kohn (1980, p.305) has concluded that 'rather than concerning himself with imperfect adaptation, Darwin's attempts to explain evolution, prior to reading Malthus, were predicated on the *ad hoc* notion that organisms directly, that is automatically, produce variants that adjust them to their changing environment.' Within that explanatory framework, Darwin could explain imperfect adaptations as the hereditary traces of what had once been acts of direct adaptation. Or, in other words, the acknowledgement of the possibility of imperfect adaptation, which for Limoges marks the decisive break with the natural theology literature, need not have had such seminal significance for Darwin, given the mechanism he was entertaining at the time.

There are in fact several good reasons why historical sensitivity requires the rejection of the conventional antithesis as the best guide to the relationship between Darwin's science and contemporary natural theology. It has, for example, become increasingly clear that natural theology was itself producing variants, some of which were better equipped to survive than the teleological argument of Paley (Bowler, 1976, ch. 3, and 1977; Brooke, 1977a; Ospovat, 1978 and 1980; Corsi, 1980a). At least two of these variants could accommodate a looser fit between the structure of an organism and its environment. The design arguments of Richard Owen, for instance, were premissed on a unity of structural type in the vertebrate kingdom, which he happily interpreted in terms of a transcendent archetypal idea – a divine blueprint for creation (Owen, 1849, MacLeod, 1965; Desmond, 1982; Brooke, 1977b, and 1983). The uselessness of male nipples could not embarrass *that* version of the design argument! A second variant was even less susceptible to attack – that which saw evidence of design in the laws governing the natural world rather than in the minutiae of specific adaptations. Robert Chambers and Baden Powell were to be two champions of that perspective (Powell, 1855; Gillispie, 1959; Millhauser, 1959; Corsi, 1980a).

Given these alternative forms of the design argument there is the question whether Darwin responded favourably or unfavourably to them, particularly during the crucial year of 1838. The first alternative appears to have left him cold. He was unmoved by a transcendental interpretation of bones. In the *Essay on Theology* for example, he considered Cuvier's explanation for abortive bones, only to reject the explanation as abortive. Cuvier had argued that the skeletal structures reflected a 'determination to adhere to a plan once adopted' and that it was 'from these very circumstances, that we become satisfied respecting an original thought, or design, pursued to its utmost exhaustion, and till it must be abandoned for another'. Darwin's comments were scathing: 'the design determiner of a God-head – the designs of an omnipotent creator, exhausted and abandoned. Such is man's philosophy, when he argues about his creator' (Gruber and Barrett, 1974, pp.417–8). And if we were left in any doubt, a subsequent entry in the same essay came clean:

> N.B. The explanation of types of structure in classes – as resulting from the *will* of the deity, to create animals on certain plans – is no explanation – it has not the character of a physical law / & is therefore utterly useless – it foretells nothing / because we know nothing of the will of the Deity . . .

Here, the emphasis on the character of physical law is striking. To insist on explanations in terms of 'laws' was not, however, incompatible with that other variant of natural theology which saw evidence of design in the laws themselves. This is a point which Ospovat (1978, 1979, 1980) has particularly emphasized. One wonders whether Darwin's hostility to the argument from structural archetypes was not occasioned in part by the very fact of his having worked out his own alternative to Paley, an alternative which the transcendentalists threatened to compromise. The fact is that there are several entries in the transmutation notebooks which indicate that Darwin was discovering a philosophy of nature which he *genuinely* believed conferred a new grandeur on the deity, despite – or rather because of – the fact that it superseded Paley.

The belief that 'the Creator creates by . . . laws' was firmly in Darwin's mind as he compiled the first transmutation notebook (de Beer, 1960, p.53). How much more simple and sublime the power of God, if by analogy with his activity in the astronomical realm, he had devised the fixed laws of generation so that, in Darwin's own words, 'let animal be created, then . . . such will be their successors'. Or again, in the second notebook: the 'end of formation of species and genera is probably to add to quantum of life possible with certain preexisting laws' (de Beer, 1960, p.98). The important point there is that, certainly in the early part of 1838, laws did not rule out ends. In the third notebook the theological point is developed further. Reflecting on the extraordinary interaction between the causal chains in the physical and biological worlds, Darwin could happily refer to 'laws of harmony' in the system (de Beer, 1960, p.132). Laws implied a legislator no less than design implied a designer. Was not the notion of God's creating by law 'far grander' than the 'idea from cramped imagination that God created . . . the Rhinoceros of Java & Sumatra, that since the time of the Silurian he has made a long succession of vile molluscous animals. How beneath the dignity of him, who is supposed to have said let there be light and there was light'.

From this angle Darwin could shout 'hurrah' whenever he found reference to 'intermediate causes' in species production (de Beer, 1960, p.165), and yet at the same time could still affirm, as he did in the *Essay on Theology,* that 'the laws of propagation were created with reference to successive development' (Gruber and Barrett, 1974, p.416). True, by the time of this *Essay* he was beginning to have doubts: there is the characteristically cautious qualification that in saying such things he was probably speaking from ignorance. Yet it is hard to deny the fact that in the period leading up to his reading of Malthus, and possibly for some time afterwards, Darwin was experimenting with his own variant of natural theology which was decidedly more positive than a mere negation of Paley.

In the first major *Sketch* of his theory (1842) this motif from natural theology has not yet disappeared. The divine laws which led to 'death, famine, rapine, and the concealed war of nature' are justified on the ground that they produce 'the highest good, which we can conceive, the creation of the higher animals' (Darwin, 1842, p.87). The existence of such laws did not diminish but 'should exalt our notion of the power of the omniscient Creator'. The positive aspect of this alternative natural theology is underlined by the strong language Darwin had used in his M notebook. To deny that God was capable of producing 'every effect of every kind' through 'his most magnificent laws' was described as an act of profanity (Ospovat, 1980, p.183). To reduce the relations between Darwin's science and his religion to the traditional antithesis clearly fails.[1]

It fails for another major reason. Precisely because the theory of natural selection emerged through dialogue with prevailing concepts of design, there are certain structural continuities between the theory and natural theology which can all too easily be overlooked. It is to those structural parallels that I now wish to turn. The claim that Darwin's theory of evolution was indebted to the natural theology literature is arguably less contentious now than twenty years ago when Cannon (1961) proposed the extravagant thesis that Darwin was more indebted to the British natural theologians than to anyone else. The claim that natural theology defined the structure of the only universe in which the mechanism of natural selection would work has been elaborated and endorsed by J. R. Moore. After charting Darwin's break with Christian orthodoxy, Moore (1979, p.322) boldy declares that all that was left of that orthodoxy was its universe – no small legacy. Similarly, J. R. Durant (1977) has shown how many of the motifs that became prominent in nineteenth-century scientific naturalism stood in such a dialectical relationship with motifs in natural theology that they could only be sustained through a period in which natural theology itself still had currency. Again among recent commentators Manier (1978, p.16) has observed that Darwin 'often employed the patterns of speech, the argumentative structures, and the basic concepts of Paley as if they were his own'. Even in the structure of the *Origin of Species,* writes N. C. Gillespie (1979, p.134; Moore, 1981), theology had 'an evident integral function'. Theses and observations of this kind are as fascinating as they are paradoxical. Although more prevalent than they once were, they remain difficult to evaluate. If theory X contains a set of propositions each of which contradicts a corresponding proposition in theory Y, one would be able to assert structural congruity despite the contradiction in content. If the relationship between Darwin's theory and Paley's theology were of that kind, then the assertion of structural continuity would be weak and little more than a restatement of the conventional antithesis. If Darwin's theory *was* more than a mirror image of Paley then, as Young (1971) has indicated, it is important to clarify what kind of structural continuity is being proposed. What follows is a rudimentary classification, but it is an attempt to distinguish five different senses in which natural theology may have been reflected in Darwin's science:

In general terms one might assert a similarity of structure

(1) in the sense that a pattern of argument may be common to the presentation of two different theories;
(2) in the sense that the one theory defines the problems that the second theory solves;

(3) in the stronger sense that certain basic presuppositions of the one theory may be discerned in the other;

(4) in the sense that concepts and metaphors drawn from the first may be used to explicate the basic concepts of the second;

(5) in the sense that the application of a new concept may be regulated or constrained by survivals from the old, thereby affecting the *content* of the new theory.

In each of these five senses there is structural continuity between Darwin's theory and natural theology – though, as one would expect, in no case is the congruence perfect. It is necessary to make these distinctions because scholars who have asserted the 'structural' parallels have not always appreciated the lack of clarity which can arise when a common but loose metaphor is employed. If the elaboration of these five categories is to have any value, two further points of caution must be noted. The affirmation of structural continuity between the arguments of natural theology and the germination of Darwin's theory must not be taken to imply that Darwin's science can be reduced to the reworking of an essentially theological thesis. Nor should the identification of intellectual parallels between scientific and theological assumptions be taken to preclude a further analysis which might relate the common structures and changes of emphasis to ulterior patterns in the organization and development of an increasingly industrial society.

Of the five types of structural continuity, the first is clearly weakest in its implications. That Darwin presented his case using patterns of argument reminiscent of Paley may tell us something about the deep impact that Paley's works had made upon him in his Cambridge days. It could hardly be the basis of serious historical revision. Yet the similarity of pattern *is* there and we know that the young Darwin was indeed charmed by the 'long lines of argumentation' that Paley had developed (Barlow, 1958, p.59). Manier (1978) has gone further than most in exploring this particular isomorphism. His point is that when Darwin read Paley's *Evidences of Christianity* he would have encountered a characteristic form of argument, prominent at the very outset where Paley sought to correct Hume on the miraculous. Hume had launched his famous argument that it was always more probable that the witnesses to a reported miracle were deceived than that the miracle actually took place. Paley's rejoinder was that although Hume may have shown the relative improbability of miracles he had not shown they were impossible. A style of argument which set out to show that the improbable need not be impossible was a prominent feature of Paley's apologia, and one can certainly detect it in Darwin. Manier's example is that Darwin found most of his contemporaries assuming that it was improbable there should be no natural limit to organic variation: Darwin showed that it was not impossible. Other telling examples might be drawn from the *Origin of Species* where, in chapter 6, Darwin was to anticipate objections to his theory. Time and again he rejoiced in accumulating improbabilities, only to show that they were not, after all, impossible. An improbability such as the transition of an insectivorous quadruped into a flying bat was shown not to be impossible after all. Tactically it was a brilliant device; objections described as 'fatal' to the theory were systematically disarmed. In Manier's précis, 'the structure of this argument: 'p' has not been proven impossible; therefore 'p' is possible, was common to Paley and Darwin' (Manier, 1978, pp.70–1).

Doubtless other examples of this kind of structural parallel could be found, not least because a form of *analogical* argument was at the core of the respective theses. In Paley's *Natural Theology* the analogy was between human artefact and divine artefact. In Darwin's *Origin of Species* it was to be between human selection (as practised on plants and animals under domestication) and natural selection (as favourable variations would tend to be preserved in the struggle for existence). The opening chapters of both works defined the base from which the analogies were projected, Paley articulating his celebrated analogy between the world and a watch, Darwin delineating the scope of variation under domestication. Let us, however, leave these rather abstract parallels for more tangible continuities of the second category. Here we must consider the suggestion that Paley's discussion defined at least some of the problems that Darwin proceeded to solve.

That Darwin and Paley shared the same explanandum, the close adaptation of an organism to its environment, goes almost without saying. But the case for structural continuity in this second sense is stronger than that. It is stronger because in his *Natural Theology* Paley had considered the very kind of explanans that Darwin was to promote. Paley had denied its cogency but the very terms of his denial defined a problem that Darwin, literally in this case, was to take on board. Paley (1802, p.24) had recognized that

> There is another answer which has the same effect as the resolving of things into chance, which answer would persuade us to believe that the eye, the animal to which it belongs, every other animal, every plant, indeed every organized body which we see are only so many out of the possible varieties and combinations of being which the lapse of infinite ages has brought into existence; that the present world is the relic of that variety; millions of other bodily forms and other species having perished, being, by the defect of their constitution, incapable of preservation, or of continuance by generation.

With the privilege of hindsight that passage can be made to appear remarkably prescient! But the crucial point is the framework within which Paley (1802, p.25) rejects the option:

> All these and a thousand other imaginable varieties might live and propagate. We may modify any one species many different ways, all consistent with life, and with the actions necessary to preservation, although affording different degrees of conveniency and enjoyment to the animal. And if we carry these modifications through the different species which are known to subsist, their number would be incalculable. No reason can be given why, if these deperdits [i.e. lost species] ever existed, they have now disappeared.

As part of the suppositional framework which supports Paley's refutation, there is the clear admission of 'different degrees of conveniency' in the modification of species, immediately juxtaposed with the impossibility of explaining incalculable extinction. Clearly Paley's refutation could have acted as a template for one of Darwin's problems: how to explain extinction if nature is geared to the preservation of adaptation.

There are, of course, qualifications. Paley was after all doing battle with the hypothesis that 'every possible variety of being has at one time or other found its way into existence'. And Darwin, both on the Beagle voyage and subsequently, was clearly in dialogue with the full body of Lyell's geology rather than the mere skeleton of Paley's logic. Yet, speaking in the most general terms, the argument does hold – not least because Lyell's *Principles of Geology* themselves bear the impress of a natural theology tradition. As Kohn (1980, pp.68–72) has stressed, Lyell's examples of ecological relations, his assumption that survival depends on close adaptation to local circumstances, and his fusion of a steady state geology with the balance of nature, all point to the fact that 'the biological portion of Lyell's *Principles* is a *Bridgewater Treatise* sanitized of the religious language of design and Designer'. To say that Darwin was more indebted to Lyell than to Paley may very well be true, but it does not delete this broad sense of structural continuity. Darwin was drawn to new solutions but to problems that had already been posed in contexts where the presuppositions of natural theology still held sway.

For the third and stronger sense of structural parallel I should like to turn to the argument that several presuppositions, characteristic of British natural theology, and Paley in particular, defined the structure of a universe, the only universe, in which natural selection could work. Cannon (1961, p.128) claimed to find no less than ten such presuppositions in Darwin which had a strict parallel in Paley, and without which a viable mechanism for evolution would not have been forthcoming. Among the presuppositions held in common were, in Cannon's paraphrase:

> The universal adaptation of living beings to their environments; and therefore . . . the usefulness of *purpose* or *conditions of existence* as a fruitful concept in biology; . . . the usefulnesses of every organ to the individual and not to some other species . . . the subservience of Malthusian superfecundity to the purposes of the system; the historical nature of the past . . . [understood as] an irreversible process [but] not merely eventuating in man; . . . the progressive nature of that development . . . asserted empirically.

This is such a condensation of Cannon's argument that one or two comments are required by way of clarification. The suggestion that both Darwin and Paley shared a historical vision of the universe may seem odd at first sight since, for Paley, a species clearly did not have the convoluted history it had for Darwin. Moreover, we tend to associate the natural theology tradition with an essentially static picture of creation – that system of flora and fauna which, for John Ray, had been fixed from the beginning. But Cannon's point was that Christianity is a religion with a distinctive view of history as an irreversible process, and this view, as Hooykaas (1957, 1963, 1966) also argued, could easily be read into nature. By the 1830s and 1840s, as natural theology absorbed the findings of the geologists, the notion of *progressive* creation through time became particularly attractive – a notion which in the works of William Whewell, for example, permitted the contemplation of future races transcending the present achievements of man. Hence the last three points in Cannon's list. Natural theology was rarely as anthropocentric as its caricaturists suggest. And a degree of support for Cannon's parallels comes from the testimony of no less a figure than Lyell. In May 1856 he admitted to himself that a progressive creationist such as Hugh Miller had been, albeit unwittingly, more of an advocate for the evolution of man out of lower grades of life than *he* had been (Wilson, 1970, pp.88–9; Moore, 1981, p.196). To Cannon's parallels others still may be added. R. J. Richards (1981) has observed that the continuity between the springs of human and animal behaviour, which meant so much to Darwin, was already taken for granted by natural theologians such as John Fleming, Henry Brougham and William Kirby, if not by Paley. In addition, both Darwin and the natural theologians shared a common aversion: that is, to the notion that some vitalistic *principle of order*, such as that mooted by Hume, could account for adaptation (Cannon, 1961; Moore, 1979, p.310).

These various parallels, mediated by a common set of presuppositions, lack neither difficulties nor critics. Cannon was correct to emphasize that the best of the natural theology literature was not as anthropocentric as is often supposed. But Darwin's own critique of anthropocentric philosophies can hardly be said to parallel that of the natural theologians, certainly not exactly, when he eventually came to believe that the very *undertaking* of natural theology was profoundly anthropocentric. The human mind, he eventually concluded, was simply not adapted to the pursuit of metaphysics.

Why should it be if it were itself a product of evolution? Some of Cannon's other parallels look shaky when the mature theory is considered (Brooke, 1974, pp.44–50). Malthusian superfecundity in Paley was subservient to the balance of nature; in Darwin it was eventually subservient to an imbalance. Again, what Darwin was to mean by 'progress' in the history of living organisms was certainly not the same as was meant by the clerical geologists, who were superimposing their progressive creationism on the fossil record. As early as 1839 perhaps, Darwin was speaking of increasing 'complication' not of progression (Vorzimmer, 1975, p.216). These qualifications are serious and must be given due weight. But the early drafts of Darwin's theory differed very considerably from the mature theory and for those early drafts much of Cannon's analysis still holds. As we shall see in a moment, and as Ospovat (1979) has been keen to point out, Darwin's *initial* absorption of Malthus did not result in the immediate overthrow of a harmonious and teleologically ordered universe.

Now to the fourth category of structural continuity: the direct transfer of concepts or metaphors from one system to assist in the explication of concepts in the other. Here the most illuminating example occurs in Darwin's *Sketch* of 1842 and his *Essay* of 1844. The context is the defence and articulation of the concept of natural selection. Because of his analogy between human selection on variants under domestication and nature's selection in the wild, Darwin's word 'selection' was to have connotations which, as R.M. Young (1971) has emphasized, created a degree of ambiguity for the interpretation of Darwin's intentions. Interpreted one way the analogy could imply intelligence working through nature, just as human intelligence was involved in selecting the most propitious variants for further breeding. In the *Origin of Species* Darwin did his best to avoid such a misunderstanding, but in so doing he found it extremely difficult to avoid personifying *nature*. The interesting point is that in the earlier drafts of the theory it is a being other than nature which is personified. 'If every part of a plant or animal was to vary', Darwin (1842, p.45) argued in his *Sketch*

> and if a being infinitely more sagacious than man (not an omniscient
> creator) during thousands and thousands of years were to select all

the variations which tended towards certain ends . . . for instance, if he foresaw a canine animal would be better off, owing to the country producing more hares, if he were longer legged and [had] keener sight – [then a] greyhound [would be] produced.

And again, from the *Essay* (1844, p.114):

> Let us now suppose a Being with penetration sufficient to perceive differences in the outer and innermost organization quite imperceptible to man, and with forethought extending over future centuries to watch with unerring care and select for any object the offspring of an organism produced under the foregoing circumstances; I can see no conceivable reason why he could not form a new race . . . adapted to new ends.

In that distinction between a 'being infinitely more sagacious than man' and an omniscient creator, Manier (1978, p.73) sees a crucial break with Paley. In any case this being, though credited with forethought, watchfulness and powers of selection, is clearly a heuristic device and to that extent imaginary. As Manier (1978, pp.173–5) contends, the device was also a convenient way of by-passing the problem of ignorance concerning the inner physiology which correlated with the imperceptible differences. And yet the break is not so sharp. It is possible that Manier may have overlooked that fascinating paragraph in which Paley had also distinguished between two beings, one of them imaginary. After noting that God prescribes limits to His power, Paley had written:

> It is as though one Being should have fixed certain rules; and, if we may so speak, provided certain materials; and afterwards, have committed to another Being, out of those materials, and in subordination to these rules, the task of drawing forth a creation . . . We do not advance this as a doctrine either of philosophy or of religion; but we may say that the subject may be safely represented under this view, because the Deity, acting himself by general laws, will have the same consequences upon our reasoning, as if he had prescribed these laws to another. (Paley, 1802, p.19; Moore 1979, p.322; Durant, 1977, pp.56–7)

Given that in the same part of the *Sketch* in which Darwin had introduced his imaginary being he continued to talk about the activity of a creator (with a capital C), it is not impossible that he had in mind a distinction between two beings similar to that drawn by Paley. In that case, even where Manier sees a critical break, there may be structural continuity. Paley's imaginary being was arguably taken over by Darwin as a vehicle for clarifying what he meant by natural selection. Of that remarkable passage in Paley, John Durant (1977, p.57) has said that 'by pushing God Himself into the background, and entrusting the enforcement of the 'rules of creation' to an intelligent subordinate ... Paley unwittingly transformed his defence of theism into a model of naturalistic explanation'.

The establishment of this structural parallel in the use of two beings is of vital importance, because just as Paley could jettison his imaginary being, indeed *had* to in order to preserve a monotheism, so too could Darwin without having to abandon an original creator. If the powers of selecting were taken away from the imaginary being and invested completely in nature, as they were in the *Origin,* if the property of foreknowledge were invested in the original creator, then a more or less coherent deism could be achieved (cf. Moore, 1979, p.324). I believe something of this process did take place in Darwin's mind because it is striking how, from the time of the *Origin* onwards, he *would* credit his creator with foresight, forethought, or foreknowledge, if not with much else. In a well-known letter to Lyell of August 1861 he was to insist that 'the view that each variation has been providentially arranged seems to me to make Natural Selection entirely superfluous'. But he went on to declare: 'I do not wish to say that God did not foresee everything which would ensue' (Darwin and Seward, 1903, vol. 1, pp.190–2). In a letter to Asa Gray, though the tone was agnostic, he felt able to credit the creator with omniscience as well as prescience: 'I can see no reason why a man, or other animal, may not have been expressly designed by an omniscient Creator, who foresaw every future event and consequence' (Darwin, 1887, vol. 2, pp.310–12). Indeed one might argue that the ascription of fore*sight* to the creator was an ingenious way of avoiding the language of fore*ordainment,* which was not only difficult to integrate with the theory, but which also landed one in what Darwin called the 'wretched imbroglio as between free will and preordained necessity'.[2]

For the fifth sense of structuring by natural theology one must turn to the major study of the late Dov Ospovat, who argued that Darwin's adherence to a harmonious view of nature was not a trivial survival from his youthful period. On the contrary it is said to inform and regulate the whole of his early speculations on transmutation. (Ospovat, 1979, p.215, 1981). In this respect the *content* of the theory betrayed a theological legacy in both senses of the word 'betray'. Ospovat (1979, p.212) shared with Kohn an interpretation of the transmutation notebooks which emphasized Darwin's commitment to a concept of perfect adaptation – a concept which was not so much rooted in an empirical examination of organisms as in a belief that all organisms were created – either directly or indirectly – by a wise and benevolent God. It was this legacy from natural theology that informed one of Darwin's earliest mechanisms for the transmutation of species – the sexual theory, as Kohn (1980, pp.81–113) has called it. The basic idea was that sexual reproduction was itself the mechanism for producing just the right variations in an organism to ensure the maintenance of perfect adaptation to an ever-changing environment. Darwin was unsure of the details of the process, but this early mechanism had the attraction of explaining why a bi-sexual method of generation was necessary or advantageous. The blending aspect of heredity was to eliminate short-term trivial changes, to allow longer-term modification in correlation with longer-term geological environmental changes (Ospovat, 1981, pp.44–5). Nature was thus regarded as a harmonious system in which transmutation was the means to an end – the preservation of adaptation. Darwin's commitment to this mechanism was apparently so strong that for a while it actually obscured a perception of natural selection (Kohn, 1980, p.68).

On this interpretation, Darwin, in July 1837, was simply incorporating the effect of time into the Paleyan world-view. A species was 'as much locked into a state of perfect fit with the environment in the case where the organism [was] smoothly and continuously compensating for gradual environmental change . . .

as in the case where neither organism nor environment [changed]'
(Kohn, 1980, p.98). Here is a clear case where natural theology
affected the content of the theory – and not just ephemerally. It was
Ospovat's contention that a belief in 'perfect adaptation' continued
to put constraints on Darwin's mechanism even after the concept of
natural selection had been articulated. The constraint arises from
the fact that perfectly adapted forms would be expected to vary
little, giving natural selection a minimal scope. Once perfect
adaptation was achieved, no further variation, and hence no
further selection, would take place unless and until the environment changed. According to Ospovat (1979, p.218) this restriction
is still to be found in the *Essay* of 1844: 'the action of natural
selection is restricted to a few situations – those in which there is
geological change, or those in which organisms are transported into
new regions'. The natural selection of new variations only became a
significant force when some major environmental change produced
pressure for further adaptation. It was still possible to see the
process in teleological terms: towards new forms of perfect
adaptation. It must be made clear that Darwin's concept of perfect
adaptation did not exclude the possession of vestigial bits and
pieces which had once been of use to a progenitor. It did, however,
exclude the concept of relative adaptation and that greater scope
for natural selection which was eventually affirmed in the *Origin*. In
1844 Darwin still believed that offspring different from their
parents only came about when the reproductive system had been
influenced by external changes (Ospovat, 1979, p.225).

That a legacy from natural theology could affect the content of
the theory for seven years or more is interesting in itself. But it
raises a further question every bit as interesting. At some stage
during those seven years – and Ospovat agreed with most scholars
in suggesting the autumn of 1838 – Darwin took the theology out of
the legacy. Though, at a more subconscious level, the concept of
perfect adaptation continued to regulate the scope of natural
selection for several years to come, explicit references to the 'great
system' of nature disappear. The question is, 'why?'. Unlike some
scholars Ospovat did not insist on the reading of Malthus as the
immediate determinant. A heightened perception of natural
selection did not itself banish final causes. Indeed, an excised

passage from the D notebook confirms that Darwin *was* prepared to absorb the Malthusian argument within a harmonious scheme: 'the final cause of all this wedging, must be to sort out proper structure, and adapt it to changes, – to do that for form, which Malthus shows is the final effect . . . of this populousness on the energy of man'. Superfecundity, in other words, had a function, a purpose: geared to the promotion of initiative in man, it would promote adaptation in beast. But if the Malthusian argument was not sufficient to destroy Darwin's sense of a purposeful system, something else presumably was. For he was soon asking whether he was being consistent in speaking of final causes, soon reminding himself that they had once been exposed as barren virgins (Gruber and Barrett, 1974, p.419). Why the change? Despite his qualifications to the traditional view, Ospovat stuck to an explanation internal to Darwin's science. The naturalist soon came to believe, Ospovat wrote (1979, pp.220–1), that natural selection could not be reconciled with the supposition that the effects of particular laws could have been precisely known beforehand. From that point on he held that the creator established 'only general laws'. Purposive intent, from having been shot through creation was effectively shot out. In my concluding remarks I should therefore like to raise the question whether Darwin's reflections on the implications of natural selection were the primary, or a sufficient, source for these new doubts. I should like to enlarge on Darwin's loss of conviction in a providentially designed system.

In one respect it seems a little strange to say that Darwin came to believe that natural selection could not be reconciled with a doctrine of prescience. Foreknowledge was, as we have seen, the one attribute Darwin *would* grant the creator, even at the time when natural selection was given its maximum scope. There was of course a difficulty. Ospovat's explanation hinged on the fact that variations which Darwin had once seen as automatically adaptive were reinterpreted as 'accidental', with consequent damage to conceptions of design. But to focus on this difficulty may be to glide over other circumstances which affected Darwin's assessment of Providence. Whilst it has always been tempting to compose a picture in which his science militated against his faith (Mandelbaum, 1958, pp.365 and 369), two considerations point to a more subtle interaction.[3]

In the first place the 'chance' or 'accidental' elements associated with natural selection as a mechanism do not appear to have been regarded by Darwin as eluding reduction to determined sequences. Both Manier (1978, p.121) and Schweber (1979, pp.187–8) have observed that when he speaks of *chance* in 1838 he seems to have in mind the intersection in space and time of separate causal chains. If Darwin was, in reality, the determinist Schweber has described then a doctrine of divine pre-vision, even pre-ordainment, would surely have been safe? As Ospovat (1980, pp.184–9) himself acknowledged, Darwin continued to write as if natural selection were fulfilling general if not specific purposes, of which the production of higher animals was the most palpable. Had Darwin wished to retain an albeit modified doctrine of Providence, natural selection alone need not have stood in his way. [4]

The second consideration stems from the structural parallels we were examining earlier. Given that Darwin, in 1842 and 1844, found it convenient to explicate natural selection by reference to his imaginary being – a being with 'forethought extending over future centuries', – it is difficult to believe that natural selection was sufficient to assassinate such a being. Schweber's suggestion (1977, p.311) that this 'being' was introduced out of concern for his wife's religious views seems to miss the point – quite apart from insulting the intelligence of Emma and the integrity of Charles. They had enjoyed an understanding from before their marriage that there would be no dissimulation. 'I thank you from my heart for your openness with me' was Emma's response in a letter of 23 November 1838; 'I should dread the feeling that you were concealing your opinion from the fear of giving me pain' (Darwin Papers, box 204, 13). For Darwin the chief argument for God's existence was always to be the 'impossibility of conceiving that this grand wondrous universe, with our conscious selves, arose through chance'. In later life he would introduce the immediate qualification: 'whether this is an argument of real value, I have never been able to decide' (Darwin, 1887, vol. 1, p.306). But it is the reason he gives for that qualification that is arresting: it is not that natural selection replaces order with chance, or necessity with accident; but rather the classic philosopher's objection that awkward questions could be asked about the cause of the supposedly 'first' cause. 'I am aware', he wrote, 'that if we admit a first cause, the mind still craves to know whence it came, and how it arose' (Darwin, 1887, vol. 1, pp.306–7).

That Darwin chose to voice that particular objection may serve as a reminder that we do now have an alternative frame of reference for discussing his loss of religious conviction. In Manier's study it is Darwin's wider, cultural resources that are emphasized rather than the implications of his science. The scepticism of Hume and the positivism of Comte are only two of many resources which, Manier suggests (1978, pp.24, 40–7, 86–9), Darwin had assimilated by the autumn of 1838. The difficulty with this approach is that there is a sense in which one is embarrassed by riches. In seeking to understand the expiry of religious conviction, Hume and Comte together might be thought to constitute an overkill! And there is the additional problem that Manier does not always show how the cultural insights dovetail into the science. There is an occasional looseness of fit between what is said of Darwin's metaphysics and what might be said about his science at a particular point in time. Pietro Corsi (1980b, p.677) has drawn attention to one aspect of this looseness. In England during the 1830s there were critiques of natural theology to be found closer to home than in Hume or Comte. Or, as another example, the spiritual affinity between Wordsworth and the young Darwin, which Manier explores (1978, pp.89–96), was arguably not as close as he wishes to imply. For Wordsworth, man's mind was at least fitted to its metaphysical quest. For Darwin that was not to be. It is also a little surprising to find Darwin's well-known aversion to doctrines of spiritual damnation subsumed under a Wordsworthian influence. The unitarianism in his family background, his association (through his atheist brother Erasmus) with Harriet Martineau and her circle of heterodox intellectuals, surely were the crucial factors here (Erskine, 1983) – both in liberating freedom of thought from moral stigma and in confronting him directly with the problem to which he later referred in his *Autobiography*, namely the fate of heterodox members of his own family (Barlow, 1958, p.87). A loathing of Christian doctrines of eternal damnation, when interpreted literally, was common to most who aligned themselves with a secular cause (Budd, 1977, pp.116–7). In short, the difficulty is that a catalogue of cultural resources, if it is too detached from the problems of Darwin's science, can easily explain too little and too much.

What follows is a far briefer, and in many respects more superficial, catalogue than Manier has proposed; but it is designed to draw attention to specific points of contact between Darwin's science and his wider philosophical and theological concerns. It is these specific points of contact that repay study. On certain issues the light which Darwin threw on and drew from nature had a frequency which resonated with the cultural input. It is these examples of resonance which may best explain his growing agnosticism. One must also assume that his growing disenchantment with Christianity could have done nothing but diminish his *desire* to project a providentialist image of nature. That assumption raises a further point which perhaps deserves comment. Reacting against the view that it was Darwin's science which destroyed his faith, some scholars have verged on what seems to me to be the diametrically opposite mistake. It is possible, certainly, to construct a scenario in which Darwin shared in that moral revolt against Christianity which was a significant feature of the intellectual life of the period. (Murphy, 1955; Moore, 1982). It is possible to see in the *Origin of Species* not so much an original attack on Christian doctrine (however veiled) as the expression, in scientific terms, of an already established rejection of the Christian revelation. Such a scenario is a valuable corrective to those cruder models of secularization which refer reductively to the impact of science on society. Darwin did have moral objections to Christianity as he understood it: that religious deviants would be condemned to perdition was one of them. In reconstructing his religious mentality one must also take into account, as Moore (1982, p.188) has recently suggested, the shattering effect of the loss of his third child in 1842 and eventually of his beloved Annie in 1851. There is, in fact, much that is valuable in the view that the *Origin* eventually brought the moral crisis of the 1840s into the open. But such theses can err if they eliminate all interaction between loss of faith and the content of Darwin's science. A stronger case can be established for *mutual* interactions.

As an example of the kind of resonance one might look for, there is that remarkable entry in his diary concerning the contrasts between the flora and fauna of two distinct islands: 'an unbeliever in everything beyond his own reason might exclaim, "surely two distinct Creators must have been at work" (Moore, 1979, p.316). One cannot but be reminded of the polytheistic possibilities that Hume had exploited. Contemplating those islands, the science and the philosophy coalesced. Darwin was himself an unbeliever of revelation, his first and foremost argument having been drawn from a source to which he had been exposed by the Beagle voyage: cultural relativism. In his *Autobiography* (Barlow, 1958, pp.85–6) he tells us that by the period 1836–9 he had come to see that 'the Old Testament was no more to be trusted than the sacred books of the Hindoos. The question then continually rose before my mind and would not be banished, – is it credible that if God were now to make a revelation to the Hindoos, he would permit it to be connected with the belief in Vishnu, Siva, &c. as Christianity is connected with the Old Testament? This appeared to me utterly incredible'. The fact that many false religions had spread like wildfire over large parts of the Earth also carried weight. His first-hand experience of the Fuegians, and the natives of Australia, equipped him with a reply to those who urged that a sense of God was universally distributed. And, of the greatest importance, it was a reply that resonated with his arguments for gradation between man and the animals. As he wrote in the second transmutation notebook (de Beer, 1960, p.111):

Hensleigh [Wedgwood] says the love of the deity and thought of him or eternity only difference between the mind of man and animals. – yet how faint in a Fuegian or Australian! Why not gradation.

It was to this point he would return for his opening remarks on religion in his *Descent of Man*. 'There is no evidence that man was aboriginally endowed with the ennobling belief in the existence of an omnipotent God. On the contrary there is ample evidence, derived not from hasty travellers, but from men who have long resided with savages, that numerous races have existed, and still exist, who have no idea of one or more gods, and who have no words in their languages to express such an idea' (Darwin, 1906, pp.142–3). Darwin had, after all, *investigated* the beliefs of the Fuegians with whom he had rubbed shoulders: 'we could never discover that [they] believed in what we should call a God, or practised any religious rites' (Darwin, 1906, p.145).

There was surely mutual interaction between Darwin's religious perspectives and his science. Doubts about revelation were clearly reinforced by his understanding of nature. With Lyell in his pocket, corals and volcanoes had contradicted a popular biblical chronology. And this was a foundation on which a further scepticism was built. In February 1837 he had written to his sister Caroline (Darwin Papers, box 154):

> You tell me you do not see what is new in Sir John Herschel's idea about the chronology of the Old Testament being wrong – I have used the word chronology in dubious manner, it is not to the days of creation which he refers but to the lapse of years since the first man made his wonderful appearance on this world. As far as I know everyone has yet thought that the six thousand odd years had been the right period but Sir John thinks that a far greater number must have passed since the Chinese [and] the Caucasian languages separated from one stock.

One cannot ignore another sense in which the categories through which he interpreted nature reinforced his critique of revelation. Miracles were excluded by the pressure from a continuity of secondary causes. It was a point to which he returned in the *Autobiography:* 'the more we know of the fixed laws of nature the more incredible do miracles become'. And of the gospel writers: 'the men at that time were ignorant and credulous to a degree almost incomprehensible by us' (Barlow, 1958, p.86). This aspect of Darwin's scepticism may have come to the fore earlier than Manier suggests. An aversion to the miraculous was expressed in the notes he made while reading Paley's *Evidences*. Manier (1978, pp.70–1) has used this set of notes to claim that Darwin was less credulous than he later imagined concerning the factual basis of Paley's case. But this is an interpretation which can only be sustained if one identifies Darwin's précis of Paley's argument with what he himself believed. This is hardly a safe thing to do when the manuscript contains an interpolation in which Darwin apparently dissociated himself from Paley's position:

> Supposing Jesus to be an enthusiast:- It is extremely improbable that his enthusiasm should have taken a line so directly contrary to his own and other people's previous opinions: but waiving this there must have been a certain degree of imposture in his miracles and prophecies, and if so the foregoing arguments apply to it.[5]

Darwin is going along with Paley to a certain extent. The arguments against Christ as an impostor carry a certain weight. But they must ultimately be defective because some imposture, so Darwin believes, was necessarily bound up with his miracles. The young Darwin was already predisposed against the disruption or suspension of natural laws. His early association of miracle with a degree of imposture suggests that the relationship between Darwin's science and loss of religious conviction was more symbiotic than unidirectional. This same form of relationship can be discerned in three other domains where scientific and religious considerations had a common focus. The three foci were those of epistemology, the problem of suffering, and what, in various contexts, has been called the 'offence of the particular'.

Emma Darwin certainly thought there might be an interdependence between her husband's scientific mentality and a religious scepticism. In a well-known letter written shortly after their marriage she enquired, 'may not the habit in scientific pursuits of believing nothing till it is proved, influence your mind too much in other things which cannot be proved in the same way, and which if true are likely to be above our comprehension' (Barlow, 1958, p.236). When Darwin did vent his spleen against the apologetic thrust of natural theology, it was usually because he was taking exception to the arrogance, as he saw it, of those who considered themselves privy to God's purposes. As Moore has implied (1979, p.318) there is almost a hint of piety in the humility which he brought to bear on metaphysical and theological questions. But the important point is that there was resonance between Darwin's critique of natural theology on epistemological grounds and his affirmation of continuity between man and the animals. It was that ultimate gradation between the *mind* of man and the *mind* of a dog which he would invoke to justify an agnosticism on the pressing questions of creation and purpose. If the mind of man were only that little higher than the mind of the brutes from which it was ultimately derived, what guarantee was there that it could decipher the riddles of existence? The interdependence of the scientific and religious reasoning is in evidence as early as the second transmutation notebook: 'man in his arrogance thinks himself a great work worthy the interposition of a deity, more humble & I believe truer to consider him created from animals' (de Beer, 1960, entry 196). Mandelbaum (1958) suggests that the argument for agnosticism based on the evolution of man's mind was a later argument in Darwin's development, but the notebook entries linking gradation with a humble stance on epistemological issues indicate that the seeds of that argument may well have been germinating earlier.

Of Darwin's hypersensitivity to pain and suffering much has been written. It was Donald Fleming's thesis (1961, p.231) that Darwin rightly intuited that 'modern man would rather have senseless suffering than suffering warranted to be intelligible because willed from on high'. There was a sense, Fleming observed, in which 'he belonged, with the Mills, to a class of God-deniers who were yearning after a better God than God.' The point is that Darwin's inner sensitivity to pain, no doubt intensified by his own celebrated illness (Colp, 1977; Winslow, 1971), resonated with an image of nature in which pain and suffering were concomitants of evolution. The presence of so *much* pain and suffering in the world he once declared to be one of the strongest arguments against belief in a beneficent deity. But, he added, it accorded well with the theory of natural selection. The personal experience, the religious reasoning and the scientific perspective all interlocked. Not that Darwin deliberately selected, as Hume might have done, only the darkest features of existence for his purpose. He was prepared to acknowledge that 'if all the individuals of any species were habitually to suffer to an extreme degree they would neglect to propagate their kind, and this would be incompatible with natural selection' (Barlow, 1958, p.88).

Finally, the offence of the particular. In July 1860, when Darwin was in correspondence with Asa Gray on the very subject of design in nature, he wrote a few sentences which are more than usually revealing (Darwin, 1887, vol. 1, p.315):

> An innocent and good man stands under a tree and is killed by a flash of lightning. Do you believe (and I really should like to hear) that God *designedly* killed this man? Many or most persons do believe this; I can't and don't. If you believe so, do you believe that when a swallow snaps up a gnat that God designed that that particular swallow should snap up that particular gnat at that particular instant? I believe that the man and the gnat are in the same predicament. If the death of neither man nor gnat are designed, I see no reason to believe that their *first* birth or production should be necessarily designed.

There would seem to be evidence in that letter that Darwin's loss of conviction in a teleological system was occasioned in part by the difficulty he experienced in rationalizing particular events in providentialist terms. And his offence surely did resonate with one aspect of natural selection, where the particulars of the evolutionary process could be handed over to 'chance'. If evolution were not true then the creation of loathsome parasites, attributable to a direct expression of divine will, would be a particularity of another kind that Darwin found offensive. He could not persuade himself that 'a beneficent and omnipotent God would have designedly created the Ichneumonidae with the express intention of their feeding within the living bodies of caterpillars' (Darwin, 1887, vol. 2, pp.310–12). As a product of evolution, such devilish works were at least comprehensible. Darwin many times said that he was inclined to believe that the general trend of evolution was the result of laws, with the details left to chance – not that the notion ever really satisfied him.

Scholars have noted that Darwin's loss of a specifically Christian faith occurred about the same time that he outlawed divine activity from his biological theory. Herbert and Ospovat have concluded that it is impossible to say whether the loss of faith preceded and made possible his 'materialism', or whether it was caused or hastened by it (Ospovat, 1980, p.193). By emphasizing these various resonances between an emerging science and an emerging unbelief, I have tried to show that it does not have to be a question of which came first. The interaction could be mutual and continuous. My suggestion is that Darwin was already experiencing these resonances to some degree by the autumn of 1838. They were all steering him away from a providentialist reading of the incipient theory. One last question, therefore, remains. Was there any other event or intellectual consideration which may have helped him to perceive what he could no longer believe? My conjecture would be that there was: his engagement to Emma Wedgwood who, with her touching importunity on religious questions – and prayer in particular – compelled her fiancé to consider the extent to which he could share her religious devotion. The timing is particularly suggestive. It was in November 1838 that they were exchanging letters on the subject of religion. Emma, already aware that she was engaged to an honest doubter, already saddened by a 'fear that our opinions on the most important subjects should differ widely', was asking favours of the utmost poignancy:

> Will you do me a favour? Yes I am sure you will, it is to read our Saviour's farewell discourse to his disciples which begins at the end of the 13th Chap of John. It is so full of love to them and devotion and every beautiful feeling. It is the part of the New Testament I love best. This is a whim of mine it would give me great pleasure though I can hardly tell why. (Emma to Charles, 23 November 1838, Darwin Papers, box 204, folio 13)

It was such a letter that Charles 'read . . . over again for the fifth time' (Charles to Emma, 27 November 1838, Darwin Papers, box 210, folio 19) – such a letter that compelled him to face up squarely to the extent of his doubts – such a letter that made him 'feel as if I had been guilty of some very selfish action in obtaining such a good dear wife. With no sacrifice at all on my part . . .'. Throughout the engagement Emma wished to see Charles 'earnest on the subject', her anxieties finding expression in one of the last letters (postmarked 24 January 1839) preceding the marriage:

> I do hope that though our opinions may not agree upon all points of religion we may sympathize a good deal in our *feelings* on the subject.

In his reply of the following day, Charles avoided the subject, as he had preferred to do on earlier occasions. But he could not have avoided it in his own mind when it was coming ever closer to home.

In this chapter I have tried to clarify some of the complex relations between Darwin's science and a legacy from natural theology which, in several different senses, helped to structure it. I have also suggested that Darwin's loss of conviction in a harmonious preordained system was not simply the result of the impact of his science on his faith. The interaction took place in both directions and on different levels. To ask how these intellectual processes were related to the social changes of the day is, therefore, to ask a question with no simple answer, a question with several interlocking components.[6]

As far as the content of Darwin's theory is concerned, it is certainly possible to see in the crucial notion of intra-specific competition a reflection of the competitiveness all too apparent in a rapidly industrializing society. It is not entirely clear that Darwin was consciously influenced by any such consideration, but it is perfectly clear, as is shown by Moore's contribution to this volume, that a message of the survival of the fittest would not run short of an audience. The disappearance of natural theology from within science cannot be understood, as I have argued elsewhere (Brooke, 1979), without an analysis of the social and theological functions which design arguments had been called upon to perform. Since one of those functions had been to make scientific theories theologically acceptable, it is one of the more ironic features of the Darwinian revolution that, whilst Darwin was making biology more 'scientific', he was gradually dismantling one of the ideological supports of science itself. Since another function had been to unite the intellectual interests of clerical scientists, it is also true, as F. M. Turner (1978) has stressed, that any account of the waning of natural theology must recognize the extent to which science became a 'professional' concern in nineteenth century Britain with standards and criteria which, during Darwin's lifetime, deliberately and fairly swiftly excluded the clerical 'amateur'. Furthermore, the arguments of natural theology had often been couched in a form which presupposed analogies between a fixed socio-political order and a fixed natural order. Since Darwin lived through a period of intense political reform it would be surprising if he had not experienced additional doubts about a God-given natural order. Analysis of his political comments might yet give substance to that possibility.

NOTES

1 There is, as Ospovat shows (1980, p.182), an interesting corollary of this positive aspect of Darwin's natural theology. The attempts to find an evolutionary explanation for man's idea of God, which have sometimes been taken as evidence that Darwin was a committed agnostic by 1838, are at least open to an alternative interpretation. In Ospovat's reading, 'the problem in giving an evolutionary explanation for the existence of the idea of God was not to show how the idea of God arose even though God does not or may not exist; rather, it was to show how God, acting not directly, but through deterministic laws, has produced in men the idea of God'.

2 Darwin and Seward, 1903, vol. 1, p.192. Darwin found it less easy to cast the problem aside than he might have wished. In a letter to J. D. Hooker of 12 July 1870 (Darwin and Seward, 1903, vol.1, p.321) he agreed that 'your conclusion that all speculation about preordination is idle waste of time is the only wise one'. But he could not refrain from adding 'how difficult it is not to speculate!'. His theology was self-confessedly a 'simple muddle', but that is not the same as non-existent. Recourse to divine foresight was clearly attractive to the scientific naturalists who wished to say *something* about Providence without getting heavily involved in philosophical theology. Thus T.H. Huxley (1892, p.33) conceded that if the doctrine of Providence

is held to imply that, in some indefinitely remote past aeon, the cosmic process was set going by some entity possessed of intelligence and foresight, similar to our own in kind, however superior in degree; if, consequently, it is held that every event, not merely in our planetary speck, but in untold millions of other worlds, was foreknown before these worlds were, scientific thought, so far as I know anything about it, has nothing to say against that hypothesis.

3 One is tempted to add a third consideration more historiographical in
  kind. In his analysis of the structural role of natural theology in
  Darwin's science, Ospovat clearly recognized that the shape of natural
  theology itself had been fashioned in response to a range of social,
  political, and religious pressures from the past. But his emphasis on the
  past allowed him to side-step the problem of assessing those same kinds
  of pressure in Darwin's *present*. Indeed he saw it as an advantage of his
  methodology 'that it avoids the difficult problems of discovering the
  social, political, and religious interests of the scientist . . . and of
  correlating them directly with his scientific ideas' (1981, pp.231–3).
  With this preconception he may have been led to place undue emphasis
  on Darwin's science as the prime determinant of his religion. Thus it
  was 'presumably as a result of reflecting on the implications of natural
  selection' that Darwin came to ascribe the details of the system to
  chance (1979, p.220).
4 The philosophical issues here are extremely complex, but the admission
  of the possibility of more than one outcome from a particular
  concatenation of circumstances need not have excluded the possibility
  that each outcome and its consequences had been 'scripted'. Even
  human playwrights have been known to script alternative endings, the
  choice being determined by the toss of a coin within the play!
5 Darwin's notes on Paley's *Evidences*, Darwin Papers, box 91, folios,
  114–8, especially the passage in square brackets on the reverse side of
  115. My own reconstruction does, however, fail if this interpolation was
  not written at the same time as the rest of the notes.
6 For an introduction to the complexities see Young (1973). On specific
  connections between concepts of a division of labour and Darwin's
  articulation of his principle of divergence see Schweber (1980).

REFERENCES

Barlow, N. (ed.) (1958) *The Autobiography of Charles Darwin*, London,
  Collins.
De Beer, G. (1959) 'Darwin's Journal', *Bulletin of the British Museum
  (Natural History)*, Historical Series **2**, part 1.
De Beer, G. (1960) 'Darwin's Notebooks on transmutation of Species',
  Bulletin of the British Museum (Natural History), Historical Series, **2**,
  parts 2–5.

Bowler, P. J. (1976) *Fossils and Progress: Paleontology and the Idea of Progressive Evolution in the 19th Century*, New York, Science History Publications.

Bowler, P.J. (1977) 'Darwinism and the Argument from Design: suggestions for a Revaluation', *Journal of the History of Biology*, **10**, pp.29–43.

Brooke, J.H. (1974) 'Precursors of Darwin?', in J.H. Brooke and A. Richardson, *The Crisis of Evolution*, Milton Keynes, Open University Press, pp.5–51.

Brooke, J.H. (1977a) 'Natural Theology and the Plurality of Worlds: Observations on the Brewster-Whewell Debate', *Annals of Science*, **34**, pp.221–86.

Brooke, J.H. (1977b) 'Richard Owen, William Whewell and the "Vestiges"', *British Journal for the History of Science*, **10**, pp.132–45.

Brooke, J.H. (1979) 'The Natural Theology of the Geologists: Some Theological Strata', in L.J. Jordanova and R.S. Porter (eds), *Images of the Earth*, Chalfont St Giles, British Society for the History of Science, pp.39–64.

Brooke, J.H. (1983) 'Middle Positions', *London Review of Books*, **5** no. 13, pp.11–12.

Budd, S. (1977) *Varieties of Unbelief*, London, Heinemann

Cannon, W.F. (1961) 'The Bases of Darwin's Achievement: a Revaluation', *Victorian Studies*, **5**, pp.109–34.

Colp, R.E. (1977) *To be an Invalid: the Illness of Charles of Darwin*, Chicago, University of Chicago Press.

Corsi, P. (1980a) 'Natural Theology, the Methodology of Science, and the Question of Species in the Works of the Reverend Baden Powell', University of Oxford D. Phil. dissertation.

Corsi, P. (1980b) Essay Review of E. Manier, *The Young Darwin and his Cultural Circle, Annals of Science*, **37**, pp.673–8.

Darwin, C. Unpublished letters and papers, Cambridge University Library Archive.

Darwin, C. (1842) '*Sketch*', in G. de Beer (ed.) (1958) *Evolution by Natural Selection*, Cambridge, Cambridge Universtiy Press.

Darwin, C. (1844) '*Essay*', in G. de Beer (ed.) (1958) *Evolution by Natural Selection*, Cambridge, Cambridge University Press.

Darwin, C. (1906) *The Descent of Man*, reprint of 2nd edn, London Murray.

Darwin, F. (ed.) (1887) *The Life and Letters of Charles Darwin*, 3 vols, 3rd edn, London, Murray.

Darwin, F. and Seward, A.C. (ed) (1903), *More Letters of Charles Darwin*, 2 vols, London, Murray.

Desmond, A. (1982) *Archetypes and Ancestors: Paleontology in Victorian London*, London, Blond & Briggs.

Durant, J.R. (1977) 'The Meaning of Evolution: Post-Darwinian Debates on the Significance for Man of the Theory of Evolution, 1858–1908', University of Cambridge PhD dissertation.

Erskine, F. (1983) 'Darwin's London Years 1836–42: A Study of his Social Relationships', paper presented to the British Society for the History of Science Conference at the Royal Institution, 31 October.

Fleming, D. (1961) 'Charles Darwin, the Anaesthetic man', *Victorian Studies*, **4**, pp.219–36.

Gillespie, N.C. (1979) *Charles Darwin and the Problem of Creation*, Chicago, University of Chicago Press.

Gillispie, C.C. (1959) *Genesis and Geology*, New York, Harper.

Gruber, H.E. and Barrett, P.H. (1974) *Darwin on Man*, New York, Dutton.

Hooykaas, R. (1957) 'The Parallel between the History of the Earth and the History of the Animal World', *Archives Internationales d'Histoire des Sciences*, **10**, pp.1–18.

Hooykaas, R. (1963) *The Principle of Uniformity in Geology, Biology and Theology*, Leiden, Brill.

Hooykaas, R. (1966) 'Geological Uniformitarianism and Evolution', *Archives Internationales d'Histoire des Sciences*, **19**, pp.3–19.

Houghton, W. (1973) *The Victorian Frame of Mind*, Yale, Yale University Press.

Huxley, T.H. (1892) 'On Providence', from 'An Apologetic Irenicon', *Fortnightly Review*, **52**, pp.557–71, reproduced in N.G. Coley and V.M.D. Hall (eds) (1980) *Darwin to Einstein: Primary Sources on Science and Belief*, New York, Longman in association with the Open University Press.

Kohn, D. (1980) 'Theories to Work by: Rejected Theories, Reproduction and Darwin's Path to Natural Selection', *Studies in the History of Biology*, **4**, pp.67–170.

Limoges, C. (1970) *La Sélection Naturelle*, Paris, Presses Universitaires de France.

MacLeod, R. (1965) 'Evolutionism and Richard Owen, 1830–68', *Isis*, **56**, pp.259–80.

Mandelbaum, M. (1958) 'Darwin's Religious Views', *Journal of the History of Ideas*, **19**, pp.363–78.

Manier, E. (1978) *The Young Darwin and his Cultural Circle*, Dordrecht and Boston, Reidel.

Millhauser, M. (1959) *Just before Darwin: Robert Chambers and 'Vestiges'*, Middletown, Conn., Wesleyan University Press.

Moore, J.R. (1979) *The Post-Darwinian Controversies*, Cambridge, Cambridge University Press.

Moore, J.R. (1981) 'Creation and the Problem of Charles Darwin' *British Journal for the History of Science*, **14**, pp.189–200.

Moore, J.R. (1982) '1859 and All That: Remaking the Story of Evolution-and-Religion', in R.G. Chapman and C.T. Duval (eds), *Charles Darwin, 1809–1882: A Centennial Commemorative*, Wellington, NZ, pp.167–94.

Murphy, H.R. (1955) 'The Ethical Revolt against Christian Orthodoxy in Early Victorian England', *American Historical Review*, **60**, pp.800–17.

Oldroyd, D.R. (1980) *Darwinian Impacts*, Milton Keynes, Open University Press.

Ospovat, D. (1978) 'Perfect Adaptation and Teleological Explanation: Approaches to the Problem of the History of Life in the Mid-19th Century', *Studies in the History of Biology*, **2**, pp.35–56.

Ospovat, D. (1979) 'Darwin after Malthus', *Journal of the History of Biology*, **12**, pp.211–30.

Ospovat, D. (1980) 'God and Natural Selection: the Darwinian idea of Design', *Journal of the History of Biology*, **13**, pp.169–94.

Ospovat, D. (1981) *The Development of Darwin's Theory*, Cambridge, Cambridge University Press.

Owen, R. (1849) *On the Nature of Limbs*, London, Van Voorst.

Paley, W. (1802) *Natural Theology* (1802), Selections, edited and with an introduction by F. Ferré (1963) Indianapolis and New York, Bobbs-Merrill.

Powell Baden (1855) *Essays on the Spirit of the Inductive Philosophy, the Unity of Worlds, and the Philosophy of Creation*, London, Longman.

Richards, R.J. (1981) 'Instinct and Intelligence in British Natural Theology: Some Contributions to Darwin's Theory of the Evolution of Behaviour', *Journal of the History of Biology*, **14**, pp.193–230.

Schweber, S.S. (1977) 'The Origin of the *Origin* Revisited', *Journal of the History of Biology*, **10**, pp.229–316.

Schweber, S.S. (1979) 'The Young Darwin', *Journal of the History of Biology*, **12**, pp.175–92.

Schweber, S.S. (1980) 'Darwin and the Political Economists', *Journal of the History of Biology*, **13**, pp.195–289.

Turner, F.M. (1978) 'The Victorian Conflict between Science and Religion: A Professional Dimension', *Isis*, **69**, pp.356–76.

Vorzimmer, P.J. (1975) 'An Early Darwin Manuscript: the "Outline and Draft of 1839"' *Journal of the History of Biology*, **8**, pp.191–217.

Wilson, L.G. (ed) (1970) *Sir Charles Lyell's Scientific Journals on the Species Question*, New Haven, Yale University Press.

Winslow, J.H. (1971) *Darwin's Victorian Malady*, American Philosophical Society.

Young, R.M. (1971) 'Darwin's Metaphor: Does Nature Select?', *The Monist*, **55**, pp.442–503.

Young, R.M. (1973) 'The Historiographic and Ideological contexts of the 19th-Century Debate on Man's Place in Nature', in M. Teich and R.M. Young (eds), *Changing Perspectives in the History of Science*, London, Heinemann, pp.344–438.

3

Herbert Spencer's Henchmen:
The Evolution of Protestant Liberals
in Late Nineteenth-Century America

Jim Moore

Today we honour Darwin for devising a theory that has trium-
phantly become scientific truth. In 1982, scholars around the world
paid solemn tribute by commemorating the centenary of his death.
Collectively, their observance was like the great funeral itself, when
international dignitaries assembled to lay Darwin's body in
Westminster Abbey. The funeral pointed up the significance of the
man and his work for professional science and religious liberalism,
for family, nation, and empire (Moore, 1982). A century later
Darwin's public reputation is undiminished. But we honour
Darwin for a great deal more, for the Victorian obsequies did not
yet signify the triumph of the theory of natural selection. Since 1859
the theory had come under attack by formidable critics. Darwin
had responded by qualifying his arguments in five revised editions
of the *Origin of Species* . Meanwhile other theories of evolution were
gaining ground, and the bewildered public routinely conflated
them with Darwin's. 'Evolution' (or as philosophers say, 'evolutionary naturalism') was the popular doctrine to reckon with in natural
history, social theory, and theology. Natural selection, by contrast,
remained the subject of academic controversy well into the
twentieth century. In assessing the public impact of evolution a
century ago, we must therefore look beyond Darwin's distinctive

theoretical contribution and consider the doctrine as held by its popularizers.

Prominent among works popularizing evolution in the nineteenth century were those of the English philosopher Herbert Spencer (1820–1903). Today scarcely anyone honours Spencer; it is left to academics to debate his discredited theories. Although he devised a 'law of evolution' that was comprehensive enough to include natural selection, by the time he died this law had done its work and his reputation was being eclipsed. In 1903 the Dean of Westminster pointedly declined a request from a large number of Spencer's 'friends, admirers and disciples' that the philosopher should be buried in Westminster Abbey. Twenty years earlier it is just possible that a different result might have been obtained. For Spencer was then at the height of his popularity. His theories in biology, psychology, and sociology were gaining international recognition, especially in the United States. In 1882, a few months after Darwin's death, Spencer crossed the Atlantic to see his theories at work. It was his first and last visit to America. On the eve of his departure home an event occurred in which he personally received greater public acclaim than at any time in his life. A century later this event indicates as much about how and why Spencer influenced the American public at the end of the nineteenth century, as the Abbey funeral reveals about Darwin's social impact in mid-Victorian Britain (Hofstadter, 1955; Russett, 1976; Bannister, 1979; literature cited in Moore, 1979, p.375, nn.45–9).

I

Date: Thursday evening, 9 November 1882;
Place: Manhattan Island, New York City;
Venue: the banqueting hall, Delmonico's Restaurant;
Guests: the leaders of national life, by invitation only.

The gathering was cultivated and brilliant by American standards, the dinner elaborate and elegant. A dozen courses and as many varieties of wine made the rounds to the accompaniment of an overbearing band. Then, as blue smoke rose about the cut glass and flowers to the chandeliers, the room reverberated with sated guffaws and hurrumphs. Belts were loosened, moustaches wiped clean, and 160 middle-aged to ageing gentlemen awaited the introduction of the guest of honour.

Natural selection had brought them together, the chairman began. The room emitted a boozy laugh. Here indeed was social Darwinism incarnate. The famous sat at every table – Otis, Libbey, Newberry, Appleton, Holt, Van Nostrand, Colgate, and Peabody. The chairman, William M. Evarts, was a former Attorney General of the United States, and recently Secretary of State under the Republican President, Rutherford B. Hayes. A former Republican Treasury Secretary and now a prominent New York lawyer, Benjamin H. Bristow, was in the audience. His predecessor in the office under Presidents Lincoln and Johnson, the financier Hugh McCulloch, had sent the organizers his sincere regrets. Elihu Root, a young corporation lawyer, was also in attendance. Later he was to serve as Secretary of War in the Republican administrations of Presidents McKinley and Theodore Roosevelt. The Republican Party was, and still is, the party of American big business. Not only its leaders but also its constituency were present in force: Cyrus W. Field, the railroad and newspaper magnate, who laid the first transatlantic cable in 1858; Chauncey M. Depew, general counsel and later chairman of the Vanderbilt railroad empire; Andrew Carnegie, the Scottish–American millionaire–industrialist; bankers and philanthropists such as Morris K. Jessup and Joseph W. Drexel; and finally the editors of the Republican press, Carl Schurz of the New York *Evening Post*, Charles A. Dana of the New York *Sun*, and Edwin L. Godkin of *The Nation*.[1]

The chairman, Evarts, proceeded with an effusive introduction. The audience interspersed laughter and applause. At length, turning to the distinguished guest, Evarts praised him for the 'penetrating intelligence' and 'thorough insight' with which he had analysed the social world, 'the world worth knowing, the world worth speaking of, the world worth planning for, the world worth working for'. His sociology was 'practical', 'benevolent', and 'reverent'. 'It aims at the highest results in virtue; . . . it treats evil not as eternal, but as evanescent, and . . . it expects to arrive at what is sought through faith in the millennium – that condition of affairs in which there is the highest morality and the greatest happiness.' 'You will please fill your glasses', the chairman concluded, 'while I propose *The health of our guest, Herbert Spencer*' (Youmans, 1883, pp.25–8).

Hearty applause followed, mingled with cheers and waving of handkerchiefs. It was all that Spencer feared. He had come to the United States strictly for a holiday. He had travelled for nearly three months, floating contemplatively about the country, as was his custom, avoiding unnecessary conversation (especially with reporters), grumbling at the service in hotels, and generally finding things, like Niagara Falls, 'much what I had expected'. Cleveland, Pittsburgh, Washington, Baltimore, Philadelphia, New York, Boston, then back to New York – the journey had been arduous for a man in his sixties. But it was the last leg, Spencer later reported, that had left him 'in a condition worse than I had been for six-and-twenty years'. Travel-weariness compounded by loss of sleep and the prospect of a rare public appearance had reactivated a persistent nervous debility, and his manic-depressive cycle had entered its latter phase. Now his usual ear-muffs could not shut out the excitement of unwanted conversation, he could not lie down, and his servant could not show the offending company to the door. Spencer steeled himself, dreading the dyspepsia and insomnia that would ensue. He raised his slender five feet ten inches to the podium and grimly chided the captains of industry for overwork. A homily on the 'gospel of relaxation' was, he admitted, 'a very unconventional after-dinner speech'. But at least it evinced his his consistent virtue of shunning pretence and cant (Spencer, 1904, vol 2, pp.390–407; Youmans, 1883, p.35).

II

Petty, monotonous, self-pitying, cantankerous – Spencer was the Eeyore of Victorian science. His life did not exemplify the sociology for which he was being honoured. That was left to its devotees. Most of them lived in the United States, and Spencer had been gracious enough in previous weeks to accept their hospitality. He stayed with Carnegie in the Alleghenies and toured his ironworks at Pittsburgh. He visited John W. Garrett, president of the Baltimore and Ohio Railroad, and accompanied him in his private steamer on

Chesapeake Bay. He inspected the Baldwin locomotive works at Philadelphia and made an excursion on the Delaware River by courtesy of G.B. Roberts, president of the Pennsylvania Railroad. All this impressed Spencer deeply – the vastness of America, its entrepreneurial spirit, its burgeoning material wealth. 'Clearly', he later reflected, 'at the present rate of progress . . . the United States will very soon be by far the most powerful nation in the world' (Spencer, 1904, vol. 2, pp.396–402).

What was the sociology behind this auspicious, or rather audacious, prediction? Roughly speaking, it was the political economy of English middle-class dissent with an evolutionary twist. As a young man in the 1840s Spencer abandoned the Christianity of his Wesleyan and Unitarian relatives and sought a basis in natural law, rather than divine revelation, for its social doctrines. By the 1850s he had conceived of Nature, including human nature and society, as a lawful and orderly system of rewards and punishments that inevitably promoted material and moral progress. Poverty, according to Spencer, resulted from individual improvidence; wealth was thus a sign of individual worth. The distribution of earthly goods followed directly from the laws of organic individuals. Progress through social conflict, on the other hand, followed from the laws of the 'social organism'. Spencer never resolved the discrepancy in his sociology between individual-ism and organicism. On the one hand he advocated individual freedom and *laissez-faire,* on the other he insisted that natural human inequality and free economic competition result in the inevitable growth of a highly differentiated but functionally integrated industrial society in which personal autonomy is freely sacrificed for the common good (Moore *et al.*, 1981, pp.6–15; Hearnshaw, 1950, pp.80–2; Wiltshire, 1978, pp.235–42). But this equivocation did not deter him from making the laws of individual and collective morality the subject of his life's work. Over a period of 40 years, beginning in 1860, he published a 10-volume *System of Synthetic Philosophy* in which ethics was grounded in sociology, sociology in psychology, psychology in biology, and biology in metaphysical first principles that were overtly religious. Spencer believed that the whole of evolution was the progressive manifest-ation of an Unknowable Power that makes for righteousness. This

Power, which is the ultimate object of scientific enquiry, he declared in 1884, 'stands towards our general conception of things, in substantially the same relation as does the Creative Power asserted by Theology' (Spencer, 1884).

Spencer's sociology had numerous appeals. It was scientific. it was religious. It was necessitarian. It was optimistic. It was systematic and comprehensive. It offered, in short, a world-view possessing marked affinities with other more explicitly theological creeds. The so-called 'robber barons', who treated the American subcontinent as one vast 'enterprise zone', were religiously high-minded men, and some commended Spencer's sociology for its justification of industrial competition as the moral equivalent of war. Carnegie's classic statement of the 'gospel of wealth' in 1889 is perhaps the best evidence of this (White, 1979; cf. Josephson, 1934, pp.317ff; Fine, 1964, pp.96–125; Bridges, 1960, pp.138–52). But the industrialists and Republican politicians who attended the farewell banquet at Delmonico's were neither the most influential devotees of Spencer's sociology nor the only defenders of American captitalism in the Gilded Age. In the late 1870s, as many historians have shown, the Protestant churches 'presented a massive, almost unbroken front in . . . defense of the social status quo' (May, 1949, p.91; Hudson, 1965, p.302). And no industrialist or politician of the period exercised a greater moral sway than the churches' leading spokesmen. Five liberal Protestants who found aspects of Spencer's creed congenial were present at the banquet. By considering briefly their careers and beliefs I want to illustrate the changing ideological function of evolution in late nineteenth-century America. This will lead in conclusion to some general remarks on the role of liberal Protestant theology in mediating between science and society.

III

M.J. Savage (1841–1918) and John Fiske (1842–1901) were Spencer's chief spokesmen on the theological left wing of American Protestantism. Both had been brought up in the narrow ways of New England Congregationalism. Both had turned against its Calvinistic theology in the 1860s and embraced the new Spencerian creed. Savage had been a pastor and missionary in the West, Fiske a tearaway at Harvard with prodigious scholarly promise. By 1874 both were firmly established in New England as publicists and preachers of evolution. Savage ministered at the Church of the Unity in Boston. His published sermons circulated widely, and by 1882 he had collected them in two books, *The Religion of Evolution* (1876) and *The Morals of Evolution* (1880), the latter of which was dedicated 'by permission to Herbert Spencer and his friend, John Fiske'. Fiske, too, had begun collecting and publishing his lectures on evolution. Having failed in an academic career, he had taken to the lecture circuit to make a living and satisfy an extravagant *goût de bon vivre*. He became popular among religious free-thinkers whose views, like his own, were shaped by the Transcendentalist rejection of orthodox Calvinism (Moore, 1975, pp.440–54; literature cited in Moore, 1979, pp.383–4, nn. 40–5). But after the national centenary in 1876, Fiske discovered the non-sectarian market for evolutionary interpretations of American history; and soon, among genteel folk of every creed, he became the foremost authority for believing that America's 'manifest destiny', led by a New England elite, was to advance the evolutionary process by which the 'Anglo-Saxon' race would eventually bring peace and prosperity to the entire globe (Berman, 1961, pp.125–7, 219).

Following Spencer's homily at the banquet there were several speeches. Fiske made his remarks after the chairman's toast: 'Evolution and religion: that which perfects humanity can not destroy religion'. As one who had drawn out the sociological implications of Spencer's doctrine of evolution even before Spencer did, Fiske now stressed the moral basis for their application in the nation's future. Natural forces, he declared, are moral forces; and the lofty moral sentiments which, at length, these 'subtle and exquisite forces' have caused to evolve in history have a 'value proportionate to the enormous effort' required for their production. 'Human responsibility is made more strict and solemn than ever, when the eternal Power that lives in every event of the universe is thus seen to be in the deepest possible sense the author of the moral law that should guide our lives, and in obedience to which lies our only guarantee of the happiness which is incorruptible' (Youmans, 1883, pp.56,57).

The moral 'pursuit of happiness', a doctrine integral to the

United States' Constitution, was a belief that Savage fully shared, although he did not speak publicly at the farewell banquet. Stressing the slowness of moral progress, as well as its naturalness, he pointed up the 'futility' of legislative attempts at social reform. 'The most that laws can do', he stated in a sermon, 'is to help on suitable conditions for the development of character' (1876, pp.89–90). These conditions lay altogether beyond human control in the cosmic process described by the *Synthetic Philosophy's* famous 'law' of evolution. Savage waxed lyrical when he pondered Spencer's law (1884, p.68, emphasis in original).

> Hear me, O jarring peoples! I am one,
>   In deep abysses or in heavens high:
> One law swings the long circuit of the sun,
>   And by one law the new-fledged birdlings fly.
> Religion binds thee to my law divine,
>   And this law binds thee to thy fellow-man.
> *'Tis one law in the market, at the shrine:*
>   *Earth, heaven – see! they're built upon one plan.*

Elsewhere Savage remarked, 'I shall be greatly mistaken if the radicalism of evolution does not prove to be the grandest of all conservatism in society and politics not only, but in religion as well' (Savage, 1876, p.46).

Savage was not mistaken, although the religious conservatism to which he referred proved to be ideological rather than theological. The reason for this was simply Henry Ward Beecher (1818–1887), the most prominent clergyman in American evangelical Protestantism between 1850 and 1880, and possibly the most famous and influential American preacher of the century. If it had been known that God were dead, a newspaper of the time observed, Beecher would have been unanimously elected by the American people to fill his place. In far-off England the Darwin family thought this comment extremely funny, but they little realized how nearly true it was (Fiske, 1894, p.276). Henry Ward Beecher was the nineteenth-century equivalent of today's electronic man-of-God, the Robert Schuller or Jerry Falwell of the Gilded Age. Since 1847 he had preached mightily to the throbbing human heart from Plymouth Congregational Church in Brooklyn, New York. He had overthrown his father's crusading Calvinism and embraced phrenology, craniology, thermodynamics, homeopathy, mesmerism, and evolution. He had joined his sister, Harriet Beecher Stowe, in condemning slavery and firing Northern patriotism during the Civil War. He had invested $15,000 in the war-profiteer Jay Cooke's notorious Northern Pacific Railroad, and had advertised the company's virtues in his very own 'family' paper, which enjoyed the largest circulation of any religious periodical in America (McLoughlin, 1970, p.46; Josephson, 1934, p.95; Brown, 1953, ch.6). He had delivered countless sermons over the years to his wealthy suburban congregation, and these, together with his twice weekly lectures, had been published in scores of newspapers across the nation, reaching tens of thousands of troubled Victorian minds. These, like his parishioners, 'would never have read Darwin or Spencer or Huxley, or understood a word of it if they had. But they came to hear Henry Ward Beecher and went away uplifted and rejoiced, with a new hope in life' (Hibben, 1942, p.310; Clark; 1978).

Beecher's view of society was a carbon copy of Spencer's, embellished with Calvinist elitism, federalist class-consciousness, and transcendentalist hero-worship. God had intended 'the great to be great, and the little to be little'; the 'American doctrine' of government was simply 'hands off', and so forth (quoted in Fine, 1964, pp.119, 120). Everything that happened in Beecher's world happened according to 'mystic yet natural laws of growth and love, laws of development and civilization, laws of elevation and perfection'. Any contradictions, explains William McLoughlin, were resolved by the liberal assumption 'that God is in control of it all, that He is ever present and working out His will in Nature and in history, that He is beneficent and seeks man's welfare, redemption, and reunion with Him'. 'Beecher's social and economic conservatism', McLoughlin continues, 'was merely the obverse side of his religious liberalism. For subjectivism in reverse was rugged individualism; science in reverse was intellectual elitism; progress was survival of the fittest; mystical experiences in art, culture, and Nature were aspects of social control. Only the highly endowed, the refined, the gifted were able to commune with God directly; only the intelligent could fathom the secret laws of the universe. The rest of mankind existed on lower rungs of the Great Chain of Being' (McLoughlin, 1970, pp.138–9, 256).

Now Spencer was Beecher's intelligent man *par excellence,* and this is why the preacher answered the chairman's toast to 'evolution and religion' by boasting that he could not reconcile Spencer's ideas with those of Augustine and Calvin, that the morality taught in the *Synthetic Philosophy* was 'entirely in agreement with the great morality taught in the sacred Scriptures', and that the doctrine of evolution was 'going to revolutionize theology from one end to the other' (Youmans, 1883, pp.58, 60, 61). Slowly, masterfully, Beecher roused his audience and himself, until at last, in an apoplectic flush, he proclaimed his emancipation from New England orthodoxy into the brave new world of theological liberalism and American free enterprise.

> I began to read Mr. Spencer's works more than twenty years ago. They have been meat and bread to me. They have helped me through a great many difficulties. I desire to own my obligation personally to him, and to say that if I had the fortune of a millionaire, and I should pour all my gold at his feet, it would be no sort of compensation compared to that which I believe I owe him; for whoever gives me a thought that dispels the darkness that hangs over the most precious secrets of life, whoever gives me confidence in the destiny of my fellow-men, whoever gives me a clearer stand-point from which I can look to the great silent One, and hear him even in half, and believe in him, not by the tests of physical science, but by moral intuition – whoever gives that power is more to me than even my father and my mother; they gave me an outward and a physical life, but these others emancipate that life from superstition, from fears, and from thralls, and make me a citizen of the universe. (Youmans, 1883, p.67)

Again the tycoons and other dignitaries applauded. It was 'entirely fitting', a biographer later jibed, that on this occasion, at Delmonico's, in 1882, 'Henry Ward Beecher should stand forth as the type of what America had to offer in the intellectual field' (Hibben, 1942, p.299). This would have been a fairer assessment, perhaps, if the intellectual field had been confined to the exponents of evangelical liberalism.

IV

Two other clergymen attended the banquet. Like Savage, neither spoke publicly, but their presence marked a sea change in American Protestantism, and thus in American society. Since 1873 the economy had wallowed in recession. Real wages fell some 25 per cent over the decade, and in 1877 a national railroad strike brought pitched battles to many cities, raising fears of anarchy and imminent revolution. The Knights of Labor, a militant organization inclined towards socialism, was increasingly active in this period. After the 'panic of 1884' its membership reached over half a million. No longer could the plight of working people be ignored. Never had the social order been at greater risk. By the time of Spencer's farewell banquet the conservatism of Savage, Fiske, and Beecher had begun to look both politically and religiously misguided. Doing nothing, or waiting for nature to take its course, was the wrong approach to curing society's ills. The right approach to social reform would have to be grounded, not in an individualistic sociology, but in an organic one. The solidarity of society, the interdependence of its members, the mutuality of their interests – here was the basis for a 'social gospel' that would mobilize the churches' massive power and resources behind a progressive industrial order. Two preachers of this new gospel were present at Delmonico's to receive from Spencer himself, as it were, a scientific legacy to invest.

Richard Heber Newton (1840–1914), the rector of All Souls in New York City, was the foremost liberal clergyman in the Protestant Episcopal Church. He had gone on record six years earlier, in *The Morals of Trade* (1876), in saying that the Church was responsible for improving the business ethics of its parishioners and that ministers, accordingly, should be trained in social science. Although he repudiated the sociology of *laissez-faire*, Newton had the 'profoundest respect' for Spencer's 'abilities and character'. Indeed, both of them foresaw (in Newton's words) 'no other basis for real religion than the truths science and philosophy yield', truths that 'turn in action into the forces of social virtue'. The measure of social virtue Newton called human 'brotherhood'.

Human brotherhood would only gradually be realized through the growth of the Kingdom of God, a universal cooperative common- wealth, he told the US Senate Committee on Education and Labor in 1885, that would be fostered best when the state's first concern was 'to see her citizens healthful, vigorous, wealth-producing factors (Hopkins, 1967, p.38; Youmans, 1883, p.88; quoted in Fine, 1964, p.183). The state's gender here notwithstanding, for Newton and other Protestant liberals the governing analogy of social relations was the patriarchal family. God the Father would bring about the brotherhood of man through the agency of his Son, immanent in the ministrations of a paternalistic Christian state (Fishburn, 1982).

In 1885 Newton became a charter member of the American Economic Association, a body devoted to economics as an objective science and to the state as an agent of the general welfare. Another charter member was the Reverend Lyman Abbott (1835–1922), editor-in-chief of Beecher's family paper, the *Christian Union,* and in 1888 his successor at Plymouth Congregational Church. Abbott was a derivative thinker, a facile writer, and by the turn of the century America's outstanding representative of theological liberal- ism. He honoured Spencer by attending the farewell banquet, no doubt, because the philosopher had assisted his liberation from Calvinist orthodoxy by enabling him to see how a 'New Theology' could be 'evolved out of the Old' (Abbott, 1892, p.134; Abbott, 1915, pp.449–50, 458). With added insights from Fiske, and from Spencer's most popular British disciple, Henry Drummond (1851–97), Abbott conceived of evolution as continuous prog- ressive change, 'from a lower to a higher condition, from a simpler to a more complex condition', by means of one Resident Force, or God, working according to laws of 'growth'. In *The Theology of an Evolutionist* (1897) he wrote (p.20):

> As God makes the oak out of the acorn, and the rose out of the cutting, and the man out of the babe, and the nation out of the colony, and the literature out of the alphabet, so God has made all things by the development of higher from lower forms . . . God is never a manufacturer, but always does His work by growth processes.

From such considerations, Abbott concluded in *The Evolution of Christianity* (1892) that the laws 'of political economy . . . of industry, of politics', are not merely enacted statutes. 'These laws are the laws of man because they are the laws of God . . . They are . . . inviolable because they are inherent in the nature of man and inherent in the nature of God'. 'So absolute and so inviolable' were the laws of social growth that Abbott was prepared to admit, 'if we could conceive that God himself were dethroned and ceased to exist, law would still go on throughout eternity, unless nature itself were dissolved into anarchy' (1892, pp.114, 115; cf. Savage, 1887, p.7).

Anarchy would not rear its ugly head if Abbott had anything to say. Mindful of the treacherous times, he abandoned Beecher's social conservatism and in the autumn of 1882 began to redirect the *Christian Union's* editorial policy away from its traditional Republicanism towards an independent stance. During the 1880s and 1880s, when there were more than 14,000 strikes and lock-outs affecting over four million workers, Abbott argued editorially that the ideal of 'industrial democracy' could be gradually achieved by means of compulsory arbitration, profit-sharing, and public regulation of enterprise. So successful were his exposures of employers' abuses, not to mention his pleas for the 'golden mean' in labour disputes, that a prominent socialist is reported to have said that the *Christian Union* did 'more to defeat radicalism than all the other religious papers combined' (Brown, 1953, pp.102, 109). What sustained Abbott's self-confidence throughout this period was an 'optimistic faith in man', a faith based on 'faith in God the All-Father', the 'infinite and Eternal Energy' of Spencer's creed. Government, he believed, was undergoing a man-made 'transition', or growth, from 'Paternalism', through 'Individualism', to 'Fraternalism'. And, quoting T.H. Huxley, Abbott urged that 'each man who enters into the enjoyment of the advantages of a polity shall be mindful of his debt to those who have laboriously constructed it, and shall take heed that no act of his weakens the fabric in which he has been permitted to live'. Industrial peace would come only through the final triumph of these doctrines of 'social and organic Christianity' (Abbott, 1892, p.188; Abbott, 1897, p.97; Brown, 1953, p.103).

V

For half a century after Spencer's departure from the United States, organicism was integral to the liberal Protestant theodicy of industrial society. The doctrine did not always come immediately from Spencer, to be sure. Organicism was rife in German academic sociology and political theory. Perhaps as many Protestant intellectuals imported it from this source as imbibed it at second hand from the functionalist social scientists in their own country who took inspiration from the *Synthetic Philosophy* (Coker, 1910; Manuel, 1972; Greene, 1981; Phillips, 1970; Young, 1981; Saccaro-Battisti, 1983). But there can be little doubt that many of the most influential spokesmen for Protestant liberalism in the period were captivated by an evolutionary and biologistic vision of a prog-ressive social order, a vision that owed more, directly or indirectly, to Spencer's philosophy than to any other single source.

Take, for instance, two of the greatest prophets of the social gospel, Richard T. Ely (1854–1943) and Washington Gladden (1836–1918). Like Newton and Abbott, both were charter members of the American Economic Association. Ely, an Episcopal layman, studied economics in Germany and became professor of political economy in the University of Wisconsin. He published numerous popular works, including *Studies in the Evolution of Industrial Society* (1903). The book begins with Spencer's premise that human society is the 'highest form of life' and, as such, it naturally evolves toward greater 'complexity and coherence'. Industrial society in America, the most advanced form of the 'social organism', manifests the complex interdependence of social classes. It has developed over many centuries and is thus 'the scientific alternative of socialism'. Any future reforms, Ely concluded, should be introduced at a rate commensurate with the proven pace of 'growth' (1903, pp.7, 9, 469).

Gladden, an activist congregational minister in Columbus, Ohio, put the same conviction to work by offering himself as an 'impartial' mediator in industrial disputes. Spencer's interpreters, Fiske and Drummond, had shown him that the basic doctrines of Christianity could be verified inductively, and in a book signifi-cantly entitled *Ruling Ideas of the Present Age* (1895) he maintained as theological truth that social relations were not contractual in character but 'vital and organic' (p.285). Love was the 'organic law' by which these relations would be transformed into the Kingdom of God.

> This kingdom that we find, here on the earth, steadily widening its dominion; growing as the dawn grows toward the perfect day that is not yet; coming as the summer comes, from the time when the first bluebird chirps upon the paling and the first greenness glints through the dead-brown grasses on the sunny bank, to 'the high tide of the year' when the roses of June are blowing and the birds are singing full chorus – this kingdom is itself a mighty witness of a Power that makes for righteousness, of a God whose name is Love. (Gladden, 1890, pp.228, 243)

Gladden's 'a priori assumption of the harmony and organic unity of society', writes his biographer, 'was almost as rigid as the laws of the laissez faire economists that he rejected'. Little wonder, then, that he was often subjected to recriminations from employers and workers alike (Dorn, 1967, pp.170–1, 220).

But it would be wrong to conclude from this that social organicism was a neutral doctrine, neither more nor less friendly to capital than to labour. As a theodicy the doctrine served, like all theodicies, to justify the ways of God and men to humankind. Spencer and his liberal Protestant henchmen were brought up in cultures massively influenced by a system of belief in the eternal transcendence, boundless power, and absolute causality of God; in the innate depravity and moral unworthiness of human creatures; in the sovereign predestination by God of some to salvation and others to eternal damnation; and in the beneficient necessity of poverty, social and sexual inequality, and a hierarchical division of labour. What remained of this Calvinist system after the Victorian revolt against the doctrines of depravity and perdition, together with their basis in an infallible Bible, were beliefs that could none the less be inferred from or applied to 'Nature' as the revelation of God: transcendent power, lawful operation, moral purpose, and the promise of future perfection to compensate for present social evil (Peel, 1971, pp.102–11).

Liberal Christians and unbelievers alike in the later nineteenth century praised Calvinism for giving 'a ground for and a sanctity to law, in its presentation of the divine Lawgiver', for testifying to 'the nature and origin of the laws by which mankind are governed' (Abbott, 1892, p.92; Froude, 1871, p.59; cf. Moore *et al.*, 1981, pp.15, 23–5). And in the *Synthetic Philosophy*, it may be argued, the naturalization of this theology achieved an appropriately grand and rigorous expression. The 'hardness of life' in Spencer's world, 'the impossibility of finding easy solutions for human ills, . . . the necessity of labor and self-denial and the inevitability of suffering' – all this, according to Richard Hofstadter, amounted to 'a kind of naturalistic Calvinism in which man's relation to nature is as hard and demanding as man's relation to God under the Calvinistic system' (1955, p.10). This, I suggest, goes a long way towards explaining the affinity between Spencer and his American henchmen, former Calvinists that many of them were. For in a world of bewildering change his sociology furnished a systematic and transcendental justification, as Calvinism had, for law and order, and hope.

The liberal theologian who most clearly understood social organicism as a theodicy was, ironically, perhaps the one least directly influenced by Spencer. Walter Rauschenbusch (1861–1918), a second-generation German-American who taught in the Baptist seminary at Rochester, New York, had been educated in German theological faculties. His own organic view of the Kingdom may have owed as much to his professors there as to the Harvard idealist philosopher Josiah Royce, whose organicism derived from the German psychologist Wilhelm Wundt. In his last book, *A Theology for the Social Gospel* (1917), written during the First World War, Rauschenbusch confronted the problem of human suffering:

The idea of solidarity, when once understood, acts as a theodicy. None of us would want a world without organic community of life, any more than we would want a world without gravitation. The fact that a careless boy falls downstairs does not condemn gravitation, nor does the existence of evil community life condemn God who constituted us social beings. The innocent suffering of great groups through social solidarity simply brings home to us that the tolerance of social injustice is an intolerable evil. The great sin of men is to resist the reformation of predatory society. We do not want God to be charged with that attitude. A conception of God which describes him as sanctioning the present social order and utilizing it in order to sanctify its victims through their suffering, without striving for its overthrow, is repugnant to our moral sense. (pp.183–4)

So far, then, Rauschenbusch puts social organicism on a par with gravitation, implying that people will occasionally fall foul of the order of nature through no fault of their own. He adds, however, that society is constituted organically, *so that* as innocent people fall foul of it, others should be motivated to eliminate the social injustice, which God either cannot, or will not, or merely strives to remove. This is obviously a pretty weak theodicy, along the lines of 'let us do evil that good may come'. But Rauschenbusch must be allowed to continue.

Both the Old Testament and the New Testament characterizations of God's righteousness assure us that he hates with steadfast hatred just such practices as modern communities tolerate and promote. If we can trust the Bible, God is against capitalism, its methods, spirit, and results. The bourgeois theologians have misrepresented our revolutionary God. God is for the Kingdom of God, and his Kingdom does not mean injustice and the perpetuation of innocent suffering. The best theodicy for modern needs is to make this very clear. (p.184)

The revolutionary overthrow of capitalism – all well and good. But since when was social organicism the 'best theodicy' for achieving it?

Rauschenbusch might have known better. From the *Synthetic Philosophy* right through the writings of the Protestant liberals, social organicism had appeared as an adjustive, palliative, and gradualist ideology (Rauschenbusch, 1907, pp.421–2; 1916, pp.58–9, 76; 1917, pp.70–1, 165). It was, indeed, the ideology of a much broader 'technocratic reform movement' at the turn of the century, a movement of secular humanitarians and intellectuals, as well as clergymen, who addressed the conflict between monopoly capital and organized labour with calls for the social regulation of economic life. Harmonious interaction, slow growth, gradual adaptation and improvement – these, after all, were the methods of evolution as well as of God. Protestant liberals, it might be said, were only the 'praying part of Progressivism' (Gedicks, 1975; Hopkins, 1967, pp.318–27; Ahlstrom, 1972, pp.796–804; cf. Noble, 1958).

There is another reason for thinking that Rauschenbusch might have known better than to propose social organicism as a theodicy for revolutionary social change. Six years had not yet passed since his own denomination, the Northern Baptist Convention, adopted under his influence and leadership a social creed that stipulated 'the gaining of wealth by Christian methods and principles, and the holding of wealth as a social trust; the discouragement of the immoderate desire for wealth, and the exaltation of man as the end and standard of industrial activity'. This creed was immediately welcomed and acclaimed by the denomination's leading layman, John D. Rockefeller, Jr (Sharpe, 1942, pp.403–4). Rockefeller's father had founded a great Baptist institution, the University of Chicago, and had endowed it with 35 million dollars. By the time of the First World War the Chicago Divinity School had become the mecca of 'scientific modernism' in American Protestant theology.

The younger Rockefeller enriched and expanded his father's religious enterprises. In 1913 he became the first president of the Rockefeller Foundation, one objective of which was the promotion of Christian ethics and Christian civilization throughout the world (R.B. Fosdick, 1952, p.29). The Rockefeller family's oil money flowed through the Foundation, and spilled more directly, into numerous selected charitable, missionary, and religious research projects, including the Federal Council of Churches.[2] A 'conspiracy of silence' has surrounded many of these dealings until quite recently – Rauschenbusch is thus partly absolved – but it now seems likely that the younger Rockefeller was intent on promoting the social ideals of Protestant liberalism on an unprecedented and breathtaking scale. His dream, for which he sought 50 to 100 million dollars from his father, was to 'administratively consolidate the denominations along the lines of big business' by means of an organization called the Interchurch World Movement. Through more efficient conduct of the churches' domestic and foreign ministries he proposed that the Interchurch should advance a practical Christianity of voluntary social welfare that would 'restore class harmony within global capitalism'. Rockefeller, who saw the growth of a business like the pruning of the American Beauty rose, likewise saw the realization of his dream as an 'evolutionary unfolding of God's love in Christ, "leading the human race to the higher sphere of health and happiness and unselfish service which I believe to be the good for which we should strive"' (Harvey, 1982, pp.201–4).

The Interchurch World Movement collapsed in 1920, suffocated in the cloud of suspicion and distrust that settled over America after the Great War. In 1921 a board member of the Rockefeller Foundation, the Reverend Harry Emerson Fosdick, tendered his resignation to make way for his brother Raymond, who later falsified Rockefeller's dealings with the Interchurch. In May 1922 Harry Emerson Fosdick preached a sermon in New York City entitled 'Shall the Fundamentalists Win?'. It was this sermon that precipitated the famous controversy between those who rejected evolution and emphasized Christianity as a mode of personal salvation, and those who accepted evolution as the basis for the harmonious social relations they believed were essential to industrial progress without revolution (Harvey, 1982, pp.205–9; H.E. Fosdick, 1957, chs 7 and 8). In 1924, as Fosdick was being hounded from his Presbyterian pulpit by the Fundamentalists in his denomination, Rockefeller invited him to become the minister of his own Park Avenue Baptist Church, in 'one of the swankiest residential areas' of Manhattan. Fosdick regretfully declined. Then, he later recalled (1957, p.178),

> Mr Rockefeller asked why, and I answered: 'Because you are too wealthy, and I do not want to be known as the pastor of the richest man in the country'. Dead silence followed, and then he said: 'I like your frankness, but do you think that more people will criticize you on account of my wealth, than will criticize me on account of your theology?'

Both men laughed. Fosdick gave in. Within six years Rockefeller had built him a national pulpit, the famous Riverside Church in Morningside Heights. There Fosdick remained until 1946, America's 'most influential Protestant preacher' (Ahlstrom, 1972, p.911).

Over the west portal of Riverside Church, with Christ triumphant above the doorway, stands a series of sculptures representing famous philosophers, scientists, and religious leaders. One of them is Darwin. Spencer does not appear. When Einstein visited in 1930 and found his image there, he exclaimed, 'that could not have happened anywhere except in America' (H.E. Fosdick, 1957, p.192). He was wrong. Darwin's gravestone lies in the pavement of Westminster Abbey; nearby on a wall the bearded patriarch peers from a memorial bas-relief. No memorial to Spencer, however, is to be found. There are several ironies in this iconography, not least that a renegade ordinand and renowned infidel such as Darwin should be commemorated in the fabric of churches. The sculptures in London and New York were erected when it was by no means certain that the theory for which we honour Darwin today would prove a triumphant success. And the philosopher who so largely inspired the quest of Protestant liberals in America for a harmonious, organically united, and progressive social order is not honoured in the noblest monument to the material and ideological success of their tradition, the Riverside Church. Had Spencer lived to see the sculptures above the west portal, no doubt he would have grumbled in his usual way about an untutored public conflating his views with those of Darwin.

Whatever Spencer might have said, those with hindsight cannot make the mistake of supposing that Protestant liberals in the twentieth century failed to distinguish the relative merits of Darwin's and Spencer's achievements. One hundred years ago this failure may have been commonplace – some liberals even ranked Spencer above Darwin as an evolutionist – but with the decline of belief in progress after the First World War, accompanied by the growing predominance in biology of Darwinian over Lamarckian theories of development (ie theories based on selection over those based on the inheritance of acquired characteristics), Spencer's sociology lost whatever status it had enjoyed as a scientific orthodoxy. The high tide of evolutionary optimism receded as rapidly as the Western powers undermined Spencer's carefully drawn contrast between militant and industrial societies. Protestant liberals who had swum in the ideological mainstream found themselves stranded, like beached whales, on the shoals of intractable human conflict. 'Many of the present difficulties of liberalism', wrote an astute observer on the eve of the Second World War, 'are explainable by the fact that in the nineteenth century special theories of development were accepted as final which have later had doubt thrown upon them or have been rejected altogether' (Williams, 1941, p.158).

It was for this reason, primarily, rather than because natural selection had been vindicated, that Protestant liberals in the early twentieth century made an icon of Darwin. He, unlike Spencer, still cut the figure of the humble, hard-working seeker after truth, the self-image of the modern scientist. And this time history was on their side. Between 1930 and 1960 Darwin's reputation as a theoretician was so completely rehabilitated that in 1964 a leading zoologist could write, 'The evolutionist today is closer to the Darwin of 1859 than at any period in the last 100 years' (Mayr, 1972, Introduction, p.viii). Two decades have passed, and the theory of natural selection has gone from strength to strength. Indeed, E.O. Wilson has recently proposed to extend the so-called 'neo-Darwinian synthesis' to include the social sciences and the humanities. *Sociobiology: The New Synthesis* (1975) is the title of his epoch-making book, a work that essays to investigate 'the biological basis of all social behaviour' in a manner redolent of Spencer's *Synthetic Philosophy*. Like Spencer among his religious interpreters at Delmonico's in 1882, Wilson appeared in 1979 at the 26th Summer Conference of the Institute of Religion in an Age of Science, held at Star Island, New Hampshire. In a modest paper entitled 'The Relation of Science to Theology' he offered liberal theologians a junior partnership in the advance of 'scientific materialism' through the insights of sociobiology. 'Liberal theology', he stated, 'can serve as a buffer', a buffer between sociobiological expertise on the one hand, and, on the other, 'one of the unmitigated evils of the world, . . . fundamentalist religion'. In contact with sociobiology, liberal theology, together with the humanities, 'will evolve into something new', enriched rather than pauperized by 'the stringencies of scientific materialism' (Wilson, 1980).

How long history will stay on the side of Protestant liberals is anyone's guess. Certainly their tradition has proven its malleability under the impact of scientific change, from Spencer's day to this. Already some liberals have been willing to let sociobiology define human values and set limits to human nature (e.g. Hefner, 1981; Peacocke, 1979). Perhaps in the future we may look to them and their colleagues for guidance as to the evolutionary constraints set by God on social aspirations under late capitalism. 'Scientific materialism' need not be radical, or even anti-theistic, after all. Many others, however, will remain unwilling to leave questions of human values to be settled by men who, as a world elite, have so largely failed to settle the basic issue of the survival of the human race. Fundamentalists, ecologists, feminists, Marxists – whatever they may be called – these dissenters will continue to seek a basis for human values transcending the present realities that society experiences as 'natural'. True religion for them consists in being neither the junior partners of evolutionists nor their henchmen, but in struggling together to build the New Jerusalem whose creator is God.

NOTES

1 My remarks are based on a preliminary analysis of the proceedings, speeches, letters, and list of subscribers contained in [Youmans], 1983. A handful of naturalists and physicians attended the banquet, as well as other cultural leaders.
2 Not all Protestant liberals approved of this. For example, Gladden preached against Rockefeller's 'tainted money' (Dorn, 1967, pp.264–7).

REFERENCES

Abbott, L. (1892) *The Evolution of Christianity,* Boston, Houghton, Mifflin Co.

Abbott, L. (1897) *The Theology of an Evolutionist,* Boston, Houghton, Mifflin Co.

Abbott, L. (1915) *Reminiscences,* Boston, Houghton, Mifflin & Co.

Ahlstrom, S.E. (1972) *A Religious History of the American People,* New Haven, Yale University Press.

Bannister, R.C. (1979) *Social Darwinism: Science and Myth in Anglo-American Social Thought,* Philadelphia, Temple University Press.

Berman, M. (1961) *John Fiske: The Evolution of a Popularizer,* Cambridge,

Mass., Harvard University Press.

Bridges, H. (1960) 'The Idea of the Robber Barons in American History', in D. Sheehan and H.C. Syrett (eds) *Essays in American Historiography: Papers Presented in Honor of Allan Nevins*, New York, Columbia University Press, pp.138–52.

Brown, I.V. (1953) *Lyman Abbott, Christian Evolutionist: A Study in Religious Liberalism*, Cambridge, Mass., Harvard University Press.

Clark, C.E. (1978) *Henry Ward Beecher: Spokesman for a Middle-Class America*, Urbana, University of Illinois Press.

Coker, F.W. (1910) *Organismic Theories of the State: Nineteenth Century Interpretations of the State as Organism or as Person*, New York, Columbia University Press.

Dorn, J.H. (1967) *Washington Gladden: Prophet of the Social Gospel*, Columbus, Ohio State University Press.

Ely, R.T. (1903) *Studies in the Evolution of Industrial Society*, New York, Macmillan.

Fine, S. (1964) *Laissez-Faire and the General-Welfare State: A Study of Conflict in American Thought, 1865–1901*, Ann Arbor, University of Michigan Press.

Fishburn, J. (1982) *The Fatherhood of God and the Victorian Family: The Social Gospel in America*, Philadelphia, Fortress Press.

Fiske, J. (1894) *Life and Letters of Edward Livingston Youmans: Comprising Correspondence with Spencer, Huxley, Tyndall, and Others*, London, Chapman & Hall.

Fosdick, H.E. (1957) *The Living of These Days: An Autobiography*, London, SCM Press.

Fosdick, R.B. (1952) *The Story of the Rockefeller Foundation*, London, Odhams Press.

Froude, J.A. (1871) *Calvinism: An Address Delivered at St. Andrew's, March 17, 1871*, London, Longmans, Green & Co.

Gedicks, A. (1975) 'American Social Scientists and the Emerging Corporate Economy: 1885–1915', *Insurgent Sociologist* **5**, pp.25–47.

Gladden, W. (1890) *Burning Questions of the Life That Now Is and of That Which Is to Come*, London, James Clarke & Co.

Gladden, W. (1895) *Ruling Ideas of the Present Age*, Boston, Houghton, Mifflin & Co.

Greene, J.C. (1981) 'Biology and Social Theory in the Nineteenth Century: Auguste Comte and Herbert Spencer', in J.C. Greene, *Science, Ideology, and World View: Essays in the History of Evolutionary Ideas*, Berkeley, University of California Press, pp.60–94.

Harvey, C.E. (1982) 'John D. Rockefeller, Jr., and the Interchurch World

Movement of 1919–1920: A Different Angle on the Ecumenical Movement', *Church History* **51**, pp.198–209.

Hearnshaw, F.J.C. (1950) 'Herbert Spencer and the Individualists', in F.C.J. Hearnshaw (ed.) *The Social and Political Ideas of Some Representative Thinkers of the Victorian Age*, New York, Barnes & Noble, pp.53–83.

Hefner, P. (1981) 'Is/Ought: A Risky Relationship between Theology and Science', in A.R. Peacocke (ed.) *The Sciences and Theology in the 20th Century*, London, Oriel Press.

Hibben, P. (1942) *Henry Ward Beecher: An American Portrait*, New York, Press of the Readers Club.

Hofstadter, R. (1955) *Social Darwinism in American Thought*, Boston, Beacon Press.

Hopkins, C.H. (1967) *The Rise of the Social Gospel in American Protestantism, 1865–1915* (rev. edn), New Haven, Yale University Press.

Hudson, W.S. (1965) *Religion in America*, New York, Charles Scribner's Sons.

Josephson, M. (1934) *The Robber Barons: The Great American Capitalists, 1861–1901*, New York, Harcourt, Brace & Co.

McLoughlin, W.G. (1970) *The Meaning of Henry Ward Beecher*, New York, Alfred A. Knopf.

Manuel, F.E. (1972) 'From Equality to Organicism', in F.E. Manuel, *Freedom from History, and Other Untimely Essays*, London, University of London Press, pp.221–41.

May, H.F. (1949) *Protestant Churches and Industrial America*, New York, Harper & Bros.

Mayr, E. (1972) 'Introduction', in C. Darwin, *On the Origin of Species by Charles Darwin: A Facsimile of the First Edition*, New York, Atheneum.

Moore, J.R. (1975) 'The Post-Darwinian Controversies: A Study of the Protestant Struggle to Come to Terms with Darwin in Great Britain and America, 1870–1900' PhD thesis, University of Manchester.

Moore, J.R. (1979) *The Post-Darwinian Controversies: A Study of the Protestant Struggle to Come to Terms with Darwin in Great Britain and America, 1870–1900*, Cambridge, Cambridge University Press.

Moore, J. R. (1981) *The Future of Science and Belief: Theological Views in the Twentieth Century*, Milton Keynes, Open University Press.

Moore, J.R. (1982) 'Charles Darwin Lies in Westminster Abbey', *Biological Journal of the Linnean Society* **17**, 1982, pp.97–113.

Moore J.R. *et al.* (1981) *Science and Metaphysics in Victorian Britain*, Milton Keynes, Open University Press.

Noble, D.W. (1958) *The Paradox of Progressive Thought*, Minneapolis, University of Minnesota Press.

Peackocke, A.R. (1979) *Creation and the World of Science*, Oxford, Clarendon Press.

Peel, J.D.Y. (1971) *Herbert Spencer: The Evolution of a Sociologist*, London, Heinemann.

Phillips, D.C. (1970) 'Organicism in the Late Nineteenth and Early Twentieth Centuries', *Journal of the History of Ideas*, **31**, pp. 413–32.

Rauschenbusch, W. (1907) *Christianity and the Social Crisis*, New York, Macmillan.

Rauschenbusch, W. (1916) *The Social Principles of Jesus*, New York, Methodist Book Concern.

Rauschenbusch, W. (1917) *A Theology for the Social Gospel*, New York, Macmillan.

Russett, C.E. (1976) *Darwin in America: The Intellectual Response, 1865–1912*, San Francisco, W.H. Freeman & Co.

Saccaro-Battisti, G. (1983) 'Changing Metaphors of Political Structures', *Journal of the History of Ideas*, **44**, pp. 31–54.

Savage, M.J. (1876) *The Religion of Evolution*, Boston, Geo. H. Ellis.

Savage, M.J. (1884) *Poems of Modern Thought*, London, Williams & Norgate.

Savage, M.J. (1887) *Herbert Spencer: His Influence on Religion and Morality*, Liverpool, W. & J. Arnold.

Sharpe, D.R. (1942) *Walter Rauschenbusch*, New York, Macmillan.

Spencer, H. (1884) 'Retrogressive Religion', *Nineteenth Century*, **16**, pp.3–26.

Spencer, H. (1904) *An Autobiography*, 2 vols, London, Williams & Norgate.

White, J. (1979) 'Andrew Carnegie and Herbert Spencer: A Special Relationship', *Journal of American Studies*, **13**, 57–71.

Williams, D.D. (1941) *The Andover Liberals: A Study in American Theology*, Morningside Heights, King's Crown Press.

Wilson, E.O. (1975) *Sociobiology: The New Synthesis*, Cambridge, Mass., Harvard University Press.

Wilson, E.O. (1980) 'The Relation of Science to Theology', *Zygon: Journal of Religion and Science*, **15**, pp. 425–34.

Wiltshire, D. (1978) *The Social and Political Thought of Herbert Spencer*, Oxford, Oxford University Press.

[Youmans, E.L.] (1883) *Herbert Spencer on the Americans and the Americans on Herbert Spencer: Being a Full Report of His Interview, and of the Proceedings at the Farewell Banquet of Nov. 9, 1882*, New York, D. Appleton & Co.

Young, R. M. (1981) 'The Naturalization of Value Systems in the Human Sciences', in M. Bartholomew *et al.*, *Problems in the Biological and Human Sciences*, Milton Keynes, Open University Press, pp.63–110.

4

Biological Evolution and Christian Theology – Yesterday and Today

Arthur Peacocke

INTRODUCTION

No assessment of the relation between biological evolution and Christian theology today can be made without an adequate historical perspective. Fortunately that perspective has been greatly enriched by historical investigations in recent decades, as well represented by other contributions to this volume, and these have resulted in a significant reappraisal of the impact of Darwin and of the Darwinians on the thought of their day. Let it suffice for me, therefore, simply to remind you that evolutionary ideas, as expounded by Darwin, were widely seen as a threat to religious belief in the mid-nineteenth century, not only by their apparent impugning of the veracity of the Scriptures, as literally read, but also by their undermining of traditional ideas about the nature and origin of human beings. Instead of dwelling on this familiar confrontation, however, I shall begin by recalling some of the more conciliatory theological responses to Darwinism in the last century. For the stage has been occupied too often by those who want to stress the negative reactions of many Christians, both theologians and lay people, to Darwinism in the Victoria era. The reconciling responses are worth recapitulating because many of them provided fruitful soil for the growth of a more coherent and constructive approach by Christian theology to evolution. In order to face contemporary issues, it will also be necessary to sketch in some of the broad features of current evolutionary theory. Then we can return to the question that is implicit in the title, namely 'What is it to be a Christian theist in a post-Darwinian world'?

CONSTRUCTIVE RECONCILING THEOLOGICAL
RESPONSES TO DARWIN

The constructive responses of those Christian theologians who, in the phrase of Gertrude Himmelfarb (1968), wished to be 'reconcilers' rather than 'irreconcilers' were not based on any mood of defeatism or any sense of accommodation of Christian truth to a new and overwhelming force. Rather, they were based on a conviction that has always motivated the best and, in the long run, the most influential theology – namely that, to be intelligible and plausible to any generation, the Christian faith must express itself in ways that are consistent with such understanding of the nature of the world as is contemporarily available. For the constructive theological responses to Darwin's ideas represent a better-established way of doing theology than some of the more extreme denials that then filled the stage (and often still fill our headlines). However, the theological questions were real enough: How could one believe in Darwin's hypothesis and still hold the account of creation in Genesis to be true? How should God's action as creator be conceived in relation to an evolutionary formation of new creatures? How could one continue to use the popular argument for the existence of God, namely, that the presence of design and apparent purpose in the mechanisms of living organisms shows them to have been fashioned by a cosmic designer of an intelligence and power attributable only to a creator God? Moreover, if human beings had evolved from the animals to a higher state of intellectual and moral consciousness, how could there be any place for the supposed historic Fall, as thought to be described in the early chapters of Genesis, and much elaborated in Augustinian strands of Christianity, both Catholic and Protestant? If human higher capacities had evolved by natural means from those of animals, how could we go on supposing that they had any special ultimate value or significance? So although Darwin himself was careful never to debate these issues in public, as his own Christian belief gradually and privately ebbed away, it is not surprising that the publication of his ideas provided a new tiltyard for those who wished to enter the lists on behalf either of supposed Christian truth or of free scientific enquiry.

Because Darwin was an Englishman writing in England, and his work was first published in London, it was inevitable that the first impact of his ideas on Christian theology was upon the Church of England. But let us begin by examining the fate of his evolutionary ideas in the German and French contexts, and the response of the Roman Catholic Church.

German readers tended to see Darwin through the spectacles of Ernst Haeckel, who held a monistic world view based on a strongly mechanistic view of evolution. For him the only viable religion was the 'monistic religion of humanity', of 'truth, goodness and beauty' (*q.v.* Daecke, 1982, p.710). It was such a pantheistic religion of immanence which alone could form a bond with *Wissenschaft* and create a unity of God and the world. At the same time, the recruiting of Darwinism into the struggle for socialism, atheism and free-thinking by Marx and Engels tied evolution into a package which most theologians inevitably rejected (see Daecke, 1982, for a fuller exposition of this aspect of German thought). Thus German theology, insofar as it did not reject all evolutionary thought but did reject both monism and Marxism, was pushed either towards a neo-vitalism, which had its roots in an earlier *Naturphilosophie,* or towards an existentialist dualism of 'belief' and 'knowledge' in the post-Kantian tradition of Albrecht Ritschl. Those who chose the former option were deeply influenced by Hans Driesch, who saw in evolution the working a non-material factor – a vital agent or *entelechie* which could interlock with the material processes of living organisms as understood by physics and chemistry, and was the source of their character as *living* entities. Seeberg (1924), for example, saw in this a way of countering a purely mechanistic interpretation of evolutionary causality and so of 'saving' the creative intervention of God. For him, as for Driesch, matter, life and spirit were transformed by the action of an inner, active, teleological principle transcending the laws of physics and chemistry. Driesch's vitalistic concept of wholeness (*Ganzheit*) was also utilized by other theologians, such as Jacob von Uexküll (1926), who regarded the organism and its environment as parts of a concerted unity, linked together by an 'immaterial factor'. Arthur Titius and Karl Heim also invoked the idea of wholeness in order to unite causal and teleological explanations. In his *Das Weltbild der Zukunft* (1904), Heim attempted to integrate the principle of natural selection with a natural theology. For both Titius and Heim mechanistic causality was not enough to explain evolution; an active purposefulness (*Ganzheitsfaktor*) was also necessary, and the introduction of this concept created a bond between science and religion. This emphasis on the *Ganzheit* principle brought both Titius and Heim close to vitalism, which in Heim's case sat rather uncomfortably with his understanding of God as personal. Titius developed the idea of *Ganzheit* to interpret God as the driving force of the cosmos, and he saw creation and evolution as different ways of conceiving the same divine activity (*q.v.* Daecke, 1982).

For a long period after the Second World War, German theology (and with it much American and European, though not English, theology) was dominated by the impressive writings of Karl Barth, for whom the relation between the realms of nature and grace, between the sphere of the corrupt human intellect and that of the pure word of God, between the created and the creator, was simply and starkly that of a 'great gulf fixed', with no possible traffic between them that man could initiate. Consequently natural theology was relegated to the wings of the theological stage, and even a theology *of* nature was not much pursued. So inevitably from the mid-1940s to about the mid-1960s there was little active consideration in Barthian circles of the relation between evolutionary ideas and Christian theology. Today, however, under the pressure of environmental problems that generate the need for a theology of nature, German theology has begun to take a new interest in the findings of science in general, and of evolutionary biology in particular. Thus we have two of Germany's leading theologians, Wolfhart Pannenberg and Jurgen Moltmann, writing on these themes. Pannenberg (1973) has carefully worked out the relation between theology and the natural and human sciences. In his view, when natural science and human understanding are emancipated from the spectre of scientific positivism, they can regulate each other in a unified perspective in which theology deals with the all-embracing totality of meaning that is implicit in them both. According to Pannenberg (1981), this entails theology asking certain questions of the natural sciences, such as, 'Is there any equivalent in modern biology to the Biblical notion of the Divine Spirit as origin of life that transcends the limit of the organism?' Whether or not this is the best way to formulate the question is open to debate, but it is clear that German theology has now really begun to come to grips with the actual content of evolutionary biology. Moltmann's work (1979) is more confessional and political in tone, dwelling on the practical tasks of understanding and transformation. But he does take account of an evolutionary understanding of what is happening in the world. He sees the natural and biological worlds as open systems with open futures, and examines what this entails for human activity, including political action.

In France, biology was dominated in the early nineteenth century by the giant figure of Georges Cuvier, a formidable opponent of the evolutionary scheme and mechanism proposed by Jean Baptiste de Lamarck. The reaction to Darwin in France was bedevilled by the French word *evolution* referring primarily to 'individual development' while 'evolution' in Darwin's sense was there referred to as *transformation* or *transformisme*. Moreover 'Ever since Ray ... the definition of the term 'species' [*Fr. éspèce*] had entailed that two different species must be *geneologically* distinct: this being so, the theory of *transformisme* could not be stated as a doctrine about 'species' at all – let alone throw light on the origin of species' (Toulmin and Goodfield, 1965, p.214). This semantic stumbling block, which worried the French more than the empirical English, has only been properly circumvented in the mid-twentieth century 'new taxonomy' wherein 'species' are defined in a much more restricted fashion that takes account of the evolutionary process (Toulmin and Goodfield, 1965, p.215).

Undoubtedly, the chief influence in French philosophy of evolution was Henri Bergson, who was born in the same year as the publication of *The Origin of Species* and who died during the Second World War. In *Creative Evolution* ([1907] 1911) Bergson invoked a vital impulse (*élan vitale*) as the cause and co-ordinator of the variations that produce new organs and new species. He postulated a dualism of life and spirit *versus* matter and regarded evolution as a process in which life and spirit diverged and unfolded from matter. Bergson differed from German neo-vitalism in that he was against 'finalism', the belief that the cosmos in general (including the biological world) was moving towards a predetermined and possibly forseeable end. For Bergson, evolution proceeded unpredictably from the one to the many. It was not a creative unification.

French Christian theology is largely Roman Catholic, and the official response of that church to Darwin may be fairly described as a cautious keeping of Darwinism at arm's length with the preserving of belief in a distinctive act of creation for the human species through two historical individuals (traditionally known as Adam and Eve). Thus the Roman Catholic church virtually 'bracketed off' the whole question of evolution until the middle of the twentieth century, when the posthumous publication of the French Jesuit Teilhard de Chardin's personal synthesis of Christian faith and evolutionary philosophy, stimulated a renewed debate about it. Teilhard was one of the most widely-read Roman Catholic thinkers to base his thinking on evolution, which he used as a theological category and as a hermeneutical principle to transpose Christian belief out of a static world-view into one that recognized the world as being in process of becoming ('cosmogenesis'). For him, the Christian God was 'a God of cosmogenesis, a God of evolution'. Rejecting Bergson's emphasis on divergence, Teilhard reinstated the idea of evolution as creative unification. In spite of the plethora of living organisms, the evolutionary process had a spearhead in the human psyche and moved towards an ultimate unification in what he called the 'omega point'. For Teilhard, cosmogenesis had taken place in the evolution of life and spirit and potentially it could become a 'Christogenesis'. In his writings an emphasis on Christ as redeemer is replaced by an emphasis on Christ as evolver; and the idea of salvation is extended from that of 'redemption' to embrace that of 'genesis'. Christ himself 'saves evolution' by being its mover, animator, guide, co-ordinator, and uniter. It is not always clear in, for example, *The Phenomenon of Man*

(1959) whether the 'God of evolution' and the 'Christ-evolver' are vitalistic, teleological factors, or whether they represent a conjunction of two ultimate but fundamentally coincident consummations in human consciousness and the evolutionary process.

Although Teilhard's ideas were rejected by the official organs of the Roman Catholic church, both during his lifetime and when they were eventually published posthumously, he has been extremely influential among lay Roman Catholics (and others), and possibly even in the deliberations of the Second Vatican Council (1962–5). Meanwhile the official response of the Roman Catholic Church to Darwinism in the last few decades may be summarized in the words of Alszeghi:

> Documents after Pius X11 touch only indirectly on the problem of evolution. Although taking account of the possibility of hominization [presumably meaning the formation of human beings or their creation] through evolution, they none the less affirm the necessity of proceeding with moderation and they insist on the fact that the question of the reconciliation of the faith with evolution cannot yet be regarded as definitely resolved. A recent allocution of Paul VI to a group of theologians characterizes evolution as no longer an hypothesis but a 'theory', and makes no other reservation for its application to man than the immediate creation of each and every human soul and the decisive importance exerted on the lot of humanity by the disobedience of Adam. . . . The Pope observes that polygenism has not been scientifically demonstrated and cannot be admitted if it involves the denial of the dogma of original sin. (p.16)
>
> A final factor which was to attenuate the diffidence of the Church towards evolution consisted in the deeper understanding of the Creator's special action in the formation of man. For, on the one hand, it is inadmissable that the human race should spring forth independently of the Creator; and on the other hand, the interpretation of the divine intervention in a determinative manner – as an action of God which is part of the same plane of secondary causes – does not fit in with an evolutionistic vision of the world. This obstacle has been overcome by conceiving the special action of God as one that works through all the generations of living beings, so that everyone shares in this special but continuous action in the great work of universal evolution. (p.17)

Alszeghi concludes that it is not at all likely that the ecclesiastical *magisterium* would 'in the concrete' declare that evolution is irreconcilable with the faith.

In a significant contribution to Roman Catholic thought on evolution, Karl Rahner (1966) has put forward a challenging interpretation of the incarnation of Christ. Rahner's Christology forms part of an immensely comprehensive and profound Christian theology, and little justice can be done to it here. Rather than attempting to summarize his position, I choose to present his ideas by some excerpts from his work that, even out of context, may perhaps serve to indicate the gist of an influential position within Roman Catholic theology that adopts a positive and welcoming approach to evolutionary ideas. We must, Rahner says

> take into consideration the known history of the cosmos as it has been investigated and described by the modern natural sciences: this history is seen more and more as one homogeneous history of matter, life and man. This one history does not exclude differences of nature but on the contrary includes them in its concept, since history is precisely not the permanence of the same but rather the becoming of something entirely new and not merely of something other. (p.166)

Thus Rahner assumes the current evolutionary view of the world, emphasizing the connections between matter and spirit, natural history and the history of man, that it implies. Because all is the creation of one and the same God, he deems it self-evident for Christian theology that matter and spirit have 'more things in common' than 'things dividing them'. This is shown *par excellence* in the unity of matter and spirit in man himself, who is not a merely temporary composite but is fundamentally so – for the starting point is the one man in his *one* self-realization. By 'spirit', Rahner means 'the one man in so far as he becomes conscious of himself in an absolute consciousness of being-given-to-himself. This man does by the very fact that he is always referred to the absoluteness of reality as such and so to its one root (called God) . . .' (pp.162, 163).

This inseparable, but irreducible, correlatedness of matter and spirit in man itself has a history; for matter develops out of its inner being in the direction of spirit, and such 'becoming' must be conceived as something 'becoming *more*' – the coming into being of more reality. This 'more' Rahner describes *inter alia* as the 'self-transcendence by which an existing and active being actively approaches to the higher perfection still lacking to it' (pp.164–5). He writes:

> If man is thus the self-transcendence of living matter, then the history of Nature and spirit forms an inner, graded unity in which natural history develops towards man, continues in him as *his* history, is conserved and surpassed in him and hence reaches its proper goal with and in the history of the human spirit. (p.168).

Based on this view of the significance of the evolutionary perspective, Rahner tries

> to see man as the being in whom the basis tendency of matter to find itself in the spirit by self-transcendence arrives at the point where it definitely breaks through; thus in this way we may be in a position to regard man's being itself, from this view-point within the basic and total conception of the world. It is precisely this being of man, seen from *this* view-point, which – both by its highest, free and complete self-transcendence into God, made possible quite gratuitously by God,and by God's communication of himself – 'awaits' its own consummation and that of the world in what in Christian terms we call 'grace' and 'glory'.
>
> The first step and definitive beginning, and the absolute guarantee that this ultimate and basically unsurpassable self-transcendence will succeed and indeed has already begun, is to be found in what we call the Hypostatic Union [the union of the human nature and divine nature in the one person of Christ]. At a first approximation, this must not be seen so much as something which distinguishes Jesus Our Lord from us, but rather as some thing which must happen once, and once only, at the point where the world begins to enter into its final phase in which it is to realize its final concentration, its final climax and its radical nearness to the absolute mystery called God. Seen from this viewpoint, the Incarnation appears as the necessary and permanent beginning of the divinization of the world as a whole. (pp.160–1)

This positive treatment of a central theological theme in relation to an evolutionary persepective by a leading orthodox Roman Catholic theologian was welcome, even if somewhat delayed, coming as it did just over a century after Darwin and Wallace announced their theory of evolution by natural selection.

Needless to say the impact of Darwinism on Christian throught was greatest in the England in which Darwin first propounded his views, though naturally the controversy soon spread throughout Britain and to the United States. Historians of the Victorian period have documented a number of particular cultural and religious features of the Darwinian debate – for example, the dominance of the argument from design within traditional natural theology, and the increasingly disturbing analysis (emanating from Germany) of the Scriptures by the criteria and methods of historical scholarship. Rather than enter into this intriguing history, study of which is revealing a greater complexity in the Christian response to Darwin and a greater flexibility and openness on the part of orthodox Christian theologians than is purveyed by the inherited mythology about this period (Moore, 1979), I wish to pick out one thread in the debate. It is that quieter and, in the end, more profound response of those Christian theists who did not reject Darwin but sought seriously to incorporate the evolutionary perspective into their theological reflection.

I am referring to that part of the theological response within the Church of England that was deeply influenced by the doctrine of the incarnation. A stress on the doctrine of the incarnation, and on a sacramental understanding of the world, had been revived (by the Tractarians) in the second half of the nineteenth century. It represented a renewal in the theology of the Church of England of an earlier emphasis on the immanence of God in nature and on the sacraments as an expression and reflection of that presence of God in the world. This goes back to the very foundations of the reformed catholicism of the Church of England. Some indication of the flavour of this theology is provided by the following selected quotations. Some thirty years after the publication of the *Origin* Aubrey Moore wrote:

> The scientific evidence in favour of evolution, *as a theory* is infinitely

more Christian than the theory of 'special creation'. For it implies the immanence of God in nature, and the omnipresence of His creative power. Those who oppose the doctrine of evolution in defence of a 'continued intervention' of God, seem to have failed to notice that *a theory of occasional intervention implies as its correlative a theory of ordinary absence.* (Moore, 1889, p.184)

The same author also wrote in the collection *Lux Mundi* (1891):

The one absolutely impossible conception of God, in the present day, is that which represents him as an occasional visitor. Science has pushed the deist's God further and further away, and at the moment when it seemed as if He would be thrust out all together, Darwinism appeared, and, under the disguise of a foe, did the work of a friend. . . . Either God is everywhere present in nature, or He is nowhere. (p.73 in 12th edn., 1891)

In the same volume, in an essay entitled significantly 'The Incarnation in relation to Development', J.R. Illingworth wrote:

The last few years have witnessed the gradual acceptance by Christians of the great scientific generalisation of our age, which is briefly if somewhat vaguely described as the Theory of Evolution. . . . It is an advance in our theological thinking; a definite increase of insight; a fresher and fuller appreciation of those 'many ways' in which 'God fulfills Himself'.

Illingworth saw Christ as the consummation of the evolutionary process:

in scientific language, the Incarnation may be said to have introduced a new species into the world – the Divine man transcending past humanity, as humanity transcended the rest of the animal creation, and communicating His vital energy by a spiritual process to subsequent generations of men. (Illingworth (1891)

Charles Gore, the editor of that same controversial volume, later in his 1891 Bampton Lectures affirmed that:

from the Christian point of view, this revelation of God, this unfolding of divine qualities, reaches a climax in Christ. God has expressed in inorganic nature, His immutability, immensity, power, wisdom; in organic nature He has shown also that He is alive; in human nature He has given glimpses of His mind and character. In Christ not one of these earlier revelations is abrogated; nay, they are reaffirmed; but they reach a completion in the fuller exposition of the divine character, the divine personality, the divine love. (Gore, 1891, pp.32–3)

In the twentieth century one of the most positive attempts to integrate evolutionary biology into Christian theology was made by Tennant (1902), who rejected the traditional pessimism about man, as it had been developed from the Bible by the combination of Genesis with the Pauline epistles. Instead, Tennant appealed from the Scriptures, understood in the light of tradition, to the evidence of the evolutionary process. In the original man, he argued, the moral consciousness awakened only slowly: there was no question of some *catastrophic* change for the worse in his relationship with God, nor was there, at a later stage in man's development, a 'radical bias towards evil' because of the Fall. It was as true to say that God was still making man as to say that God had made him. Similarly the origin and meaning of sin were to be sought in the process of becoming. This emphasis on the 'process of becoming' was also a major strand in the philosophy of Whitehead (1929). The theologians Temple (1934) and Thornton (1928) were contemporaries of Whitehead and were deeply influenced by him; like Tennant, they drew upon the tradition of evolutionary interpretation that went back to *Lux Mundi*.

The last name I want to mention in this specifically Anglican tradition is that of Charles Raven, formerly Regius Professor of Divinity in the University of Cambridge, and one whom his biographer, Dillistone (1975) dubbed as 'naturalist, historian, theologian'. Raven's whole life was devoted to integrating the evolutionary perspective of biology with his Christian theology, for he embraced evolution whole heartedly and believed that it could serve as the conceptual framework for religious expression (Raven, 1953). He strove to enhance the place of the life sciences in man's understanding of the universe, then largely dominated by physics, and pioneered in emphasizing the need for ecologically wise policies of conservation. The living world was for him the many splendoured sacrament of the activity and presence of the living God. His last words from the pulpit, which I was privileged to hear, expressed with characteristic eloquence his vision of the unity of Christian insight and aspiration with a perspective on the cosmos that was deeply informed by the natural sciences and above all by that of evolution. Such a vision pervades this 'immanentist' tradition of Christian theology in Britain, and this may help to explain why the ideas of Teilhard de Chardin and of Whiteheadian 'process theology' have been generally less significant for an indigeneous tradition that was already integrating science and religion, but not under the sway of one dominating metaphysic.

In contrast, process theology is that particular development of American natural theology which, utilizing the metaphysical system of Whitehead, incorporates both the idea of the natural world as 'in process of becoming' and an emphasis on organicism. The process theologians have taken more seriously than almost any others in recent decades the problem of explicating God's action in a world for which all is describable in terms of law-like evolutionary processes. In process thought, God in His 'primordial nature' is regarded as providing 'aims' for all actual occasions, the ideals which they are striving to become, and in this aspect God is the envisager and fund of universals – he is eternal, absolute, unchangeable. In his 'consequent nature' he is responsive love and is temporal, relative, dependent and constantly changing in response to new unforeseen happenings. Process theology is closely interlocked with pan-psychism, a view of the world which sees mental and physical aspects in all entities and events. Although I find the postulate of pan-psychism to be logically flawed (Peacocke, 1979, pp.125–7), there is no doubting the seriousness with which process theology takes the evolutionary perspective. Process thought has had considerable influence, particularly as developed by Charles Hartshorne at Chicago, and it has subsequently proliferated elsewhere, especially at the Center for Process Studies at Claremont, California. It is still the dominant form of natural theology in America today.

An even more complete welding of theology and evolutionary

ideas occurs in the 'scientific theology' of Burhoe. Burhoe regards the sciences of human nature and the increasingly accepted role of religion in human evolution as capable of providing the major religious traditions with the means of interpreting themselves in harmonious relation both to science itself and to one another. He even goes so far as to claim that it makes 'little difference whether we name it [the power that created the earth and life] natural selection or God, so long as we recognise it as that to which we must bow our heads or adapt' (Burhoe, 1981, p.21).

This has now brought us up to the recent past in our survey of constructive theological responses to evolution. But science never stands still and there is a continuous need to rethink our understanding of the relation of nature, man and God as our perceptive upon the natural world changes.

BIOLOGICAL EVOLUTION TODAY

Let us review some features of contemporary evolutionary theory which will have to be taken into account in formulating any viable Christian theological response.

Evolution – 'Fact' or 'Theory'?

Much play has been made by 'creationists' of the proposal that the evolutionary account of biological relationships is 'only a theory'. There are a number of confusions locked up in such a view. Any scientific account of the past has to be based on inferences from present-day observations. On such reckoning the whole of historical geology and much of modern cosmology is 'only a theory'. However, inferences of this kind can lead to near-certainty and then it becomes proper to speak of these inferences as describing what actually happened. The idea of biological evolution refers principally to the past, and, in its general form, simply affirms the existence of genetic relations between the different organisms we now see on the Earth or know from fossils to have been there in the past. The relationship inferred is that, to use Darwin's phrase, of 'descent with modification', *by whatever mechanism*. That the mechanism is natural selection is another matter and must be substantiated by other means. Whatever controversies there may be about the mechanism and speed of evolution there is no dispute among biologists about the *fact* of evolution itself.

It is true that when Darwin propounded his theory the evidence for evolution was circumstantial rather than direct. But twentieth-century biochemistry, notably in its phase of 'molecular biology', has now demonstrated fundamental similarities at the molecular level between all living organisms from bacteria to man. Not only is nucleic acid (DNA or RNA) the prime carrier of hereditary information in all living organisms but the code that translates this information from base sequences in DNA, via messenger RNA, to amino acid sequences in proteins (and thence to their structure and function) is the *same* code in *all* living organisms. This code is arbitrary with respect to the relations of the molecular structures involved and its universality is explicable and comprehensible only as the result of evolution: the code now universally operative is the one which happened to be present in the living matter that first successfully reproduced itself fast enough to outnumber all other rivals. Molecular biology has provided another independent and powerful confirmation of evolutionary relations through its ability to compare the amino acid sequences in proteins with the same chemical function (e.g. cytochrome C) in widely different organisms. The striking fact is that such comparisons entirely and independently confirm (and often illuminatingly amplify) the evolutionary relationships previously deduced on morphological and palaeontological grounds. (For example, such studies have provided direct biochemical evidence concerning the degrees of relatedness between man and the other living primates.)

Again and again, the evolutionary hypothesis (if that is what we still prefer to call it) has survived the test of consistency with observations of a kind unthinkable even four decades ago when the 'modern synthesis' of neo-Darwinism first emerged. This does not preclude controversy about the tempo of, mode of and constraints upon evolution, but it renders it entirely reasonable for us to base our philosophy and theology on what we can presume to be the 'fact' of biological evolution, including that of man, who is regarded as being entirely within the world of nature with respect to both the biological and molecular aspects of his existence relevant to his origins.

Cosmic Evolution

Darwin himself, T.H. Huxley and the first generation of Darwinists saw biological evolution in the context of a much wider cosmic process embracing the development of the solar system and of the galaxy. Today we can place biological evolution in a cosmic context that involves a continuous development of the forms of matter from the original 'hot big bang', through atoms and molecules, to those complex structures that could self-reproduce their pattern of organization and can be properly designated as 'living'. This gives us a new incentive to reflect on the cosmic significance of the process of evolution. We now know that it is not confined simply to the development of life, but that the potentiality of matter to develop new forms of organization, according to the prevailing conditions, stretches back beyond the beginning of living forms, and may well stretch on into the future beyond their eventual demise on the surface of the Earth.

Chance, Law and the Origin of Life

Until the recent past, chance and law (necessity, or determinism) have often been regarded as alternatives for interpreting the natural world. But the interplay between these principles is more subtle and complex than the simple dichotomies of the past would allow. Jacques Monod (1972) contrasted the 'chance' processes which bring about mutations in the genetic material of an organism with the 'necessity' of their consequences in the law-abiding, well-ordered, replicative mechanisms that constitute an organism's continuity as a living form. However, there is no reason why the randomness of molecular event in relation to biological consequence has to be raised to the level of a metaphysical principle, as Monod tended to do. In the behaviour of matter on a larger scale many lawful regularities arise from the combined effect of random microscopic events. The involvement of chance at the level of genetic mutation does not preclude these events manifesting law-like behaviour at the higher levels of organisms, populations and biosystems. Rather, it would be more consistent with observation to assert that the full gamut of the potentialities of living matter could be covered only through the agency of the rapid and frequent randomizations that are possible at the molecular level of DNA. This role of chance is what one would expect if the universe were so constituted that exploration of all the potential organized forms of matter (both living and non-living) were to occur.

Since Monod wrote *Chance and Necessity*, there have been developments in theoretical biology that cast new light on the interrelation of chance and law in the origin and development of life (for a recent account see Peacocke, 1983). The Nobel Laureate Ilya Prigogine and his colleagues at Brussels have been able to show that there exists a class of open systems, 'dissipative structures', which can maintain themselves in an ordered steady state far from equilibrium. Under certain conditions they can undergo fluctuations that are no longer damped, as they are near to equilibrium, but are amplified so that the system switches to a *new* ordered state in which it can again become steady. It turns out that many plausible 'proto-living' systems, which must have involved complex networks of chemical reactions, are likely to undergo such changes. Thus it is now possible to regard as highly probable the emergence of ordered, self-reproducing molecular strutures. To this extent, the emergence of life was inevitable, but the form it was to take remained entirely open and unpredictable.

Similar conclusions have been reached by another Nobel Laureate, Manfred Eigen: ' . . . the evolution of life, it it is based on a derivable physical principle, must be considered an inevitable process despite its indeterminate course . . . it is not only inevitable "in principle" but also sufficiently probable within a realistic span of time' (Eigen, 1971, p.519). These studies demonstrate that the mutual interplay of chance and law is creative, for it is the combination of the two which allows new forms to emerge and evolve. If this is so, it looks as though evolution proceeds not like an engineer working from scratch but rather by 'tinkering, *bricolage*', that is, working on what already exists, 'managing with odds and ends' (Jacob, 1983, p.131). In other words, natural selection appears to be opportunistic. Nevertheless its end result is the kind of complex conscious life that we see in the higher mammals. including the primates and man.

In recent years there has also been a renewed understanding of the close relation of the possibility of the existence of life, and therefore of human life, to the fundamental parameters and laws of the cosmos. This raises the intriguing question of whether or not this universe, in a run of possible universes, just happens to be the one which can generate within itself creatures who can observe it and report on its own character and nature! This is the Chinese-box puzzle that lurks inside the so-called 'anthropic principle'.

Continuity and Emergence in Human Evolution

As the investigations of man's biochemistry, physiology, nervous system and behaviour patterns burgeon, striking similarities and continuities are more and more being observed between what had previously been regarded as uniquely human characteristics and parallel characteristics of the higher mammals, especially the primates. But it is also becoming increasingly apparent that there is a distinctive transition in passing from the most intelligent primates, or dolphins, to human beings. The most Herculean efforts of devoted investigators rarely seem to be able to train a highly domesticated chimpanzee beyond the level of that of an 18-month-old child. Distinctive transitions have, of course, occurred at other stages in evolution and have given rise to the notion of 'emergence' – the recognition that, with the development of new forms of life, there arise new modes of existence, new activities and new kinds of behaviour, and that new modes of investigation and new conceptual language are required for their proper and appropriate understanding. All will agree that there has been a general increase in the complexity of the organization of living systems through time. Moreover, it is clear that evolution has occurred concomitantly with increasing levels of consciousness and that in man self-consciousness emerged. In this connection, the judgement of the evolutionary biologist G.G. Simpson is pertinent:

Man has certain basic diagnostic features which set him off most sharply from any other animal and which have involved other developments not only increasing this sharp distinction but also making it an absolute difference in kind and not only a relative difference of degree. . . . Even when viewed within the framework of the animal kingdom and judged by criteria of progress applicable to that kingdom as a whole and not peculiar to man, man is thus the highest animal. (Simpson, 1971, pp.258–9)

Because of our ability to transmit culture in mankind, evolution has become 'psycho-social' as Julian Huxley used to put it; that is to say, in the case of man we have a creature that shapes its own evolution by willingly shaping its own environment. With man biology has become history.

The Problem of Reduction

Most molecular biologists would now agree with Sidney Brenner when he wrote of the upshot of their endeavours: 'I think it is now quite clear what the enterprise is about. We are looking at a rather special part of the physical universe which contains special mechanisms none of which conflict at all with the laws of physics' (Brenner, 1974). No conflict at all with the laws of physics – agreed; but does this mean that all accounts of biological systems are to be subsumed into physics? Does the triumph of molecular biology really imply the final victory for a reductionist interpretation of biology? Is the ultimate aim of biology, in the words of Francis Crick (1966, p.10) 'to explain *all* biology in terms of physics and chemistry'?

Here we come up against an important issue raised by modern biology not only for theology but for philosophy in general. This is the question of reductionism. This is too large a question to examine here; but the pertinent point is that it is possible to be anti-reductionist (that is against the kind of reductionism defined by Crick) without being a vitalist. The anti-reductionist position requires no mystical affirmations of the existence of 'non-natural' forces or agencies operating in living organisms. But it does require a recognition of the need for autonomous concepts and theories at each level of complexity of the natural world, including the biological. There simply are *not* just grades of 'reality' such that atoms are the 'most real', biological entities less so, and persons the least (for a fuller discussion, see Beckner, 1974; Peacocke, 1976; Wimsatt, 1981).

Ecology

One feature of the contemporary biological scene has been a re-discovered awareness of the ecological integration of living systems. 'It is hard to be a reductionist ecologist' according to Dr Norman Moore, an eminent ecologist, and this increasingly important branch of biology – amazingly *un*fashionable even two decades ago – certainly qualifies as one in which the study of composite wholes is essential. For ecology is the study of the interdependence of all living forms within their physical, organic and social environment. This inter-connectedness of living systems on the surface of the Earth and their interaction with their physical environment can be regarded as one expression of a more general unity and interdependence of all things and events in the cosmos.

The Role of Behaviour in Evolution

The statistical interplay between genetic mutation and environmental pressures as the sole mechanism of evolutionary change has appeared increasingly inadequate to some biologists. This mechanism, even in its most sophisticated contemporary form, represents evolution as an 'unfolding' of the basic internal genetic programme of the organism, a programme that is already present in the genes. However, some biologists have urged that 'unfolding' is an inappropriate metaphor for development. For example, the geneticist Richard Lewontin (1983) stresses that organisms are consequences of *themselves*, that is, of their state at any given moment, with all its dependence on historical accidents – *as well as* of their genotype and environment. Thus the evolution of organisms cannot be understood as a movement towards a fixed point; organisms are not climbing an "adaptive peak" with a fixed summit but rather, Lewontin suggests, walking on a trampoline that changes with the impact. In so speaking, Lewontin is close to an earlier stress of Sir Alister Hardy (1965, pp.161ff., 189ff.) on the role of behavioural patterns in evolution. This debate still continues and we have not heard the end of it yet. But it is worth drawing attention to it, to show that even amongst biologists a purely mechanistic account of evolution has its critics among those who favour more holistic and 'compositionist' interpretations.

WHAT IS IT TO BE A CHRISTIAN THEIST IN A POST-DARWINIAN WORLD?

The previous section has indicated, all too briefly, how our perspective on human life is altered by evolution (and the change would be even greater if advances in psychology, sociology and anthropology were also included). But religion in general, and Christian theology in particular, has its own distinctive perspective which may best be indicated by reminding ourselves of the actual character of the experience of human beings of their life in the natural and social worlds. As far as we can tell, *Homo sapiens* is the only organism that asks itself questions about the meaning of its existence, questions like the penetrating title of the famous story by Tolstoy 'What do men live by?'. This is a question about man's needs. Of course, man has biological needs, and the pursuit of their satisfaction has shaped human history. But even when these basic needs have been met man is not necessarily happy. For he has a restlessness which stems from his failure to satisfy other needs which he seems *not* to share with other animals. Human beings need to come to terms with their awareness of their own death, to come to terms with their finitude, to learn how to bear suffering, to realize their potentialities, and to determine their own directions. It is to the satisfaction of needs such as these that the religious quest of mankind has always directed itself, and this is true *a fortiori* of what I prefer to call the Christian experiment. These fundamental questions about human existence have to be raised because it is as a response to them that the Christian experience has developed and the theological enterprise has unfolded as reflection upon this experience. But *our* particular world is informed and dominated by the evolutionary perspective that we have expounded. So 'What *is* it to be a Christian theist in a post-Darwinian world'?

To ask such a question is to ask how Christian theology is to be related to scientific knowledge, and there are many answers to that particular question. In another context, I have delineated at least eight different ways in which modern science and Christian faith can interact in relation to their intellectual content and epistemology (Peacocke, 1984). Like most scientists, I am a sceptical, qualified realist with respect to my scientific knowledge; and since I take this same stance with respect to theological affirmations, my approach is to regard science and theology as interacting approaches to the same reality (Peacocke, 1984). I want to affirm that *both* the scientific *and* the theological enterprises are explorations into the nature of reality. The former is widely assumed, but less frequently the latter. I heartily endorse the initial and controlling statement in the report of the Doctrine Commission of the Church of England on *Christian Believing*, which opens as follows: 'Christian life is an adventure, a voyage of discovery, a journey, sustained by faith and hope, towards a final and complete communion with Love at the heart of all things' (1976, p.3). Let me therefore indicate the lines along which I think Christian theology and evolutionary ideas may be incorporated into a coherent view of nature, man and God. Inevitably, this can be only a mere sketch of a style of theological reflection that takes seriously the evolutionary perspective (for a fuller exposition see Peacocke, 1979).

Nature, Man and God

Nature. The sciences of the twentieth century have confirmed what many in the nineteenth century believed, but without adequate evidence, and what in the eighteenth century was only intimated, namely, that the whole cosmos is in a state of evolution from one form of matter to another, and that a significant point in this evolutionary process has occurred on the surface of the Earth where the conditions were such that matter was able to become living. This process is of a kind that it does not require the postulate for its occurrence of any factors external to the world itself. Our understanding of matter has been enormously enhanced as a result of this perspective, for matter turns out to be capable of organizing itself into self-reproducing systems that are capable of receiving signals and storing and processing information from their environment. Gradually, and only along certain lines in this development, matter in the form of living organisms manifests behaviour to which we attribute consciousness, and self-consciousness when it takes the form of the human-brain-in-the-human-body. These manifestations are as real at their own level as any chemical reaction or sub-atomic interaction at theirs. Self-consciousness cannot lightly be set on one side, and by the very nature of the activity itself cannot but appear to us as being one of the most significant features of the cosmos. Paradoxically, man's arrival as a product of nature must give us pause in thinking we know all about what matter is 'in itself', for it shows the potentialities of matter in a new light.

Man.   We have already seen that man is to be conceived as a part of nature. Yet in his self-consciousness he transcends nature, perceiving the outside world and parts of his body as objects for his understanding and attention. In man, part of the world has become conscious of itself and consciously responds to its surroundings; in man a new mode of interaction in the world is introduced. Oddly, however, this product of evolution, unlike any other, is strangely ill at ease in its environment, Man alone amongst living creatures individually commits suicide. Somehow, biology has produced a being of infinite restlessness, and this certainly raises the question of whether human beings have properly conceived of what their true 'environment' is. In the natural world, new life can arise only from the death of the old, for the death of the individual is essential to the possibility of new forms evolving in the future. To man this is an affront and he grieves over his suffering and his own personal demise.

God.   The postulate of God as creator of all-that-is is not, in its most profound form, a statement about what happened at a point in time. To speak of God as creator is a postulate about a perennial or 'eternal', that is to say, timeless, relation of God to the world – a relation which involves both differentiation and interaction. God is differentiated from the world in that he is totally other than it. 'God' is postulated in answer to the question 'Why is there anything at all?'. He is the 'ground of being' of the world: that without which we could neither make sense of the world having existence at all, nor of its having that kind of intellectually coherent and explorable existence which science continuously unveils. All of this is included when we say that God in himself must be 'transcendent'.

This affirmation has had to be held in tension with a sense of God's immanence in the world; for if the world is in any sense what God has created and that through which he acts and expresses his own inner being, then there is a sense in which God is never absent from his world and he is as much in his world as, say, Beethoven is in his Seventh Symphony during a performance of it. What is happening today is that our reinforced understanding of the world as continuously in process of creating new kinds of entities, new modes of existence – supremely, as we have seen, in the biological and human worlds – is leading us to reaffirm the conception of God as continuously creative, as *semper Creator*. Creation is continuous – it is a *creatio continua*. The ongoing cosmic processes of evolution are God himself being creator in his own universe. If I had to represent on a blackboard the relation of God and the world, including man, I would not simply draw three spheres labelled respectively 'nature', 'man' and 'God' and draw arrows between them to represent their interrelation. Rather, I would denote an area representing nature and place that entirely within another area representing God, which would have to extend to the edges of the blackboard and, indeed, point beyond it. When I came to depict man, I would have to place him with his feet firmly in nature but with his self-consciousness (perhaps represented by his brain?) protruding beyond the boundary of nature and into the area depicting God.

The view I have just been describing is sometimes denoted by the inelegant word 'pan-en-theism'. The basic affirmation here is that all-that-is, both nature and man, is in some sense *in* God, but that God is more than nature and man and there is more to God than nature and man. God in his being transcends, goes beyond, both man and nature. Either God is in everything created from the beginning to the end, at all times and in all places, or he is not there at all. What we see in the world is the mode of God's creativity in the world. The analogy with Beethoven's Seventh Symphony as an expression of Beethoven's own inner creative being is, I think, a fair one. In the actual processes of the world, and supremely in human self-consciousness, God is involving himself and expressing himself as creator. However, since man has free will we have also to recognize that God put himself 'at risk', as it were, in creatively evoking in the natural world a being who has free will and who can transcend his perceived world and shape it in his own way.

The Relationships between Nature, Man and God

God and nature. In speaking of God as creator, and as *semper Creator*, we have inevitably been thinking of God's relation to all-that-is. But there is more to be said. We now see in a new way the role in evolution of the interplay between random chance micro-events and the necessity which arises from the stuff of this world having its particular 'given' properties. These potentialities a theist must regard as written into creation by the creator himself in order that they may be unveiled by chance exploring their gamut. God as creator we now see as somewhat like a composer who, beginning with an arrangement of notes in an apparently simple tune, elaborates and expands it into a fugue by a variety of devices. In this way the creator may be imagined to unfold the potentialities of the universe that he himself has given it, selecting and shaping by his providential and redemptive action those that are to come to fruition – an improviser, we may suggest, of unsurpassed ingenuity.

We have found that the processes of the universe are continuous and that in them there are emergent new organizations of matter-energy. Such new levels of organization require epistemologically non-reducible concepts to articulate their distinctiveness. Any new meaning which God is able to express in such new levels of organization is thus not discontinuous with the meanings expressed in that out of which it has emerged. So we anticipate continuity, with new meanings emerging out of the old, subsuming them, perhaps, but not denying then. *Both* continuity *and* emergence are inherent features of the observed world. The processes of that world are also open-ended and so we have to develop the notion of God as 'exploring' in creation, of actualizing all the potentialities of creation, of improvising fugally all the derivations inherently possible from the tune he originally called (for a recent discussion, see Bartholomew, 1984).
God and man: in the light of the scientific perspective. Evolved man

seeks meaning and intelligibility in the world; that is (from a theological point of view) he seeks to discern the meanings expressed by God in his creation. These are meanings which, alone among created organisms, man has evolved to be capable, not only of consciously discerning, but also of freely appropriating to give purpose and meaning to his life. Although God is not more present at one time or place than at others, nevertheless man finds that in some sequences of events in nature and history God unveils his meaning more than in others. Though in one sense God as creator acts in all events, not all events are received as 'acts of God'. Some events will be more revealing than others. In any survey of events we have to recognize the existence of a natural hierarchy (or, rather, hierarchies) of complexity. The aspect of God's meaning expressed by any one level in these hierarchies is limited to what it alone can itself distinctively convey. The meanings of God unveiled to and for man will be the more partial, broken, and incomplete the more the level of creation being examined departs from the human and personal, in which the transcendence of the 'I' is experienced as immanent in our bodies. Thus although God is, in some sense, supra-personal, we may well expect that in the personal – in history, in personal experience, in personal encounter – we shall find meanings of God unveiled in a way that is not possible at the impersonal levels of existence with which we have hitherto been principally concerned. For the more personal and *self*-conscious is the entity in which God is immanent, the more capable it is of expressing God's supra-personal characteristics, and the more God can be immanent personally in that entity. The transcendence-in-immanence of man's experience raises the hope that uniquely in man there might be unveiled, without distortion, the transcendent -creator-who-is-immanent; that is, that in man (in *a* human being, or human being*s*) the presence of God the creator might be revealed with a clarity and in a glory not hitherto perceived.

Nature, man and God in a Christian perspective. There is in the long tradition of Christian thought, going back to Jesus's own actions and words, a way of relating the physical and the personal worlds which avoids any stark dichotomy between them, seeing them rather as two facets of the same reality. This way of thinking is generally denoted by the word 'sacramental'. In the Christian liturgy, things in the universe – bread, wine, water, oil sometimes – are taken as being both symbols of God's self expression and as instruments of God's action in effecting his purposes. This mode of thinking can be extended more widely to the universe as a whole, which can then be seen as both a symbol of God's self-expression, and thus a mode of his revelation of himself, and also the very means whereby he effects his purposes in his own actions as agent. In this century this view has been expressed particularly by William Temple (1934). It provides, I think, a deeper perspective on the world described by the sciences than the sciences alone can afford – a perspective in which the world's continuous and seamless web of self-development, of self-organizing by its own inherent properties, generates forms of matter that are capable of being persons and perceiving meaning, those meanings, indeed, with which the creator imbued his creation.

CONCLUSION

In the history of the people of Israel, God was always raising up apparent scourges, such as Cyrus, that were in reality blessings in disguise leading his people through the trauma that would alone enable them to apprehend new truths. So it is too with evolutionary biology which in the words of Aubrey Moore (1891, p.73), for Christian theology 'under the disguise of a foe, did the work of a friend'. For it has brought to light again and reinvigorated an older, immanentist aspect of the Judeo–Christian doctrine of creation that was in danger of being submerged. It is this strand in that doctrine which, in the *Logos* terminology of John 1, is the basic conceptual framework in Christian theology for articulating, however inadequately, its distinctive docrine of the Incarnation, of the 'Word of God' becoming 'flesh' of man.

Contemporary evolutionary biology continues to raise new questions and so continues to provide a stimulus for that rebirth of images without which any living theology soon becomes, in a rapidly changing cultural milieu, the mere inner musings of a religious ghetto. Thus Christian theology continues to be vastly indebted to that view of the transformations of the living world into which Darwin initiated us.

REFERENCES

Alszeghi, Z.(1967) 'Development in the Doctrinal Formulations of the Church concerning the Theory of Evolution', *Concilium*, **6** no.3, pp.14–17.

Bartholomew, D.J. (1984) *God of Chance*, London, SCM Press.

Beckner, M. (1974) 'Reduction, Hierarchies, and Organism', in A.J. Ayala and T. Dobzhansky (eds) *Studies in the Philosophy of Biology*, London, Macmillan pp.63–76.

Bergson, H. [1907 L'Evolution creatrice] (1911) *Creative Evolution*, Engl. transl. A. Mitchell, London, Macmillan.

Brenner, S. (1974) 'New Directions in Molecular Biology', *Nature*, **248**, pp.785–7.

Burhoe, R.W. (1981) *Towards a Scientific Theology*, Belfast, Christian Journals.

Crick, F.H.C. (1966) *Of Molecules and Man*, Seattle, University of Washington Press.

Daecke, S. (1982) 'Entwicklung', in *Theologische Realenzyklopädie*, Berlin, Walter de Gruyter.

Dillistone, F.W. (1975) *Charles Raven: Naturalist, Historian and Theologian*, London, Hodder & Stoughton.

Doctrine Commission of the Church of England (1976) *Christian Believing*, London, SPCK.

Eigen, M. (1971) 'The Self-organization of Matter and the Evolution of Biological Macromolecules', *Naturwissenschaften*, **58**, pp.465–523.

Gore, C. (1891) *The Incarnation of the Son of God*, Bampton Lectures, London, Murray.

Hardy, Sir Alister (1965) *The Living Stream*, London, Collins.

Heim, Karl (1904) *Das Weltbild der Zukunft*, Berlin, C.A. Schwetschke.

Himmelfarb, Gertrude (1968) *Darwin and the Darwinian Revolution*, New York, Norton Library.

Illingworth, J.R. (1891) 'The Incarnation in Relation to Development', in C. Gore (ed.) *Lux Mundi*, London, Murray, pp.132, 151–2.

Jacob, F. (1983) 'Molecular Tinkering in Evolution', in D.S. Bendall (ed.) *Evolution from Molecules to Men*, Cambridge, Cambridge University Press, pp.131–44. See also, F. Jacob (1977) 'Evolution and tinkering', *Science*, **196**, pp.1161–6.

Lewontin, R.C. (1983) 'Gene, organism and environment', in D.S. Bendall (ed.) *Evolution from Molecules to Men*, Cambridge, Cambridge University Press, pp.273–85.

Moltmann, J. (1979) *The Future of Creation*, London, SCM Press.

Monod, J. (1972) *Chance and Necessity*, London, Collins.

Moore, A.L. (1889), *Science and Faith*, London, Kegan Paul, Trench & Co.

Moore, A.L. (1891), 'The Christian Doctrine of God', in C. Gore (ed.) *Lux Mundi*, London, Murray.

Moore, J.R. (1979) *The Post-Darwinian Controversies*, Cambridge, Cambridge University Press.

Pannenberg, W. (1973) *Wissenschaftstheorie and Theologie*, Frankfurt am Main, Suhrkamp Verlag.

Pannenberg, W. (1981) 'Theological Questions to Scientists', in A.R. Peacocke (ed.) *The Sciences and Theology in the Twentieth Century*, London, Oriel Press; Notre Dame, University of Notre Dame Press.

Peacocke, A.R. (1976) 'Reductionism: a review of the epistemological issues and their relevance to biology and the problem of consciousness', *Zygon: Journal of Religion & Science*, **11**, pp.307–34.

Peacocke, A.R. (1979) *Creation and the World of Science*, Oxford, Clarendon Press.

Peacocke, A.R. (1981) Introduction to A.R. Peacocke (ed.) *The Sciences and Theology in the Twentieth Century*, London , Oriel Press; Notre Dame, University of Notre Dame Press, pp.ix–xviii.

Peacocke, A.R. (1983) *An Introduction to the Physical Chemistry of Biological Organization*, Oxford, Clarendon Press.

Peacocke, A.R. (1984) *Intimations of Reality: Critical Realism in Science and Religion*, Notre Dame, University of Notre Dame Press.

Rahner, K. (1966) 'Christology within an Evolutionary view', *Theological Investigations* **V(III)**, Ch. 8, pp.157–92. Tr. K.-H. Kruger London, Darton, Longman & Todd.

Raven, C.E. (1953) *Natural Religion and Christian Theology*, Gifford Lectures, **I**, Science and Religion. **II**, Experience and Interpretation, Cambridge, Cambridge University Press.

Seeberg, R. (1924) *Christliche Dogmatik*, **1**, Erlangen/Leipzig.

Simpson G.G. (1971) *The Meaning of Evolution*, New Haven, Yale University Press and Bantam Books.

Teilhard de Chardin, P. (1959) Engl. Tr. B. Wall, *The Phenomenon of Man*, London, Collins.

Temple, W. (1934) *Nature, Man and God*, 1932–33 and 1933–34 Gifford Lectures. London, Macmillan.

Tennant, F.R. (1902) *The Origin and Propagation of Sin*, Hulsean Lectures, Cambridge, 1901–2. Cambridge, Cambridge University Press.

Thornton, L.S. (1928) *The Incarnate Lord*, London, New York & Toronto, Longmans, Green & Co.

Toulmin, Stephen and Goodfield, June (1965) *The Discovery of Time*,

London, Hutchinson.

Von Uexküll, J. (1926) *Theoretical Biology*, New York, Kegan Paul, Trench, Trubner & Co. Ltd.

Whitehead, A.N. (1929) *Process and Reality*, New York, Macmillan; Cambridge, Cambridge University Press.

Wimsatt, W.R. (1981) 'Robustness, Reliability and Overdetermination', in M. Brewer and B. Collins (eds.) *Scientific Inquiry and the Social Sciences*, San Francisco, Jossey-Bass, pp.124–63.

5

The Effects of Religion on Human Biology

Vernon Reynolds and Ralph Tanner

How does membership of a religious group, or belief in a religious faith, affect individuals' chances of survival and their reproductive success? This is the central question in our current studies (Reynolds and Tanner, 1983), and in this chapter we summarize some of our ideas and conclusions. Religions, we assume, are a part of human culture in general, and are thus the product of human inventiveness (Reynolds, 1980). The ideas underlying them are to some extent akin to 'memes' (Dawkins, 1976) or 'culturgens' (Lumsden and Wilson, 1981). Richard Dawkins coined the term 'memes' to refer to the units of selection in cultural evolution, by analogy with 'genes', the units of selection in organic evolution. He discussed the similarities and differences between the process of transmission of genes and that of memes. In the case of genes, transmission is possible only from parent to child by physical reproduction between parents, whereas memes (ideas, beliefs, or practices) can pass from any individual to any other by imitation or instruction. Thus memes can spread much faster than genes. But in each case there is a common factor – competition – which exists between genes and between memes, and it is the successful ones only that are transmitted. Charles Lumsden and Edward Wilson coined the term 'culturgens' to refer to the units of which cultures are composed, by which they mean the set of alternatives open to an individual in deciding on a course of action in any given situation. Depending on the choices made, the problem of survival will become either easier or harder, and individuals will tend to adopt those choices that are most compatible with their biological capabilities in the prevailing environmental circumstances. Thus cultures will evolve through competition between culturgens and under the twin constraints of genetic structure and environmental opportunity.

A problem we see with these approaches to culture is that terms such as 'meme' and 'culturgen' tend to reify and isolate the components of cultures, as if they were natural entities in competition with each other. Social anthropology, by contrast, tends to emphasize the interdependence of facets of culture, treating them as components of rule-governed systems. Cultural rules are dependent on the structure of the culture in question, on its history, on inputs from other cultures, and also on environmental conditions. Whether or not they are 'adaptive' to the environment is a subject for investigation. Certainly any naive functionalism is doomed; but it remains possible that quite complex systems of rules might have an adaptive or functional relationship with the environment. In order to investigate this, we need to be aware of what processes might signal the existence of adaptive relationships.

The process of religious adaptation is not likely to be a simple one. It is not as simple, for instance, as the wearing of more clothes in cold regions. With religions humans have re-created their environments. They do not, strictly speaking, *need* to pray before they plant their crops, yet in many areas of the world they do so, for example in the Trobriand Islands (Malinowski, 1944). And in our own culture we still give thanks for the harvest. Why? We pray for our armies and for our rulers; we give thanks for our food. The reason is that we have invested our whole environment with sacred properties; we are not wholly in control of events, but believe we can improve our control by access to those powers that truly are in control. Religions are thus rule books for improving our grip on life. Even the so-called 'fatalistic' religions of the east are full of rules and associated practices for the arranging of the human life-cycle and the agricultural cycle. For instance, Hindu rituals are performed frequently to appease household spirits that may be causing sickness, or poor crops, or drought (Berreman, 1963). People of many of the world's major religions pray for personal fertility, sometimes worshipping at special shrines, as in Thailand where some Buddhist shrines are adorned with giant phalluses.

The world's great religions, and the many lesser ones too, all present us with a complex set of images, linked together by an internal logic that often defies that of everyday intercourse. Miracles and myths play an important part in validating more down-to-earth rules of action. In religion, the emic and the etic (Harris, 1968) are often sharply distinct. By 'emic' we mean the view of things from the inside, that is the understanding or explanation of events held or given by the people actually involved in those events. Thus an Azande might consider that a person injured by a falling branch was a victim of witchcraft. The branch was due to fall anyway, but that it fell on just *this* person is explained by reference to the action of some person (whose identity then has to be ascertained). By 'etic' is meant the interpretation of an outsider. Thus a Western anthropologist (in the above case, E.E. Evans-Pritchard) might feel that the happening was an accident or a mere coincidence.

This distinction has led some anthropologists to look carefully behind emic explanations for some adaptive etic functional explanation. The attitude of Hindus to the cow involves notions of purity and impurity that make the idea of being a shoemaker thoroughly polluting; but it has also been claimed that those who conserve cattle gain many survival advantages – it provides milk in the diet, traction for agriculture and dung for fuel. Thus cow-sanctity is adaptive and may have evolved by a complex process involving, to some extent, differential survival by natural selection (Harris, 1966).

Several theories of cultural adaptiveness have been developed (Harris, 1966; Vayda, 1976; Rappaport, 1968). A more biologically direct approach has been to see how cultural practices influence reproductivity *per se* (Irons, 1979; Chagnon, 1979; Dickemann, 1979; Wilson, 1978). Thus, Chagnon (1979) has examined the relationship between lineages and lineage heads among the Yanomamö tribe of Venezuela. He found that lineages were intensely competitive with each other, and adopted a variety of tactics to increase their own numbers at each other's expense. In strictly biological terms some such process operating in a group of animals would be seen as the result of a process known as 'kin-selection'. This is a particular form of natural selection, in which behaviour evolves because it favours the survival of closely related (and therefore genetically similar) individuals, wheras unrelated individuals are discriminated against or even attacked. Again, in male-dominated human societies such as those of Hindu India, we find evidence of a greater emphasis on the need for sons than for daughters (Dickemann, 1979). Sons are treated gently, daughters made to work; and in the past female infanticide was widespread, especially among higher castes. Now animal studies have shown that parental investment of time and effort in offspring varies between species, so that sometimes parents may invest more in the offspring of one sex than the other, and even that in some species high-ranking parents may invest more in one sex and low-ranking ones more in the other. In such cases, explanations have been found in terms of genetic success: offspring are cared for to the extent that they are likely to survive and reproduce. In the human example, we might see the attention lavished on sons, especially in high castes, as a reflection of their anticipated reproductive success, while daughters would be viewed as something of a liability because of the large dowries required to marry them off, so that surplus daughters might in fact be unmarriageable and thus totally infertile.

Reproduction may be optimized rather than maximized in the animal world. This is an important distinction. The concept of 'maximization' implies that each member of a species tries to produce as many offspring as he or she can. On this basis a male would go from female to female, and a female would resume reproduction as soon as she had given birth. In fact we do not normally find such arrangements in the animal world. Male gibbons, for instance, stay with one female partner for life, and do not copulate for long periods of the year. Female chimpanzees, though capable of reproducing at yearly intervals, in fact space out their offspring with a birth interval of 2.5 to 3.5 years. The reason is that natural selection has eliminated those individuals (and their genes) that reproduced too rapidly to enable their offspring to survive during periods of food shortage, or those whose mating habits were less successful in the long run than others.

This brings us to a consideration of r and K selection

(MacArthur and Wilson, 1967; Pianka, 1970). These terms refer to a pair of alternative reproductive strategies whose existence has long been recognized amongst plants and animals. r and K selection are both forms of natural selection, either of which may occur depending on ecological circumstances. In an unstable environment, with alternating good periods during which there is plenty of food and bad ones when food is scarce, it may 'pay' parents (genetically speaking) to produce large numbers of offspring during the good times, because this will maximize the chances of a few of them surviving the bad times. The optimal reproductive strategy here is to maximise reproductive effort during the good season. Where we find such a strategy (as for instance in many insect species, which over-reproduce enormously in the spring only to have their offspring eaten by predators, or starved or frozen to death later in the year) we see it as the result of r selection (selection for maximal reproduction). By contrast, in a non-seasonal, stable environment things are very different. Whereas the seasonal environment alternates between overcrowding and emptiness, the non-seasonal one is permanently fully occupied, with species occupying all the available niches. Such environments are typical of the tropical and equatorial regions. Here there is no advantage to rapid reproduction; many offspring would *all* die. Instead, parents must aim to reproduce slowly and if the population is stable can barely do more than replace themselves during a lifetime. This slow strategy is a result of 'K' selection (the symbol 'K' stands for the 'carrying capacity' of the environment, that is the number of individuals it can sustain, which in this case is at saturation point and is the factor determining the reproductive strategy).

r selection is associated with very little parental care, while K selection favours prolonged and devoted parental care by one or very often both parents. Religions, too, vary according to the emphasis they place on reproductivity; and we can use the symbols $r^{c}+$ and $r^{c}-$ to describe pro-natalist and anti-natalist cultural rules respectively. (The symbol K presents problems because of humankind's ability to manipulate the carrying capacity of the environment, and we have not used it. The letter 'c' stands for 'cultural rules').

Religions take a great interest in the reproductive activity of each and every individual. They establish the right and wrong conditions for conception to take place, and the rights and wrongs of abortion or infanticide; they control the circumstances of birth; they control adolescent sexuality; they regulate marriage, re-marriage, divorce and widowhood; and their preoccupation with death can, in a variety of ways, sanction the rules of everyday behaviour. In view of the existence of both pro-natalist (r^c+) and anti-natalist (r^c-) rules, we have drawn up a table (table 1) showing how religious rules might approach these life situations.

In fact no religion conforms precisely either to an r^c+ or an r^c- pattern, but there is no doubt that when the world religions are compared with each other they differ considerably with respect to these issues. If we take age at marriage, for instance, the *Laws of Manu* (Buhler (tr.) 1969) state than an eight-year-old bride is suitable for a Brahmin man of 24 years. Such a rule is clearly pro-reproductive. If followed, it implies that a girl will be married by the start of her reproductive period and will be likely to commence childbearing as soon as she is fertile. In contrast, modern Christianity leaves marriage until some years after the commencement of the menstrual cycle.

This difference has side effects, notably the phenomenon of illegitimacy. Delayed marriage is sanctioned in Christianity by a taboo on premarital intercourse, and illegitimacy is stigmatized. By contrast, there are African societies in which premarital pregnancy is valued because it is a sign of fertility. Thus we see how religiously encoded differences affect reproduction, and we can seek for the causes of these differences in environmental factors. We might, for instance, hypothesize that where environmental hazards are great, with consequent high levels of infant mortality and indeed general mortality, religious rules favouring the production of larger numbers of offspring would tend to be transmitted, while in conditions of relative security or affluence, with a high standard of public health, large numbers of offspring *per se* would tend to become disadvantageous because of the cost of high living standards, and so rules favouring a more cautious approach to reproduction would arise.

It should not be thought that religious ideas (such as the

TABLE 1 *Predictions for religious rules based on r^c- and r^c+ selection*

The life-cycle	r^c- selection	r^c+ selection
Conception	Few better	Many better
Infanticide and abortion	Approved of	Disapproved of
Birth and childhood	Few births, more care	Many births, less care
Adolescence	Delayed reproduction	Early reproduction
Marriage	Late marriage	Early marriage
Celibacy	Approved of	Disapproved of
Divorce and widowhood	Remarriage disapproved of	Remarriage preferred
Middle and old age	Refrain from reproduction	Reproduction continued
Death and disposal of the dead	Shock, separation, denial	Acceptance as routine

concepts of premarital chastity or the sinfulness of illegitimacy) play a minor role in human reproductive decisions. Not so – they play a major role. For instance, a comparative study of premarital conception rates in Utah, Indiana and Denmark (Christensen, 1960), has shown how religious ideas of legitimacy radically affect the pattern of human reproductive behaviour. In all cases rates of premarital conception were lower for those married in religious than in civil ceremonies.

Because survival rather than mere birth is important, even pro-natalist religions have rules governing the rate of reproduction. Islam lays down that children should be nursed for two full years (Koran, Sura 2.233), and contemporary data show that Muslims in Pakistan nurse continuously for an average of 21 months (Potter *et al.* 1974). Very probably this delays the return of ovulation. Moreover, Islam does not approve of sexual relations for new mothers until weaning; and this again tends to lengthen the interval between births. The sexual attentions of husbands in polygynous marriages are thus directed towards childless and post-weaning wives.

Contraception as such is not explicitly upheld by any major religion. Hinduism emphasizes the need to beget and rear a son to ensure the salvation of the father (Laws of Manu 2,28; 9, 137–8); this will act against contraception until several children have been born and at least one son has prospered. Buddhism is inexplicit, but is in general opposed to taking life; further it has been argued that contraception is interfering with rebirth, the working out of a person's destiny (Ling, 1969; Ryan, 1953). Traditional Islam has emphasized the positive value of a large family and thus tacitly opposed contraception, though modernist 'liberated' Moslems have from time to time supported it in circumstances of industrial progress and the 'demographic transition' – the process, seen in many countries, by which modernization leads first to decreased mortality and then to decreased fertility shortly afterwards. Protestant Christianity in general is fairly tolerant; although it emphasizes the family, it lays unusual stress on the husband–wife relationship, and a Christian marriage is considered complete even if there are no children. This is exceptional. Roman Catholicism differs from the rest of Christianity in having quite explicitly banned contraception. Modern Catholic moral theology allows family limitation by the 'rhythm method' so long as both partners concur (Ford and Kelly, 1963, pp.2, 430); this is in contrast with earlier views (Pius XI, *Casti Connubii*, 1931), which state that 'every attempt on the part of the married couple during the conjugal act or during the development of its natural consequences, to deprive it of its inherent power and to hinder the procreation of a new life is immoral'. Parents are, however, counselled to show restraint rather than to bring unwanted children into the world.

TABLE 2 *Premarital conception rates (%)*

Type of ceremony	Utah County, Utah	Tippecanoe County, Indiana	Copenhagen, Denmark
Civil	16.6	21.0	37.0
Religious	1.1	9.9	13.5

Source: Christensen, 1960

These complex guidelines indicate the deep involvement of religions in the reproductive process. They reveal people working out their strategies, formulating rules and validating them with the strongest possible sanctions. In the case of Roman Catholicism a central authority attempts to dictate God's wishes not only to affluent fellow-Europeans and Catholics in North America but also to vast numbers of very poor people in South America and elsewhere. The orthodox policy is pronatalist; but in the West 'liberal' Catholics face a personal dilemma, and there is evidence (Westoff and Ryder, 1977) that an increasing number of Catholic women are not conforming to Church teaching (table 3). In this non-conformity we see a pressure to change the rules, a pressure that presumably arises out of changing environmental conditions. The existence of a central dogma, centuries old, is an anomaly; modern circumstances in some countries call for new rules, but so far this step in cultural evolution has not occurred.

Just as religions have rules relating to conception and contraception, so too they concern themselves with survival during pregnancy and after birth. Abortion raises interesting questions about when life begins, or when the spirit enters the body. The teachings of the Gautama Buddha state that 'rebirth takes place when a

TABLE 3 *White Catholic women
not conforming to church teaching
on birth control (%)*

| Year of birth | Age of women | | | | |
	20–4	25–9	30–4	35–9	40–4
1916–20	—	—	—	28	45
1921–25	—	—	30	46	43
1926–30	—	37	40	52	50
1931–35	30	40	50	50	—
1936–40	43	54	68	—	—
1941–45	51	74	—	—	—
1946–50	78	—	—	—	—

Source: Westoff and Ryder (1977)

father and a mother come together, and the one to be born is present' (Suriyabongse, 1954). A modern study in Sri Lanka (Ryan, 1953) quotes a Buddhist as saying, 'if a dead "soul" wishes to be born into your family, it would be a terrible sin to prevent its birth'. Hinduism, too, has a philosophy of reincarnation and opposes abortion at any stage after conception. By contrast, Aristotle (*Politics*, vii, xiv) not only approved of early abortion ('before the embryo has acquired life and sensation') but also gave his reason: the need for 'a limit to the production of children'.

Judaism, Christianity and Islam all oppose abortion unless it is necessary to save the mother's life. Islamic scholars have divided pregnancy into two stages, before and after the instillation of life, which normally occurs at four months. In Islamic law, abortion is an offence against the husband, who, at marriage, 'buys' the future contents of his wife's womb. Wilful abortion is thus punishable by compensation, the amount depending on the age of the foetus (Hathout, 1972). In Christianity abortion became punishable in the fourth century AD; St Augustine made a distinction between a formed and an unformed foetus which is widely held today.

If the matter of abortion were purely secular, it would be relatively uncomplicated. Considerations of family size, population size, health or education could settle each case. But we inhabit a moral world in which secular attitudes are often involved in a constant struggle with spiritual ones. While increasing secularization will tend to promote abortion and other population-stablizing policies, religious revivals (such as the one in Iran in the late nineteen seventies) will tend to exacerbate population growth, unless their rules change. These rules mostly date back to periods of high mortality and can even in some cases (such as Islam) be seen as expansionist. An adaptive theory of cultural evolution would predict that religions will encompass practical policies when conditions make it expedient to do so. Some evolution has certainly occurred: Japan, for example, has integrated the idea of abortion on demand easily into its Buddhist–Shinto thinking. How this change came about is not understood, but flexibility is seen in other sectors of Japanese culture too, for example in industrialization, where conservatism has not blocked the spread of new ideas. Efforts to explain this have sometimes been based on Japan's sudden transition from feudalism to modernity (Morton, 1970). For the student of cultural evolution, and the role of religion within it, there must be much to be learned from Japan.

The next major event after conception for the surviving child is birth. Religions set up rules for this occasion. Among them are rules for life-and-death choices during parturition. Judaism holds that when there is a question of saving the mother or the child, the latter should be destroyed on the grounds that it is the most viable life that gets preference if a choice has to be made (Levine, 1968). Islam, Hinduism and Buddhism all save the mother and sacrifice the child. Roman Catholicism states that neither mother nor child has a better right to life than the other (Davis, 1946, 2, pp.166–7), and that it is morally indefensible to sacrifice the child in order to save the life of the mother, even when this sacrifice is the only means of doing so. There has been a series of decrees from the Holy Office to this effect (1884, 1889, 1895, 1898, 1902).

Many rituals surround the events of birth. In Buddhist Thailand, delivery should take place in a favourable astrological alignment during which the midwife says magical words (Hanks, 1968). Hindu midwives are of low caste since confinement is a situation of impurity. Because cloths used during delivery must be thrown away, old ones, often soiled, are used. The midwife in certain districts does not wash her hands, and has been said to be callous and impervious to the mother's suffering (Lankester 1924, p.5). In Christianity the newborn in danger of death is quickly baptized. In Burma a Buddhist monk's orange robe is often wrapped around a baby to prevent misfortune (Spiro, 1971, p.236). Many cultures isolate the mother. The Hindu mother does not become pure until after a ritual, which is held 40 days after the birth of a girl, 30 days after a boy, though this period is shorter for lower castes (Rose, 1907). Special foods, prayers, and magical spells are available for mother and child all over the world.

In such ways religions mark this event, again involving themselves in the biological process. Their role is more than passive – it is active participation, even to the point of taking over the entire event. In many societies religious rather than what we would call medical functionaries attend and control the events of birth. The birth situation, the mother's actions, and the social setting are prescribed in sacred books or verbal tradition. Much follows from this. Female infanticide was regularly practised in India until the last century (Pakrasi, 1970), and it is also reported from many pre-literate societies (Chagnon, 1977; Rasmussen, 1931). Infant mortality rates can be very high: 272 per thousand in lower castes in Bombay from 1938 to 1946 (Chandrasekhar, 1959, p.105). All over the Third World, birth is very much a time of crisis, and the result is a lower live-birth rate than would be the case under modern medicine, all other things being equal.

But if religious functionaries are not always motivated by considerations of hygiene, their interests may in some cases lead to the survival of unwanted or orphaned children. Christian institutions for foundlings have undoubtedly saved many lives, though their record has not always been good (Fortier, 1963). In Jewish law, where there is no parental estate the community has the obligation to support orphans by providing communal funds for a boy to rent and furnish a house and for a girl's clothing and the minimum dowry necessary for marriage (*Encyclopedia Judaica*, 1971). Hindu religious law requires a man to adopt a son if he has none of his own. Adoption by the husband of the wife's children by former marriage is automatic upon marriage in Islam. Orphans are supported by several passages in the Koran, which stress the need to care for them and not to misuse their property. In such ways religious rules can very signficantly affect the survival prospects of children who might otherwise die.

There are a great many other ways in which religious rules affect both survival and reproduction. The difficulty is, of course, in finding a theory that will account for their diversity. Certainly the concept of adaptiveness should not be rejected until it has been thoroughly explored, and there is every reason to test the hypothesis that, where religions touch on the basic processes of human biology, they say things that make adaptive sense now or that have made adaptive sense in the past. We suggest that the emphasis religions place on reproductivity, that is on bearing children, on early marriage, on teaching about and promoting sexual activity, on condoning divorce and approving remarriage, is directly proportional to the instability or unpredictability of prevailing ecological circumstances. To test this idea we have attempted to grade the world's major religions on a scale of 'reproductivity', based on their attitudes to relevant biological processes.

Christianity has a predominantly negative attitude to premarital and extramarital conceptions. There is an illegitimacy 'stigma', a concept of sex for its own sake as 'sin', and a strong feeling that the sex urge should be controlled, especially when it is at its most urgent, in adolescence. Celibacy is seen as close to godliness, divorce and remarriage disapproved of, especially in the Catholic church. Children, once they have arrived, are however most attentively cared for; such life as exists is sacred and there is much emphasis on hygiene and good medical care. These features place Christianity at the r^c- end of the scale: it has a negative attitude to many aspects of the reproductive process, and this is more marked in the Protestant than the Catholic form.

In contrast, Islam seems to stand at the opposite end. Muslims aim for, enjoy, and take pride in large families. The father has high status, his religion enjoins polygyny, and he may be head of a very large household indeed, up to four wives being allowed. Sex is encouraged during the nights of Ramadan (Koran 2: 183), and erotic instruction is available in religiously sanctioned sex manuals such as the *Perfumed Garden*. Widows are expected to remarry, and divorce is a simple affair. Betrothal is early, as is marriage; but premarital sex is not allowed, nor is adultery by the woman. Celibacy is not encouraged for men and is unthinkable for women. We can put Islam at the r^c+ end of the scale.

Hinduism places great emphasis on conception and, being a male-dominated religion, on the need for sons. Family size tends to be large, but infant mortality is high, not least because of religious attitudes to the birth process, which is considered polluting and impure. Betrothal and marriage occur early for girls, and sexual instruction is enjoined by the religion in such books as the *Kama Sutra* as well as on the carvings of well-known temples. Polygyny is permitted among the wealthy. Adultery is forbidden for wives, and marital fidelity reaches its world apogee with the phenomenon of suttee, in which a widow is burnt with the corpse of her dead husband. Although suttee is now almost extinct, widows are still in an anomalous position, and remarriage is often frowned upon.

TABLE 4   *Religious emphases*

r^c+ end	Grade 1	Islam
	Grade 2	Hinduism
	Grade 3	Judaism
	Grade 4	Buddhism
	Grade 5a	Christianity: Roman Catholicism
r^c- end	Grade 5b	Christianity: Protestantism

Hinduism has many pro-reproductive features, and can perhaps be placed second to Islam in this respect.

Buddhism is not outspoken on issues such as abortion, infanticide or contraception, but is mildly opposed to them all. There is no special religious encouragement for marriage and child-bearing; celibacy is given a great deal of encouragement and in some regions of Tibet celibate monks once comprised up to a third of the men in the community, though this varies a lot from place to place. Polygyny (marriage between one man and several women), polyandry (marriage between one woman and several men) and monogamy are all found; overall the religion seems less pronatalist than its neighbour, Hinduism.

Finally, Judaism differs from Christianity in a number of respects. It has no rules against contraception. Widows are actively encouraged to remarry. Abortion raises the same problems as are encountered by Roman Catholicism: traditionally abhorred, it is seen by younger 'liberals' as a necessity in the modern world. Marriage is enjoined for all, rabbis included; sex is highly approved of in marriage, which is monogamous; celibacy is not approved of; children are given great attention and their life stages marked with rituals. Judaism is pronatalist, more so than Buddhism and Christianity, though less so than Hinduism and Islam. The resulting scale is thus as shown in table 4.

We have taken 45 countries in which one or other of these religions is dominant (table 5) and obtained two ecological measures for each of them: *per capita* energy consumption, and *per capita* gross national product (*United Nations Statistical Yearbook,*

1978). These measures have then been compared with the foregoing reproductivity grades. The results are shown in tables 6 and 7, which show a strong positive correlation ($p<0.001$ in each case).

TABLE 5   *Religion, energy consumption and*
gross national product (GNP) for 45 countries
(data for 1975 and 1976)

Country	Predominant world religion	GNP per capita (US dollars 1975)	Energy consumption per capita (kg coal equiv. 1976)
Nepal	Hindu	110	11
Bangladesh	Muslim	100	32
Afghanistan	Muslim	100	41
Burma	Buddhist	90	49
Sri Lanka	Buddhist	230	106
Vietnam	Buddhist	150	124
Sudan	Muslim	150	143
Pakistan	Muslim	130	181
India	Hindu	130	218
Indonesia	Muslim	150	218
Morocco	Muslim	430	273
Thailand	Buddhist	300	308
Philippines	RC Christian	310	329
Egypt	Muslim	280	473
Malaysia	Muslim	660	578
Peru	RC Christian	710	642
Colombia	RC Christian	510	685
China	Buddhist	300	706
Iraq	Muslim	970	725
Algeria	Muslim	650	729
Brazil	RC Christian	900	731
Turkey	Muslim	690	743
Chile	RC Christian	820	987
South Korea	Buddhist	470	1,020

Mexico	RC Christian	1,000	1,227
Iran	Muslim	1,060	1,500
Argentina	RC Christian	1,900	1,804
Spain	RC Christian	1,960	2,399
Israel	Judaism	3,019	2,541
Venezuela	RC Christian	1,710	2,838
South Africa	Prot. Christian	1,200	2,985
North Korea	Buddhist	1,390	3,072
Italy	RC Christian	2,770	3,284
Hungary	RC Christian	2,140	3,553
Japan	Buddhist	3,880	3,679
France	RC Christian	5,190	4,380
Poland	RC Christian	2,450	5,253
United Kingdom	Prot. Christian	3,360	5,268
West Germany	Prot. Christian	5,890	5,922
Netherlands	Prot. Christian	4,880	6,224
Australia	Prot. Christian	4,760	6,657
East Germany	Prot. Christian	3,430	6,789
Czechoslovakia	RC Christian	3,220	7,397
Canada	Prot. Christian	6,080	9,950
USA	Prot. Christian	6,640	11,554

Sources: Broek, J.O.M. & Webb, J.W. (1978). *A Geography of Mankind,* New York, McGraw Hill. United Nations Statistical Yearbook (1978), New York, United Nations. The Israeli Embassy, London

TABLE 6 *Per capita energy consumption of countries in relation to religious emphasis on reproductivity*

Religion	r^cstatus			Energy consumption (kg of coal equivalent)			
		<100	100–249	250–999	1,000–2,499	2,500–4,999	5,000+
Islam	r^c+++	2	3	6	1		
Hinduism	r^c++	1	1				
Judaism	r^c+					1	
Buddhism	r^c–	1	2	2	1	2	
Christian (RC)	r^c– –			5	3	4	2
Christian (Prot.)	r^c– – –					1	7

Source: UN Statistical Yearbook (1978)

TABLE 7 *Per capita GNP of countries in relation to religious emphasis on reproductivity*

Religion	r^c status		Per capita GNP (US $)				
		<250	250–499	500–999	1,000–2,499	2,500–4,999	5,000+
Islam	r^c+++	5	2	4	1		
Hinduism	r^c++	2					
Judaism	r^c+					1	
Buddhism	r^c−	3	4			1	
Christian (RC)	r^c−−	1	1	4	6	1	1
Christian (Prot.)	r^c−−−				1	5	3

Source: UN Statistical Yearbook (1978)

This conclusion indicates that the instructions religions give to individuals may well be 'adaptive'. Where available energy is low and *per capita* GNP is small, environmental unpredictability is bound to be great and individuals will be constantly harassed by both high levels of mortality and uncertainties about food supply. In these circumstances religions appear to emphasize the need to reproduce, not to contracept, not to practise abortion, to marry young, and to have a positive attitude to sex. They thus enhance the reproductive success of people following the rules; but this happens in a somewhat 'Malthusian' way, by the constant production of more offspring than are expected to survive, with consequent overpopulation when modernization improves survival rates. In the case of countries with high levels of available energy and GNP *per capita,* where high survival rates have become the norm and people expect their offspring to outlive them, religions are more inclined to emphasize later marriage, to play down the need for children (but to place great emphasis on the care of those who are born), to accept contraception and in some cases abortion, and often to have a diffident or even negative attitude to sex. They thus encourage a slower rate of reproduction.

Are the religious differences we have discussed really the outcome of differential ecological pressures, acting via survival and reproductive success to fashion moral attitudes and rules regarding sex, reproduction and child-rearing?

Let us examine some of the principal objections. First, we have apparently ignored the undoubted fact that religions themselves shape the human environment. Thus while an animal is something of a slave to its food supply (with some exceptions), people not only re-create (or at least augment) what nature provides, but they use religious means to do so, for instance by placating and revering the elements, enabling them to practise conservation and achieve sustained yields, and so on. Nevertheless, it is arguable that in the final analysis the environment is the independent variable, culture the dependent one.

Second, ever since Max Weber's *Protestant Ethic and the Spirit of Capitalism,* it has been argued by many historians that Protestant Christianity has been the *source* of material progress and social reorganization, that it is the prime mover of the affluence certain countries have achieved. Such an explanation appears to be in direct contrast with our own, which places religion at the receiving end of material progress, to which it 'adapts'. Clearly, both arguments cannot be wholly right. But if Protestantism has to some extent been the cause of capitalist 'progress', it could still be that some of its features (such as the deferred gratification emphasized by Weber) may have been causal, while others (such as those emphasized in this chapter) may have been adaptations to material life.

Third, and surely more seriously for our argument, we seem to have omitted a proper diachronic analysis of religious rules. Protestant Christian countries may be affluent today, but they were not always so. Nor were Islamic societies always poor. The Mughals, the civilizations of North Africa and the Middle East, all produced fine poetry and paintings and were wealthy in their time, while Britain had its Dark Ages and its plagues. Our omission is obvious, and yet we must ask for data of the appropriate kinds before we can make a proper assessment. To begin with we need to know how widespread wealth may have been in times of 'high civilization' elsewhere; were the ordinary individuals living around Agra at the time of the Taj Mahal enjoying any luxuries at all, or were they much the same as the agricultural labourer or city pauper are today? And second, were there any detectable alterations in attitudes to sex and reproduction on the part of ecclesiastical authorities coinciding with periods of poverty and plenty?

Fourth, we have somewhat misrepresented the 'world religions' as if each had some global unity, when in fact Islam is different in say, Saudi Arabia and Java, or Hinduism in North India and Bali, or Catholicism in South America and Belgium, or Buddhism in Sri Lanka and Tibet. Not only this, but religion in any one country will contain contradictions within its own theology. In defence, we point out that for all its contradictions and peregrinations a religion does not change completely. It maintains its central tenets, especially those that distinguish it from its rivals. Again, more data are needed. When a religion occurs in both an affluent and a poor zone, can we see differences in religious attitudes and rules concerning sex and reproduction, and are they in the predicted directions?

These questions are at present unanswered and call for further research. Work is also needed to refine the methods by which ecological comparisons are made between countries, for the use of such measures as GNP or *per capita* energy consumption may possibly be misleading. Effort is also needed to incorporate more religions into the picture, and perhaps even such 'anti-religions' as Humanism and Marxism. Finally, the undoubted tensions between changing medical and socioeconomic conditions and religious values need to be more fully explored.

Much, therefore, remains to be done if the complex relationship between human religions and the biological processes of human existence is to be further elucidated. The ecological approach we have suggested will surely need considerable modification in future; its hypotheses may be falsified one by one, in which case it will disappear. But even if that were to happen, one thing would remain very clear, namely that religions everywhere take a very close interest in human biology. From conception to death, religion enters into the decisions made by ordinary people the world over in myriad different ways. From the perspective of the anthropologist we have several problems: why are religions so deeply involved? what are religions doing? why should it be religions that are doing it? and how has it come about that particular religions present us with particular rules of action rather than others?

We have presented a comparison with animal ecology. As always, such comparisons are fraught with difficulty. Nevertheless, if a start is to be made in trying to relate the complex and poorly understood processes of human culture with those equally complex processes that underlie the evolution of the social behaviour of all life, then the theory of r and K selection seems a useful starting point. It is to be hoped that further studies will illuminate some of the dark areas that pervade the present enquiry.

REFERENCES

Aristotle (1962) *Politics*, vii, xiv, tr.T.A. Sinclair, Harmondsworth, Penguin.

Berreman, G.D. (1963) *Hindus of the Himalayas,* Berkeley, University of California Press.

Chagnon, N.A. (1977) *Yanomamö: the Fierce People,* New York, Holt, Rinehart & Winston.

Chagnon, N.A. (1979) 'Mate Competition', in N.A. Chagnon and W. Irons (eds) *Evolutionary Biology and Human Social Behaviour,* Duxbury, Duxbury Press.

Chandrasekhar, S. (1959) *Infant Mortality in India, 1901–55,* London, Allen & Unwin.

Christensen, H.T. (1960) 'Cultural Relativism and Premarital Sex Norms', *American Sociological Research,* **25,** pp.53–9.

Davis, K. (1946) *Moral and Pastoral Theology,* London, Sheed & Ward.

Dawkins, R. (1976) *The Selfish Gene,* Oxford, Oxford University Press.

Dickemann, M. (1979) 'Female Infanticide, Reproductive Strategies and Social Stratification: A Preliminary Model', in N.A. Chagnon and W. Irons (eds) *Evolutionary Biology and Human Social Behaviour,* Duxbury, *Encyclopedia Judaica* (1971) Keter, Jerusalem.

Ford, J.C. and Kelly, G. (1963) *Contemporary Moral Theology,* Cork, Mercier Press.

Fortier, B. de la (1963) Les 'enfants trouvés' à l'hôpital général de Montréal, 1754–1804, *Laval Médical,* **34,** pp.442–53; **35,** pp.335–47; **36,** pp.351–9.

Hanks, J.R. (1968) *Maternity and its Rituals in Bang Chan,* Cornell Thailand Project Report No. 6, New York, Cornell.

Harris, M. (1966) 'The Cultural Ecology of India's Sacred Cattle', *Current Anthropology,* **7,** pp.51–66.

Harris, M. (1968) *The Rise of Anthropological Theory,* New York, Crowell.

Hathout, H. (1972) 'Abortion and Islam', *Journal Medicine Libanais,* **25,** pp.237–9.

Irons, W. (1979) 'Cultural and Biological Success', in N.A. Chagnon and W. Irons (eds) *Evolutionary Biology and Human Social Behaviour,* North Scituate, Mass., Duxbury Press.

Koran, The (1960) tr. R. Bell, Edinburgh, Clark.

Lankester, A. (1924) *Lecture on the Responsibility of Men in Matters Relating to Maternity,* Simla, Government of India Press.

Laws of Manu (1969) tr. G. Buhler, New York, Dover.

Levine, R.R. (1968) 'Judaism and Some Modern Medical Problems', *Journal of the Medical Society New Jersey,* **65,** pp.638–9.

Ling, T.O. (1969) 'Buddhist Factors in Population Growth and Control. A Survey Based on Thailand and Ceylon', *Population Studies,* **23,** pp.53–60.

Lumsden, C.J. and Wilson E.O., (1981) *Genes, Mind and Culture,* Cambridge, Mass, Harvard University Press.

MacArthur, R. H. and Wilson, E.O. (1967) *The Theory of Island Biogeography,* Princeton, Princeton University Press.

Malinowski, R. (1944) *The Scientific Theory of Culture,* New York, Oxford University Press.

Morton, W.S. (1970) *Japan, its History and Culture,* Newton Abbot, David & Charles.

Pakrasi, K.B. (1970) *Female Infanticide in India,* Calcutta, Editions Indian.

Pianka, E.R. (1970) 'On *r*- and *K*- Selection', *American Naturalist,* **104,** pp.592–7.

Pius XI (1931) *Casti Connubii,* London, Catholic Truth Society.

Potter, R.G., New, M.L., Wyon, J.B. and Gordon, J.E. (1964) *Symposium on Research Issues in Public Health and Population Change,* Pittsburgh, University of Pittsburgh.

Rappaport, A. (1968) *Pigs for Ancestors,* Yale, Yale University Press.

Rasmussen, K. (1931) *Report of the Fifth Thule Expedition 1921–4,* Copenhagen, Gylendalske Boghandel.

Reynolds, V. (1980) *The Biology of Human Action,* Reading and San Francisco, Freeman.

Reynolds, V. and Tanner, R.E.S., (1983) *The Biology of Religion,* London, Longman.

Rose, H.A. (1907) 'Hindu Birth Observances in the Punjab', *Journal of the Royal Anthropological Institute,* **37,** pp.220–36.

Ryan, B. (1953) 'Hinayana Buddhism and Family Planning in Ceylon', *Milbank Memorial Fund Conference,* New York.

Spiro, M.E. (1971) *Buddhism and Society,* London, Allen & Unwin.

Suriyabongse, L. (1954) 'Human Nature in the Light of the Buddha's Teachings', *Journal of the Siam Society,* **42,** pp.11–22.

United Nations Statistical Yearbook (1978), New York, United Nations.

Vayda, A. (1976) *War in Ecological Perspective. Perspective, Change and Adaptive Processes in three Oceanic Societies,* New York, Plenum Press.

Weber, M. (1930) *The Protestant Ethic and the Spirit of Capitalism,* Translated by Talcott Parsons, London, Allen & Unwin.

Westoff, C.F. and Ryder, N.B., (1977) *The Contraceptive Revolution,* Princeton, Princeton University Press.

Wilson, E.O. (1978) *On Human Nature,* Cambridge, Mass, Harvard University Press.

6

The Religion of Evolution

Mary Midgley

THE KALEIDOSCOPE RE-SHAKEN

Evolution is the creation-myth of our age. By telling us our origins it shapes our views of what we are. It influences not just our thought, but our feelings and actions too, in a way which goes far beyond its official function as a biological theory. In calling it a myth, I am not of course saying that it is a false story. I mean that it has great symbolic power, which is independent of its truth. Is the word religion appropriate to it? This will depend on the sense we give to that very elastic word. I have chosen it deliberately, because I want to draw attention to the remarkable variety of elements which it covers, and to their present strange behaviour. While traditional Christianity held those elements together in an apparently changeless and inevitable grouping, we did not notice how diverse they were. But now that the violent changes of modern life have shaken them apart, they are drifting about and cropping up in unexpected places. Ambiguity of the same fruitful but dangerous kind affects the names of other complex human concerns – names such as *morality, politics, art, sport* and indeed *science*. The ambiguity is dangerous when we do not properly understand it, when we treat these complex conceptual groupings as if they were plain, single ideas. Confusion gets worse when displaced elements migrate from one main grouping to another. And today, a surprising number of the elements which used to belong to traditional religion have regrouped themselves under the heading of science, mainly around the concept of evolution.

The first thing I want to do here is to draw attention to this phenomenon – an alarming one, surely, for those who hold that getting rid of religion is itself a prime aim of science. If the fungicide shares the vices of the fungus, something seems to have gone wrong. But the phenomenon is of wider interest than this to all of us. Why does it happen? Why is this kind of cosmic mythology so strong and so persistent? The simplest explanation, no doubt, is mere force of habit, the residual influence of Christian conditioning. This however, is no longer a plausible story. The days of really confident Christian education are simply too far behind us, and the leading myth-bearers are themselves too rebellious, too critical, too consciously and resolutely anti-Christian. If they are indeed the mental prisoners of their opponent, and that in an age when so much change is so easily accepted, there has to be a special reason for it.

In trying to understand the mythologization of science, we shall do best if we detach ourselves as far as possible from the old Voltairean notion of a ding-dong battle between science and religion. Enquiring more calmly, we shall find that there is not one all-embracing reason why religious elements persist, but many more or less distinct ones. Religion, like other complex human concerns, seems to be built up out of a wide set of natural tendencies which can be variously combined, so that it varies enormously in character according to the way in which we relate them. The same is true of science and also of art. If we want to get rid of the evils which afflict any special grouping we need to study it carefully, to sort its more permanent from its passing elements, and to work out realistically what changes are needed and possible. The attempt to investigate religion in this way will help us to understand both its rise and the rise of other comparable aspects of human life, including the ambitious abstractions which today hope to replace it. Perhaps indeed the concept of religion may be asked to go back to the temple of Delphi and look again at the inscription; know thyself. But if it does, the concept of science should certainly be asked to follow it.

We had better start by glancing at a few typical cases of the phenomenon in question – occasions when science appears to be stealing its supposed opponent's clothes. I shall concentrate on prophecies, because they provide a specially clear example. It is a standard charge against religion that it panders to wish-fulfilment, consoling people for their present miseries by promising wonders in the future, thus dishonestly gaining support by dogmatic and unwarranted predictions. With this charge in mind, let us look at the concluding passage of an otherwise sober, serious and reputable book on the chemical origins of life on earth. William Day's *Genesis on Planet Earth; The Search for Life's Beginning* (1979) reviews the evolution of intelligence, and then turns its attention to the future. Mankind, Day says, is likely to throw up a new, distinct and more intelligent type:

> He (Man) will splinter into types of humans with differing mental faculties that will lead to diversification and separate species. From among these types, a new species, Omega man, will emerge either alone, in union with others, or with mechanical amplification to transcend to new dimensions of time and space beyond our comprehension – as much beyond our imagination as our world was to the emerging eucaryotes . . . If evolution is to proceed through the line of man to a next higher form, there must exist within man's nature the making of Omega man . . . Omega man's comprehension and participation in the dimensions of the supernatural is what man yearns for himself, but cannot have. It is reasonable to assume that man's intellect is not the ultimate, but merely represents a stage intermediate between the primates and Omega man. What comprehension and powers over Nature Omega man will command can only be suggested by man's image of the supernatural. (pp.390–1)

But is there time? Time is a difficulty for Day because major steps in evolution have been occurring at steadily decreasing intervals, and the next step may be due shortly. It must be the one he is waiting for. 'On such a shortened curve, conceivably Omega man could succeed man in fewer than 10,000 years.' Ordinary evolution, however, is too slow to allow this startling development. So what is to be done?

How then can Omega man arise in so short a time?
The answer is unavoidable.
Man will make him. (Day, 1979, p.392)

This is apparently a reference to genetic engineering, something specially important to those whose faith leans heavily on the dramatized idea of evolution. They demand from that idea, not just a satisfying account of the past, but also hope for continued progress in the future. But there is a real difficulty about expecting the human race to evolve further in a literal, biological sense. Human social arrangements, even in simple cultures, block natural selection. And the more elaborate they get, the more they do so. Nineteenth-century social Darwinists attacked this problem with a meat-axe, calling for harsh commercial competition and deliberate eugenic selection so that the race could continue to progress. As we now know, however, these schemes were not just odious but futile. Commercial competition has no tendency to affect reproduction. As for 'positive eugenics', it is not possible to identify desirable genes nor to force people to breed for them; and even if it were, their spread would still be absurdly slow. The natural conclusion is that such schemes should be dropped, and that the human race should take itself as it is and learn to make the best of its existing capacities. But this thought is unbearable to those whose faith in life is pinned to the steady, continuing, upward escalator of evolution. 'If evolution is to proceed through the line of man to a next higher form', as Day puts it, there simply has to be another way. That wish, rather than the amazingly thin argument he produces about recurrent evolutionary steps, is evidently the ground of his confidence in the emergence of 'Omega man'.

THE ILLICIT ESCALATOR

This confidence, it should be noticed, is no part of orthodox, Darwinian theory. The idea of a vast escalator proceeding steadily upward from lifeless matter through plants and animals to man, and inevitably on to higher things, was championed by Lamarck and given currency by Herbert Spencer under his chosen name, 'evolution'. Darwin utterly distrusted the idea, which seemed to him a baseless piece of theorizing, and avoided the name. As far as Darwin could see, 'no innate tendency to progressive development exists . . . It is curious how seldom writers define what they mean by progressive development' (Darwin and Seward, 1903, pp.338–48; cf. Moore, 1979, p.151). His theory of natural selection gives no ground for it and does not require it. As has been pointed out, it arranges species in a radiating bush rather than on a ladder, interpreting all kinds of change equally as limited responses to particular environments. Darwin saw no reason to posit a law guaranteeing the continuation of any particular change, nor did he pick out any one trend, such as increase in intelligence, as the core of the whole process. Spencer, by contrast, believed firmly in a law of inevitable progress, and 'brief inspection made it manifest that the law held in the inorganic world, as in the organic and the superorganic' (Duncan, 1908, p.556). Accordingly, as one of his followers pointed out with pride, 'the Theory of Evolution dealing with the universe *as a whole,* from gas to genius, was formulated some months before the publication of the Darwin–Wallace paper' (Armstrong, 1904, p.48) – a priority claim which Darwin had no wish to dispute.

From that time to this Spencer's bold, colourful and flattering picture of evolution has constantly prevailed over Darwin's more sober, difficult one, not only in the public mind, but also surprisingly often in the minds of scientists who have reason to know its limitations. That very reputable scientist, J.D. Bernal, shaped it in a way which bears some relation to Day's in a remarkable Marxist utopia published in 1929. Pointing out that things might get a trifle dull after the triumph of the proletariat and the withering away of the state, Bernal predicted that only the dimmer minds would be content with this placid Paradise. Accordingly, 'the aristocracy of scientific intelligence' would give rise to new developments and create a world run increasingly by scientific experts. Scientific institutions would gradually become the government and thus achieve 'a further stage of the Marxian hierarchy of domination'. The end result would be that scientists 'would emerge as a new species and leave humanity behind' (Bernal, 1929, pp.68, 69, 71, 73. See Easlea, 1981, p.20).

DIVERGING HUMAN IDEALS

What made this idea seem sensible was surely the prior belief that scientists ought to form a caste apart, running the world without any possibility of interference by politicians, historians, voters or members of any other alien and intrusive group. This idea was strongly promoted by H.G. Wells, and was altogether rather popular in the inter-war years. It is still often found in science-fiction, and permeates other literature. Since a training in physical science does not of itself qualify people as administrators, the word 'science' tends to get a rather odd meaning here. It often seems to centre on membership of the club or tribe of scientists, and rejection of other competing clubs or tribes, rather than on theories or even methods of enquiry. This usage is delightfully shown in B.F. Skinner's utopia, *Walden Two*. Skinner repeatedly and devoutly claims that his utopian world is scientific, but the only sense in which this bizarre place could possibly be called scientific is that its founders think of themselves as scientists, that is, as members of the laboratory-based tribe, united against, e.g., historians. Their curious schemes are not based on discoveries or arguments drawn from any science, but on simple wish-fulfilment about ways of life which would be convenient for scientists. For instance, babies in Walden Two are brought up in almost total isolation in air-conditioned cells up to the age of a year, and still spend much of their time there until they are three. This treatment is so successful that thereafter they are perfectly adjusted members of society and their emotional development gives no further trouble. This, Skinner explains, is the only good way of producing sane, balanced adults. The founder of Walden Two can therefore fully excuse his own rather obvious emotional deficiencies by the agonized cry, 'Can't you see? I'm not a product of Walden Two!' (Skinner, 1948, pp.96–103, 248–9). Now the really staggering thing about these arrangements is that they are contrary to a central tenet of Skinner's scientific beliefs – namely that, since people possess no instincts, behaviour can only be produced by other behaviour. Conditioning is essential. If that tenet is right, the children should come out of their cells even more stunted and helpless than the rest of us would expect – indeed, almost exactly as they went into them three years earlier. That they can come out in an admirable state of emotional development is simply a miracle, explicable only by a far stronger theory of innate tendencies than those against which Skinner constantly fought. In other words, *Walden Two* is the dream of a shy and unsocial scientist; but it is not a scientific dream.

At least Skinner did not propose that his enlightened scientists should form a hereditary caste, reproductively isolated from the proles. Since the Second World War, a certain embarrassment has surrounded this kind of proposal, and it is no longer widely supported. Instead, the emphasis is usually placed on increasing intelligence. But it is clear that this is often seen as equivalent to the proposal to produce more and better scientists. At least, this interpretation seems the only possible explanation of the strange lack of interest in the problem of conflicting ideals. What sort of intelligence are we to aim for? Indeed, more basically still, why is intelligence as such to take precedence over all other human ideals? Such problems are by-passed entirely. Thus, the Nobel-prize-winning biologist J. Lederberg writes in *Towards Century 21*, 'Now what stops us making supermen? The main thing that stops us is that we don't know the biochemistry of the object that we are trying to produce' (Walla (ed), 1978, p.52). It does not seem to strike him, any more than it struck Day, that we cannot identify or conceive that supposed object at all, because of the relation in which we stand to it. Do we want Supereinstein, Supernietzsche, Superbeethoven, Superconfucius, Superdarwin, Superbuddha, Supernapoleon, or some sort of highest common factor (designed by a committee) between these and all other human eminences? How are the superwomen to be fitted in? Even if we somehow made an arbitrary choice, the whole idea of the lesser designing the greater is surely incoherent. Could a child invent an adult, or a crook invent an honest person? Everybody projects their faults into their work, and the more ambitious the work, the more glaring the faults become. We see these limitations plainly when we look back at the past, or outward at other cultures. If each previous century had been given the chance to put its ideals in concrete form – to produce its own supermen – we know just what faults we should expect to find in the products.

Superman-buffs today commonly hope to escape this kind of partiality by assuming first, that what is needed is simply more of a single timeless abstraction – intelligence, measured by intelligence tests – and second that that abstraction is a genetically distinct characteristic, controlled by its own gene or genes. Both these ideas, however, are indefensible. What we normally mean by intelligence is not just cleverness. It includes such things as imagination, normal feelings, good sense and decent aims – things far too complex to appear in tests or to be genetically isolated. What intelligence-testers measure is merely a convenient fiction invented for use in the social sciences – handy no doubt for many purposes, but quite unrelated to the biological complexity of nerves and brain, and a non-starter as a discrete and heritable characteristic.

SCIENTIFIC PROPHECY AND SCIENTIFIC FAITH

If I seem to be telescoping possible arguments somewhat briskly, I apologize. The only point which concerns me here is that the authors cited do not give any arguments at all, but present their assumptions openly as matters of faith. In general, if one questions such things as the possibility of genetically engineering improved hominids, or of producing them by artificial intelligence, one is usually accused of lacking faith. It is pointed out that in the early days of locomotives people did not believe that it was possible to travel at more than 20 miles an hour. The moral, it seems, is that we ought to have more faith, as George and Robert Stephenson and their backers had faith in the possibility of railways. This is very strange reasoning. The Stephensons were specialists, highly pragmatic and experienced engineers who tested their work every step of the way. But this is not at all the position of those who call upon us to have faith in the biological improvement of the human race. Rather than offering clear designs and concrete demonstrations, the prophets of superman simply ask us whether we are really so mean-spirited and so lacking in vision as to deny to the human race the crown which is promised to it.[1] But in what way is it so promised? The answer will usually be some Spencerian theory about evolution. Intelligence ought to go further – it will go further – it *must* go further – but this time the matter is in our hands. Dare we let it slip?

The first thing I find striking about this argument is its likeness to the one which has commonly been seen as a defect in the writings of the Evangelist St Matthew. Matthew often says that certain things were done 'that it might be fulfilled which was foretold by the prophets', and this is generally thought not to be a very sensible aim. The idea of a duty to produce the inevitable is certainly an odd one. However, if we avoid this kind of appeal by resting the case for superman-building on its inherent desirability, then it must compete on its merits with other proposals. When this is done, its most striking feature seems to be its irrelevance to all current or foreseeable human needs. It is not going to arrest any of the shouting ills of the present. It is not the answer to the problems of East *versus* West and North *versus* South. But neither does it have the merit, which usually belongs to more remote ideals, of helping to guide our present conduct. Notions like perpetual peace or the brotherhood of man are real ideals; they can change our aim in the present even if we think them unattainable. But the idea of a superman-blueprint somewhere in the pipeline does not seem to have any possible moral application, except to demand resources and perhaps to make us shelve immediate problems in the hope that the superpeople will solve them. It is not an ideal at all but an expedient, and one which could not be put in hand until existing clashes of ideals had been resolved – a condition which itself probably presupposes the millennium.

Theodosius Dobzhansky holds a much more clear-headed, sensitive and humane variant of the same general faith, and he is seriously worried by the thought that those of us outside the laboratories may not find that the evolutionary process gives our lives much meaning:

> Are the multitudes supererogatory? They may seem so, in view of the fact that the intellectual and spiritual advances are chiefly the works of elite minorities. To a large extent, they are due to an even smaller minority of individuals of genius. The destiny of a vast majority of humans is death or oblivion. Does this majority play any

role in the evolutionary advancement of humanity? (Dobzhansky, 1967, p.132)

He concludes that it does; we are not just 'manure in the soil in which are to grow the gorgeous flowers of elite culture'. Rather 'it is imperative that there be a multitude of climbers. Otherwise the summit may not be reached by anybody. The individually lost and forgotten multitudes have not lived in vain, provided that they too made the effort to climb!' Will this metaphor do for most of the human race? Scarcely. But their situation is not in the end quite so dreary as this passage makes it sound, since after some hesitation Dobzhansky signs up with Teilhard de Chardin for the 'Nöosphere', taking the final ideal to be, not the intellectual perfection of a separate caste, but brotherly love achieved by the whole human race. And brotherly love is something that can be immediately practised, not just planned as a biochemical possibility for the future. Nevertheless, the dismal limitations of an ideal which is both centred on a narrow set of intellectual faculties and placed entirely in the future are evident in the passage just quoted. Moreover, in the work of prophets like Day the position of outsiders is not considered at all. The scientists can find fulfilment in the superman-project, for they mean to be inside the laboratory designing him, not only to their own specifications but in their own (improved) image. For them, it is a matter of self-worship. But what anybody else might get out of the project it is impossible to imagine.

CLAIMS FOR THE FUTURE OF SCIENCE

Let us turn now to a slightly different kind of prophecy, concerned mainly with the rosy future of science itself, but involving incidentally surprising predictions about other aspects of life. It is from the sociobiologist Edward O. Wilson, who writes:

When mankind has achieved an ecological steady state, probably by the end of the twenty-first century, the internalization of social evolution will be nearly complete. About this time biology should be at its peak, with the social sciences maturing rapidly . . . cognition will be translated into circuitry. Learning and creativeness will be defined as the alteration of specific portions of the cognitive machinery regulated by input from the emotive centers. Having cannibalized psychology, the new neurobiology will yield an enduring set of first principles for sociology . . . Skinner's dream of culture predesigned for happiness will surely have to wait for the new neurobiology. A genetically accurate and hence completely fair code of ethics must also wait. (Wilson, 1975, pp. 574–5)

This sort of dogmatic confidence is interesting, because scrupulous moderation in making factual claims is commonly taken to be a central part of the scientific attitude. Listing the bad habits which infest religion, Julian Huxley naturally mentioned 'dogmatism' and 'aspiring to a false certitude' among them, and explained that science corrects these vices (Huxley, 1927, p.372). Remarks like those just quoted do not on the face of it seem to meet this standard. When I have complained of this sort of thing to scientists, I have found that some of them make a rather surprising defence. They reply that these remarks appear in the opening or closing chapters of books, and that everybody knows that what is found there is not to be taken seriously – it is just flannel for the general public. The idea seems to be that supplying such flannel constitutes a kind of a ritual. If so, it must surely strengthen our present uneasiness, since addiction to ritual is another supposed fault of religion. The point might of course be the different and more practical one of simply selling books. But if grossly inflated claims to knowledge of the future are being inserted for that reason, then either there is common dishonesty for personal profit, or there is an attempt to advance the cause of science by obviously unworthy methods. Putting these prophecies in a special part of the book does not disinfect them, unless the particular public for which the book is intended is clearly warned to take them as fiction, and clearly told just what part fiction plays in the work as a whole. It cannot be more excusable to peddle groundless predictions to the general public, who are ill-equipped to recognize them for what they are, than it is to propagate them amongst one's professional colleagues, who are in a better position to identify the particular bees infesting one's bonnet.

These few examples may be enough to show that the contrast between science and religion is unfortunately not as plain, nor the relation between them as simple, as is often believed. Thoughtful scientists have often said this, but a great many of their colleagues, and the public generally, have not seen the point, so I think further discussion is justified. What often seems to happen is that a large number of different antitheses are mixed together indiscriminately, to give force to the idea of a general crusade of light against darkness. We could group them roughly as follows:

1		Superstition
		Partiality
		Error
		Magic
Science	vs.	Wish-fulfilment
		Dogmatism
		Blind Conformism
		Childishness
2 Common sense		
Science		Mysticism
Rationalism	vs.	Faith
Logic		
		Idealism
		Animism
Materialism	vs.	Vitalism
		Common-sense dualism
3 Progress	vs.	Tradition
The future	vs.	The past
Empiricism	vs.	Rationalism
		Metaphysics
Scepticism	vs.	Credulity
Reason	vs.	Feeling or emotion
Objective	vs.	Subjective

Experience	vs.	Reason
Physical Science	vs.	Other intellectual disciplines ('the humanities')
Realism	vs.	Reverence
Prose	vs.	Poetry
Clarity	vs.	Mystery

The antitheses in the first group seem the most promising for crusaders. In them science stands opposed to something unquestionably bad. But in these cases physical science is not the only opponent of the evils in question. Superstition, partiality, and so forth find their opposites in clear thinking generally, and a particular superstition is as likely to be corrected by common-sense or history as by one of the physical sciences. The second group deals in ideas which are more ambitious, more interesting, but also much more puzzling, because we at once need definitions of the terms involved, and it is not easy to give these without falling into difficulties. The odd tendency of both rationalism and common-sense to jump the central barrier is only one example of these difficulties. In the third group, the contrasts are a good deal clearer. But they do not seem to provide material at all suitable for a crusade. They describe pairs of complementary elements in life and thought, pairs in which terms could scarcely be identified except in relation to each other. We should not use that truculent little 'vs' to divide such terms. They go very well together, and crusaders must avoid trying to set them at loggerheads. Thus it does not matter here that 'reason' appears on both sides; it is no longer possible to reduce all these pairs to a single underlying contrast. The distinctions overlap one another, and different ones are needed for different purposes.

The difficulty of relating these various antitheses clearly can be seen in Bertrand Russell's very interesting and influential book *Mysticism and Logic* (1917). Russell's main enterprise was an admirable and serious attempt to move the whole debate into our group three – to show apparently warring elements as both necessary and complementary:

Metaphysics, or the attempt to conceive the world as a whole by means of thought, has been developed, from the first, by the union and conflict of two very different human impulses, the one urging men towards mysticism, the other urging them towards science . . . In Hume, for instance, the scientific impulse reigns quite unchecked, while in Blake a strong hostility to science co-exists with profound mystic insight. But the greatest men who have been philosophers have felt the need both of science and of mysticism; the attempt to harmonize the two was what made their life, and what always must, for all its arduous uncertainty, make philosophy, to some minds, a greater thing than either science or religion . . . Mysticism, is, in essence, little more than a certain intensity and depth of feeling in regard to what is believed about the universe . . . Mysticism is to be commended as an attitude towards life, not as a creed about the world. The metaphysical creed, I shall maintain, is a mistaken outcome of the emotion, although this emotion, as colouring all other thoughts and feelings, is the inspirer of whatever is best in Man. Even the cautious and patient investigation of truth by science, which seems the very antithesis of the mystic's swift certainty, may be fostered and nourished by that very spirit of reverence in which mysticism lives and moves. (Russell, 1917, pp.9, 10, 16)

Russell got a lot of things right here. He 'got in', as they say, many items from the right-hand column of our antitheses in legitimate relation to science. He saw that, far from being a menace to science, emotion of a suitable kind may be necessary to it; and he saw that something similar is necessary for metaphysics too. The word metaphysics here is not used in the abusive sense, to mean mere empty vapouring. Rather, it is used in its proper sense of very general conceptual enquiry, covering such central topics as the relation of mind and matter, free-will and necessity, meaning, truth and the possibility of knowledge, all in an attempt to make sense of the world as a whole. In this sense, not only particular views like materialism and empiricism but also more generally sceptical enquiries are all parts of metaphysics. Empty vapouring is just bad metaphysics.

Russell had the advantage of having started his philosophical life as a disciple of Hegel, and he was not tempted (as were Hume and his disciples) to suppose that metaphysics is really just a matter of cutting down one's thoughts on such topics to a minimum. He knew that even highly constructive metaphysicians like Plato and Heraclitus, Spinoza and Hegel were not merely self-deluded; rather, they had something important to say. Yet having converted to empiricism, Russell did not want to leave the constructors any more scope than was absolutely necessary. His solution was to concentrate on the emotional function of this large-scale, constructive metaphysics, and on the intellectual function of sceptical philosophy and science. Thus mystical, constructive metaphysics was to supply the heart of the world-grasping enterprise, while science supplied the head.

THE COMPLEXITY OF SCIENCE

This is a bold and ingenious idea, but something has gone wrong with it. Russell has fitted the head of one kind of enquiry onto the heart of another. Constructive metaphysics has its own thoughts, and science its own motives. If the word *science* means what it seems to mean here – primarily the search for particular facts – then it is powered by the familiar motive of detailed curiosity. But if it means the building of those facts into a harmonious system, then it draws upon a different motive – the desire for intellectual order – which is also the motive for constructive metaphysics. Without this unifying urge, science would be nothing but mindless, meaningless collecting. At the quite mundane level of science, and quite apart from any question of mystical contemplation, the system-building tendency, with its aesthetic criteria of elegance and order, is already involved. Scientific hypotheses are not generated by randomizers, nor do they grow on trees, but on the branches of these ever-expanding thought-systems. This is why the sciences continually go beyond everybody's direct experience, and do so in a direction quite different from that of common-sense, which has more modest systems of its own. And because isolated systems are always incomplete and may conflict with each other, inevitably in the end they require metaphysics, 'the attempt to conceive the world as a whole', to harmonize them.

Long before that stage is reached, however, these intellectual constructions may present lay people with problems of belief quite as difficult as those presented by religion, and they may be equally firm in demanding faith as a response to them. They do so at present over relativity, over the size of the universe, over quantum mechanics, over evolution, and many other matters. Believers are expected to bow to the mystery, admit the inadequacy of their faculties, and accept paradoxes. If a mystical sense of reverence is, as Russell suggests, the right response to the genuinely vast and incomprehensible universe, then science itself requires it, since it is a means of access to this universe. It cannot therefore be right to call mysticism and science, as Russell does, two distinct, coordinate 'human impulses'. Mysticism is a range of human faculties, science a range of enquiries which can, at times, call these faculties into action. But long before it does so, it has parted company with common-sense, transcended experience and begun to ask for faith.

In *Mysticism and Logic*, Russell writes as if science, common-sense and experience were virtually the same thing – a kind of downright everyday truthfulness about the facts, straightforwardly opposed to the extravagant Hegelian metaphysics which flows from treating mystical emotion as a source of knowledge. Yet in his earlier *Problems of Philosophy* (1912), he points out the deep gaps between them. Our common-sense beliefs go far beyond our own individual experience, and are often at odds with it. And fully-developed science tells a quite different story from both. Much hard conceptual plumbing is needed if we are to connect them all in a watertight manner. Russell's mention of Hume in *Mysticism and Logic* as someone in whom 'the scientific impulse reigns quite unchecked' shows strikingly how far he had for the moment forgotten this kind of difficulty. Hume was no less deeply sceptical about physical science than he was about every other intellectual enterprise. Because he was so determined an empiricist, so resolute in accepting nothing but experience, he thought the idea of natural regularity extremely fishy, and sharply criticized his predecessor Locke's credulity. 'If we believe that fire warms, or water refreshes, it is only because it costs us too much pains to think otherwise' (Hume, 1978, p.270). British empiricism did not move from this sceptical position towards any real acceptance of modern science until Mill wrote his *Logic*. This still left many difficulties, some of which Russell himself did a great deal to remove. But there is a formidable pile of them left today, providing work for anyone (scientist or philosopher) who wants to understand what the sciences are really doing, and to see how to deal with their conflicts. Within the notion of science itself there are large, unresolved clashes – notably between the idea that it is simply a vast memory-store, a register of facts, and the quite different one that it is an intellectual system constructed by reasoning as a means to understanding the universe. These problems are of course no discredit to science. But they are a real obstacle to inscribing its name on a banner as a simple sign to fight under.

ON HAVING FAITH IN REASON

These divisions bring us to another key issue, rationalism. This means confidence in reason, and people's attitude to it naturally depends on what reason is supposed to be opposing at the time. When the opposite is superstition or some other member of our first right-hand column, there is no problem; all intellectuals are supposed to be united against it. But what of the less simple situation in which reason is opposed to experience – where people's perceptions seem not to accord with what they believe must be true, as for instance over the size of the stars, the shape of the earth, or the solidity of matter? Science is by no means always on the side of experience, as is plain when unexpected results are dismissed as experimental error, or in cases like parapsychology where scientists unite to refuse to look at certain groups of data at all. This may be perfectly reasonable, but the point we have to notice about it here is the strong faith which it testifies in a general, theoretical, *a priori* view of the universe.

Perhaps some such faith is an intellectual necessity. In that case, the important thing seems to be not to take it for granted, but to be conscious of it, to distinguish its various elements, and to see on what grounds we can choose between them when there are alternatives. Moderate rationalism – a certain degree of confidence in reason against experience – can be perfectly sensible. It need not commit us, as the stronger rationalism of Plato and Hegel does, to regarding the world of experience as in any way unreal or delusive. But what it does mean is that we cannot defend our theories by treating them simply as matters of direct experience. They depend also on faith, on a choice of how to regard the universe. It must follow that faith is not just something to be got rid of, but something to be rightly directed.

Is it reasonable, for instance, to have faith that the universe as a whole is lawful and regular? Two objections to this are currently influential, but I believe neither of them carries much real weight. They are first scepticism, and second logical atomism, and I shall deal with them in turn. In the conclusion of the first volume of his *Treatise of Human Nature*, Hume expressed a devotion to scepticism as such, a conviction that any belief is something of a sinful indulgence. He sceptically accepted his inability to live up to these principles, but regarded this as a mere weakness. He has had some imitators and still more admirers, but the ground for their admiration needs attention. The trouble is not just that Hume's position is self-destructive, demanding as it does an unsceptical confidence in one's own memory and powers of reasoning. Much worse, it rests on a piece of arbitrary moral dogmatism, namely a conviction that the vices attending disbelief are less grave than those attending belief. Chronic, habitual believers are not more prone to complacency and laziness than chronic, habitual disbelievers are to arrogance, perversity and self-dramatization. At best, in its own day, Hume's move merely substituted the vices of youth for those of age. But now, when disbelief has long been fashionable, sceptics can give us the benefit of both sets of vices at once. Both sets are equally distracting and dangerous. Since disbelief, as much as belief, is a positive, chosen attitude, parsimony cannot settle the matter. It makes no sense to opt for either belief or disbelief wholesale, as a general policy. We must keep both options open, assessing particular propositions on their merits.

Logical atomism is rather subtler. It is the view that all truths are particular truths, and that general propositions about the universe as a whole have no meaning whatsoever. Thus Russell, reacting sharply against the bold Hegelian view that the universe was essentially one, ruled (with equal boldness) that the very notion of a universe was illicit. 'I believe that conception of "the universe" to be, as its etymology indicates, a mere relic of pre-Copernican astronomy. . . The apparent oneness of the world is an undiscussed postulate of most metaphysics . . . Yet I believe that the apparent oneness of the world is merely the oneness of what is seen by a single spectator or apprehended by a single mind' (p.76).

This principle would veto all talk about the universe as a whole and thus prevent our expressing any general view of it, such as, for instance, the idea that it is lawful and regular. Logical atomism is a specialized form of scepticism, but it is one to which we need not bow, for it rests on a confusion. The particular propositions which it treats as ultimate could not have been formed without the framework of wider concepts which serve as their background and provide their terms. As Wittgenstein saw, particular propositions cannot always be prior to general ones. Both are elements in language, which is itself an element in our whole system of behaviour (Wittgenstein 1953, Part I). In a crucial sense, the whole is always prior to its parts. And unquestionably this kind of belief in a law-abiding universe – which is a real belief, not just a policy – is a precondition of any possible physical science.

AWE, REVERENCE AND MYSTERY

In what spirit, then, is it rational for a scientist to confront the universe in which he has this kind of confidence? Julian Huxley answered without hesitation that the spirit should be a religious one, simply because of the situation of our species as a tiny part of it. In man, he wrote,

> for the first time life becomes aware of something more than a set of events; it becomes aware of a system of powers operating in events . . . Man frames his own idea of these powers . . . We call it religious when on the one hand it involves some recognition of powers operating so as to underlie the general operation of the world, and, on the other hand, when it involves the emotions. (Huxley, 1923, pp.209–10)

In such a situation, awe and reverence were entirely appropriate emotions, and Huxley insisted that an investigator who lacked them would make a bad scientist. Russell, though he did not use the word religion as widely, made a very similar point:

> In religion, and in every deeply serious view of the world and of human destiny, there is an element of submission, a realization of the limits of human power, which is somewhat lacking in the modern world, with its quick material successes, and its insolent belief in the boundless possibilities of progress. 'He that loveth his life shall lose it', and there is danger lest, through a too confident love of life, life itself should lose much of what gives it its highest worth. The submission which religion inculcates in action is essentially the same in spirit as that which science teaches in thought. (Russell, 1917, p.29)

More recently, Dobzhansky wrote as follows:

> Rejecting vitalism in no way conflicts with what Albert Schweitzer has called 'reverence for life'. Man's conscience, the existence of life, and indeed of the universe itself, all are parts of the *mysterium tremendum* ... There is no more succinct, and at the same time accurate, statement of the distinctive quality of human nature than that of Dostoevsky: 'Man needs the unfathomable and the infinite just as much as he does the small planet which he inhabits' ... In every known human society ... peoples have arrived at some system of religious views concerning the meaning and the proper conduct of their lives ... Religion enables human beings to make peace with themselves and with the formidable and mysterious universe into which they are flung by some power greater than themselves. (Dobzhansky, 1967, pp.25, 63, 92)

This attitude owes a good deal to the fact that Dobzhansky, like Einstein, was the kind of scientist who emphasized the inevitable slightness of the whole scientific achievement and its absurd disproportion to the vastness of what there is to be known, rather than the kind who claims that the job is nearly finished. Contrast Dobzhansky's outlook with that of Francis Crick:

> While a scientist is sobered by the economic and political problems

he sees all around him, he is possessed of an almost boundless optimism concerning his ability to forge a wholly new set of beliefs, solidly based on both theory and experiment, by a careful study of the world around him and, ultimately, of himself and other human beings . . . The feeling is that within a few generations we shall have got to the heart of the matter. (Crick, 1981, p.165)

The matter in question is 'the intricacies of the brain', but Crick is equally cheerful about all other branches of scientific enquiry, including 'major efforts to improve the nature of man himself' (p.118). Readers will inevitably tend to divide themselves here into those who think that the difference between these two groups of scientists is due to the startling scientific progress made in the decade or two between their times of writing, and those who explain it, more simply, by a sharp decline in the quality of scientific education. The point I am currently making about the idea of 'the universe as a whole' is that, if one means by it not much more than what already is written down in scientific books, one is less likely to be deeply impressed with its vastness and mystery than if one regards those books as small mirrors reflecting only some of its more superficial aspects.

Is it in order for Dobzhansky and Huxley to describe their world-view as religious, or even as a religion? It is obviously not a religion if by this we mean something that a recruit can put down in the appropriate column of his army form and expect suitable provision for worship. But, as I suggested at the outset, some of the elements combined in Christianity and its more familiar alternatives seem to be dispersing, and many other religions never combined them all in the first place. In their original forms, Buddhism had no god and Judaism no doctrine of immortality. Stoicism, which also lacked both and had no ritual either, clearly served most of the functions of a religion for its followers. So does Marxism, which has a good deal in common with the evolutionist faith.

In his great book *The Varieties of Religious Experience*, William James concluded that an attitude could usefully be called religious so long as it was one directed to the world as a whole, 'about which there is something solemn, serious and tender' (James 1902, p.56).

He argued that the attitude must be one of acceptance, not rejection, and that this acceptance should be not grudging but enthusiastic. Such acceptance rested on 'belief that there is an unseen order', and flowed from 'that fundamental mystery of religious experience, the satisfaction found in absolute surrender to the larger power', a surrender which was based in turn on the sense that all things work together for good. Because this kind of attitude had had such a bad press in Western thought since the eighteenth century, James spent a great deal of his book pointing out that it would not do for empiricists, of all people, to dismiss so potent an element in human life unexamined. Empiricism, he said, demanded that religious experience be examined seriously and open-mindedly rather than defined in advance in ways designed to pre-empt it of all significance.

TWO WAYS OF EXALTING EVOLUTION

In this chapter I have of course not tried to duplicate James's work, but I have attempted to trace the path by which scientists, merely by being scientists, can find themselves resting in an attitude which is in a plain sense religious. The intellectual attitude necessary for science, if given its full scope and not reduced artificially to a mere mindless tic for collecting, is continuous with a typically religious view of the world. It is one of the varieties of religious experience. When this fact is noticed, however, very fishy conclusions are sometimes drawn from it, which tend to produce the bizarre and occasionally monstrous prophecies that have been cited. Scientists who see that they are in some sense neighbours of religion are sometimes moved, not to an exploration of shared interests, but to the hope of loot and plunder. Julian Huxley often noted with exasperation that orthodox religion, of a kind which he himself found pointless, seemed still to retain its force, while science, even when believed, had much less influence. He wanted a transfer of spiritual assets. In our own day Edward O. Wilson wastes no time complaining, but spits on his palms to set the matter right:

The time has come to ask; Does a way exist to divert the power of religion into the services of the great new enterprise that lays bare the sources of that power? . . . Make no mistake about the power of scientific materialism. It presents the human mind with an alternative mythology that until now has always, point for point in zones of conflict, defeated traditional religion. Its narrative form is the epic, the evolution of the universe from the big bang . . . (Wilson, 1978, p.196)

Wilson's attitude here may look superficially rather like Dobzhansky's, but they differ profoundly. Dobzhansky expressed his own highly complex faith, and was much concerned with its difficulties. Wilson, in a manner all too familiar to Christians, is asking, 'What faith does the age require?' He is in no doubt about the answer, which he gives in the conclusion of *On Human Nature:*

The true Promethean spirit of science . . . constructs the mythology of scientific materialism, guided by the corrective devices of the scientific method, addressed with precise and deliberately affective appeal to the deepest needs of human nature, and kept strong by the blind hopes that the journey on which we are now embarked will be farther and better than the one just completed. (p.209)

Wilson is chiefly concerned with how best to make converts. Dobzhansky, being deeply interested in other people's faiths and the problems which surround them, recognizes at once the religious elements in his own position, and maps out the various religious and non-religious paths which neighbour his own, considering them as real options. For Wilson the word 'religion' seems to be little more than the banner of an alien tribe whose assets are to be stolen. He seldom mentions any manifestation of religion which is not openly crude and contemptible. Dobzhansky sees that science and religion cannot, properly speaking, be in competition. For him, 'Science and religion deal with different aspects of existence. If one dares to overschematize for the sake of clarity, one may say that these are the aspect of fact and the aspect of meaning' (p.96). Dobzhansky deals with many local conflicts between views on both sides, but aims steadily to bring both into focus together. Wilson never doubts that there is direct competition or that it has been won, since science (in the form of sociobiology) has 'explained' religion, while religion cannot explain science (Wilson 1975, pp.559–62, 1978, p.192). This is a profoundly mistaken view. Causal explanation (which is the only kind offered) is not relevant to the value of the thing explained, as can be seen by thinking about the parallel case of a possible 'causal explanation of mathematics'. What Wilson is really trying to do is to account for the existence and power of religion, on the uncriticized assumption that its content is nothing but a load of humbug. Some people approach questions about the existence and power of sociobiology in the same spirit. In neither case does this seem to be a useful way to understand the phenomenon.

One last contrast – Dobzhansky really does understand the difference between predictions and ideals, and Wilson does not. Prophets can fairly deal in both these wares, but it is vital that they should grasp the distinction. Predictions get their support from factual evidence. Ideals get theirs from considerations of value. From its outset, the Wellsian tradition of prophecy, centring on a distorted, emotive notion of 'science', has mixed these methods. It has tended to represent its own chosen conception of the future as obligatory because it was inevitable, and also *vice versa*. The roots of this bad habit go back to Nietzsche, who first suggested answering the question 'Why should we do this?' by saying 'because the future calls for it'. Nietzsche's main point was that this is a better answer than 'because we have always done it in the past'. Even if this is true – which is none too obvious – plenty of other alternatives are available.

The confusion between predictions and ideals launches, under the banner of science, a fearful jumble of ideas which are as indefensible scientifically as they are morally, and which carry all the drawbacks of a religion with none of its advantages. In this chapter I have dealt chiefly with a particular range of prophecies whose remoteness both from genuine biological theory and from humanity's present moral problems is exceptionally plain. But there are plenty of other areas where the confusion is just as bad. A central one is the distortion of Darwinian theory to justify callous and egoistic individualism by the use of ideas, and still more of language, which dramatizes natural selection in an indefensible way. I have discussed this repeatedly elsewhere (Midgley, 1978, pp.113–58; 1979; 1980; 1981, pp.19–24; and 1984). Social Darwinism, which is really Spencerism, is not yet dead. The theory of evolution is, as I said at the outset, our creation-myth. Because it tells us how we got here, we expect it to tell us what we are. Up to a point it can indeed do this. And because it has this real explanatory force, distortions can also be used to misinform us in a disastrous way.

This capacity for damage is much increased by a confusion among many scientists about the boundaries between science and religion. They assume that, once they are outside the borders of strictly scientific reasoning, all intellectual standards cease to apply. General discourse, such as that found in the last chapters of books, seems to some of them just a free-for-all, a license for propaganda and emotional engineering. Religions appear to them merely the current holders of this licence, fortunate monopolists engaged in raising and exploiting irresponsibly certain childish emotions. Unquestionably childishness is widespread and takes many forms. Arrogance and over-confidence are no less clear symptoms of it than dependence. What should be obvious, however, is that the great religions do not exist to create or indulge the strong emotions they channel, but to discipline and control them. To call such emotions in themselves childish, as the Victorians so unhesitatingly did, is scarcely open to us today. We are no longer confident enough to declare that we are the only adults among the human race. Those emotions are no less strong and prevalent in our supposedly more mature culture than in others, they are merely less well recognized and understood. We venerate an extraordinary range of things – from speed to mechanical ingenuity – and use the name of science in a manner quite unrelated to its proper function, as a general banner for our veneration. Thus, what has been ceremonially ejected at the front door re-enters at the back one in a different guise. The ideas collected into the cult of evolution are a prime case of this and urgently need our attention.

NOTES

1 Thus Francis Crick prophesies: 'provided mankind neither blows itself up nor completely fouls up the environment, *and is not overrun by rabid anti-scientific fanatics,* we can expect to see major efforts to improve the nature of man himself' – i.e. more genetic engineering – 'within the next ten thousand years.' (1981, p.118, my italics). The use of the word 'we' here is interesting.

REFERENCES

Armstrong, A.C. (1904) *Transitional Eras in Thought, with Special Reference to the Present Age,* New York, Macmillan.

Bernal, J.D. (1929) *The World, The Flesh and the Devil,* London, Cape.

Crick, F.(1981) *Life Itself, Its Origin and Nature,* New York, Simon and Schuster.

Darwin, F. and Seward, A.C. (1903) *More Letters of Charles Darwin; A Record of his Work in a Series of Hitherto Unpublished Letters,* London, John Murray.

Day, W. (1979) *Genesis on Planet Earth; The Search for Life's Beginning,* Michigan, House of Talos.

Dobzhansky, T. (1967) *The Biology of Ultimate Concern,* London, Rapp and Whiting.

Duncan, D. (1908) *The Life and Letters of Herbert Spencer,* London, Williams and Norgate.

Easlea, B. (1981) *Science and Sexual Oppression,* London, Weidenfeld & Nicolson.

Hume, D. (1978) *Treatise of Human Nature* (ed). Nidditch, Oxford, Oxford University Press.

Huxley, J.S. (1923) *Essays of a Biologist,* London, Chatto and Windus.

Huxley, J.S. (1927) *Religion Without Revelation,* London, Benn.

James, W. (1902) *The Varieties of Religious Experience,* New York, Longmans.

Midgley, M. (1978) *Beast and Man; The Roots of Human Nature,* New York, Cornell University Press.

Midgley, M. (1979) 'Gene-Juggling', in *Philosophy,* **54,** no. 210, reprinted in Montagu, ed. (1980), pp.108–34.

Midgley, M. (1980) 'Rival Fatalisms; The Hollowness of the Sociobiology Debate', in Montagu, ed. (1980) pp.15–38.

Midgley, M. (1981) *Heart and Mind; The Varieties of Moral Experience,*

Brighton, Harvester Press.

Midgley, M. (1984) 'De-Dramatizing Darwinism' in *The Monist*, **67**, no. 2, April.

Montagu, A. (ed.) (1980) *Sociobiology Examined*, New York, Oxford University Press.

Moore, J.R. (1979) *The Post-Darwinian Controversies*, Cambridge, Cambridge University Press.

Russell, B. (1912) *The Problems of Philosophy*, Oxford, Oxford University Press.

Russell, B. (1917) *Mysticism and Logic*, London, Allen and Unwin.

Skinner, B.F. (1948) *Walden Two*, New York, MacMillan.

Walla, C.S. (ed,) (1978) *Towards Century 21*, New York, Basic Books.

Wilson, E.O. (1975) *Sociobiology: The New Synthesis*, Cambridge, Mass., Harvard University Press.

Wilson, E.O. (1978) *On Human Nature*, Cambridge, Mass., Harvard University Press.

Wittgenstein, L. (1953) *Philosophical Investigations*, Oxford, Blackwell.

7

Let There Be Light: Scientific Creationism in the Twentieth Century

Eileen Barker

It is naive to suppose that the acceptance of evolution theory depends upon the evidence of a number of so-called 'proofs'; it depends rather upon the fact that the evolutionary theory permeates and supports every branch of biological science, much as the notion of the roundness of the earth underlies all geodesy and all cosmological theories on which the shape of the earth has a bearing. Thus anti-evolutionism is of the same stature as flat-earthism.

Sir Peter Medawar

INTRODUCTION AND HISTORICAL BACKGROUND

Amongst the 'educated public' of post-war England, it has only recently been realized that people *could* believe, on what they considered to be scientific grounds, that the creation story of Genesis is literally true. The confrontation between Thomas Huxley and Samuel Wilberforce in 1860 seemed as much a thing of the past as Galileo's being forced to abjure Copernican theory or Bruno's being burned at the stake – it was something that happened long ago, and had no conceivable place in the modern world.

In England, major debates about the scientific respectability of evolution were effectively over well before the end of the nineteenth century. Darwin's *Origin of Species* had certainly met with considerable opposition in the 1860s and 1870s, but the rediscovery in 1900 of Mendel's earlier work on genetics heralded a twentieth century dominated by Darwinian or neo-Darwinian perspectives in biology.

Of course, the Genesis story was not completely disavowed; but the majority of British Christians came to regard the Bible as a source of moral and spiritual (rather than scientific) revelation. In this view, the Old Testament account of creation was seen as a myth that had explained their origins to peoples who had no access to the revelations of modern biology. God was still recognized as creator perhaps; but it was generally agreed that his method had been naturalistic and evolutionary. Darwin himself had written:

> When I view all beings not as special creations, but as the lineal descendants of some few beings which lived long before the first bed of the Cambrian system was deposited, they seem to me to become ennobled . . . There is a grandeur in this view of life, with its several powers, having been originally breathed by the Creator into a few forms or into one; and that . . . from so simple a beginning endless forms most beautiful and most wonderful have been, and are being evolved. (Darwin, 1929 pp.407–8).

As the century progressed, dissent from this view became confined to small, sectarian protests that were scarcely noticed by the general public. Evolution was not so much argued about as taken for granted; and it was taught without protest in biology classes in both state and private schools throughout Britain. By the 1980s, the conventional wisdom was captured in the Church of England's somewhat cursory entry under the doctrinal section on creation/ evolution in the *International Church Index:* 'There was an historical debate in the middle years of the last century. This is not now an issue concerning anyone' (Facey, 1981 p.88) None the less, in the same *Index* there are to be found entries by, for instance, the Assemblies of God, the Brethren, the Christadelphians, the Mormons, the Elim Pentecostal Church, the Jehovah's Witnesses, and the Seventh-day Adventists, all of whom strongly reject the theory of evolution in favour of a literal acceptance of the Genesis account of creation.[1] It is difficult to estimate the precise numbers of British people who belong to these more or less 'fundamentalist' faiths, but it is unlikely to be more than a few hundred thousand (Brierley, 1982 pp.14, 28; Currie *et al,* 1977 pp.35–7, 156–60).

The situation in Britain could not be more different from that in the United States of America. The extent of the difference may be illustrated by the fact that early in 1977 the English local authority of Hertfordshire upheld the dismissal of the head of one its schools' religious education departments because he refused to teach the county's agreed syllabus, which treated the creation story as a myth. The teacher believed in a literal interpretation of Genesis, and had declared that he wanted the children to hear this other point of view. At the very same time, the local authority in Dallas, Texas, was *insisting* that the story of Adam and Eve be taught as historical fact to children in its schools (*Sunday Telegraph*, 6 February 1977).

The history of the reception of evolution in the United States is instructive. Darwinism found early acceptance amongst American academics, and it was even introduced into classrooms during the nineteenth century (Davidheiser, 1969, pp.121–35). However the North American educational system has several features not found in the British system. Among other things, the First Amendment to the United States Constitution has been interpreted to imply that

> neither a state nor the Federal Government can . . . pass laws which aid one religion, aid all religions, or prefer one religion over another. . . . No tax, large or small can be levied to support any religious activities or institutions, whatever they may be called, or whatever form they may adopt to teach or practice religion. (*Everson* v. *Board of Education*, 1947, 330 U.S. 1, 15–16)

While the 1944 Education Act in England provided that all children in county or voluntary schools should receive religious instruction and take part in a daily corporate act of worship unless their parents wished them to be withdrawn, in the United States it was declared in 1948 that

> the preservation of the community from divisive conflicts, of Government from irreconcilable pressures by religious groups, of religion from censorship and coercion however subtly exercised, requires strict confinement of the State to instruction other than religious, leaving to the individual's church and home, indoctrination in the faith of his choice. (*McCollum* v. *Board of Education*, 1948, 33 U.S. 203, 216–7)

In America each state has jurisdiction over what is taught and which textbooks are used in its public (state-run elementary and secondary) schools. After the First World War, the fundamentalists, having enjoyed success in their campaign for Prohibition, started lobbying for legislation which would ensure that their beliefs were not attacked by the science taught in the public schools. Oklahoma passed a law banning evolutionary textbooks, and, in 1925, Tennessee made it a crime to teach evolutionary ideas. One consequence of this law was the famous 'Monkey Trial', in which a young teacher, John Scopes, was brought to court for teaching evolutionary ideas in high school. Scopes was supported by the American Civil Liberties Union, and his defence lawyer Clarence Darrow fought a famous battle with Prosecution attorney William Jennings Bryan.

Although Scopes was found guilty, the trial was considered a moral victory for the evolutionists, and it seemed as though *de facto*, if not *de jure*, the fundamentalists had lost their case. But the Tennessee 'Monkey Law' remained on the statute books for a further 40 years. Furthermore, similar laws were passed in Mississipi and Arkansas. While it might have seemed that Darrow had routed the anti-evolutionists,

> the word 'evolution' or the name of Darwin can scarcely be found in text books published in the 1930s. A national survey made in 1942 indicated that fewer than half of all high school biology teachers even mentioned evolution in their courses. (Nelkin, 1976, p.33)

THE EMERGENCE OF SCIENTIFIC CREATIONISM

In 1957 the Russians launched their first sputnik, which made many Americans worried about the quality of the science being taught in their public schools. The National Science Foundation designed a programme of new curricula and textbooks for science teaching. Those dealing with physics, mathematics and chemistry were generally welcomed; but the introduction of the biology and the social science curricula gave rise to opposition from fundamentalists, and the old conflict was revived (Nelkin, 1982, ch. 3 ff). As recently as 1968 the Supreme Court ruled in the case of

Epperson v. *Arkansas,* that a state could not forbid the teaching of evolution on religious grounds. But by this time, a new kind of challenge to evolutionary theory had begun to emerge. Increasingly, anti-evolutionists were claiming *scientific* justification for the proposal to give 'equal time' to the teaching of the idea of creation in the public schools. The position taken by these 'scientific creationists' was that evolution was not a fact but rather a theory, a hypothesis, or a belief, and that the *factual* evidence actually supported a more or less literal interpretation of the Genesis account of creation.

Soon after the Supreme Court ruling of 1968, Tennessee amended its monkey law so as to require any treatment of evolution to state that 'it is a theory . . . and is not to be represented as a scientific fact.' Textbooks had to give 'commensurate attention' and 'equal emphasis' to 'other theories, including, but not limited to, the Genesis account in the Bible'. In fact, this new law was rejected by both state and federal courts; but the battle was by no means over. For example the *Epperson* ruling was invoked by a federal district court to reinstate a student teacher in North Carolina after her dismissal for giving an evolutionary answer to a question about the origin of life (O'Neil, 1982 pp.2–4); and more recently, it was invoked in the case of *Rev. Bill McLean* v. *Arkansas Board of Education,* after the Governor of Arkansas had signed into law Act 590 of 1981, which began with the words 'Public schools within this State shall give balanced treatment to creation-science and to evolution science'. There was a quick and sharp reaction. A suit was filed challenging the constitutional validity of Act 590. The plaintiffs included local parents, taxpayers, the National Association of Biology Teachers, and representatives of a large number of religious bodies including Methodist, Episcopal, Roman Catholic, Southern Baptist, and Presbyterian churches as well as the Jewish community. An impressive array of scientists and other intellectuals were called to give evidence, and in the event the hearing became arguably the most significant confrontation between evolutionists and creation-scientists that has ever taken place.

As in now well known, Arkansas lost the case. The court was of the opinion that creation-science was not science, but 'that the *only* real effect of Act 590 is the advancement of religion' – a conclusion which would invalidate the Act under the 'establishment of religion' clause of the First Amendment. Accordingly, US District Judge William Overton ordered that an injunction should be entered permanently prohibiting the enforcement of Act 590.[2] But a further 22 states still had before them bills which would mandate the teaching of creation with evolution; there are many school boards which have equal-time policies; and there are teachers in Oklahoma who have opposed the idea of an equal-time bill because this would mean they would have to *start* teaching evolution! A similar situation has arisen in Canada; it appears that creationism alone is taught in parts of Alberta, and at least one school board in British Columbia gives it equal time in biology classes (Ruse, 1982, p.123).

Britons who read about the Arkansas and similar cases tend to assume that these must be brought merely through the efforts of some minority fringe group which is sufficiently well organized to threaten the wishes of the vast majority of the American population. But this is patently not the case. In a national Gallup survey conducted in 1982, 44 per cent of Americans said that they believed 'God created man pretty much in his present form at one time within the last 10,000 years'; 38 per cent believed 'man has developed over millions of years from less advanced forms of life, but God guided this process, including man's creation'; and 9 per cent believed 'man has developed over millions of years from less advanced forms of life. God had no part in this process'. The rest held some other belief, or said they did not know. When the respondents were asked which version should be taught in the schools, 38 per cent said creationism; 33 per cent evolution (with God); 9 per cent evolution (without God); 4 per cent volunteered 'all three'; another 4 per cent volunteered 'none'; and 12 per cent fell into the 'other/don't know' category (Princeton Religion Research Center, October 1982).

Not altogether surprisingly, the Gallup survey found that creationism was strongest in the South. This is confirmed by another survey carried out in the summer of 1981 by the Center for Social Research at the University of Texas at Arlington. Seven hundred white, middle-class, urban, home owning US citizens in the Dallas-Fort Worth area were asked a series of questions about their beliefs. Sixty-two per cent of them agreed with the statement 'the scientific theory of evolution should be taught in school'; but 73 per cent agreed that 'The Biblical account of creation should be taught in school'. In other words, a signficant proportion thought *only* the Genesis account should be taught. A more detailed breakdown according to denominational affiliation is given in table 1.

If, however, one looks at the United States as a whole, it is clear that, with a few significant exceptions (such as President Ronald Reagan), the 'top people' are not in favour of and have little respect for 'scientific creationism'. It is the *federal* courts that overrule the *state* laws supporting creationism. Within academic circles, there is a growing concern over the success that the creationists have had. In 1982, the American Association for the Advancement of Science produced a strong statement indicting creationist mandates as 'a real and present threat to the integrity of education and the teaching of science' (O'Neil, 1982, p.21); and almost the whole of

TABLE 1   *Percentage agreeing that*
(a) genesis account of creation
(b) evolution should be taught in schools

	(a) Agree Creation	(b) Agree Evolution	% sample
'Fundamental': Assemblies of God, all Pentecostal groups, Seventh-day Adventists, some non-Southern Baptists	92	32	13
'Conservative': Southern Baptists, Church of Christ, all Lutherans, Christian (Disciples of Christ)	82	55	42
Roman Catholics	72	73	15
'Moderates': all Methodists, all Presbyterians, Episcopalians	63	75	30
Total			100

Source: Stacey *et al.* (1982) pp.25, 26

the March/April issue of *Academe,* the Journal of the American Association of University Professors, was devoted to 'Countering the Creationists'. The polls indicate a strong relationship between education and attitudes to evolution. For example, the Gallup survey showed that college graduates were more than twice as likely to believe in evolution as those who had only passed through grade school; and the Texas survey found that people in white-collar occupations were more likely to be in favour of evolution being taught than were those in blue-collar work. In another poll of well over a thousand 'opinion leaders', selected at random from *Who's Who in America,* it was found that 73 per cent believed in evolution, and only 13 per cent believed in the theory of creation (compared with the 44 per cent in the national survey). A further 14 per cent were undecided, or thought that both might be true (Princeton Religion Research Center, November 1982).

As indicated earlier, scientific (as opposed to purely religious) creationism has gained currency only within the last two decades. The Creation Research Society (CRS) was founded in 1963, partly because of the dissatisfaction felt by some of its members with the growing acceptance of theistic evolutionism within the American Scientific Affiliation (which had been founded in 1941 'out of a concern for the relationship between science and Christian faith'). Within ten years the CRS was claiming 450 voting members (possessing post-graduate degrees in science), and over 1600 non-voting members, all of whom subscribed to the belief that 'the account of origins in Genesis is a factual presentation of simple historical truths.'[3] The society believes that 'science should be aligned within the framework of Biblical Creationism', and to this end it started publishing a quarterly journal in 1964.

The early 1970s saw the foundation of the Institute for Creation Research (ICR) which aims 'to provide authoritative, well documented materials and textbooks to support the scientific evidences of Biblical Creation'. By the middle of the decade, the ICR was claiming that it was already 'recognized internationally for its leadership in the scientific creationism movement' (ICR pamphlet, no date). It has sponsored some research (such as looking for Noah's Ark on Mount Ararat and for other fossil anomalies), but its main preoccupations have been evangelization and the production of creationist literature. The literature ranges from leaflets and posters to beautifully produced biology textbooks and teachers' handbooks. Lecturers from the Institute give talks, and sometimes debate with evolutionists through the media and in public forums, particularly on university campuses.

The number of creationist organizations grew steadily throughout the 1970s. Cavanaugh (1982) lists 24 groups or publications in the USA; five in Canada; five in Australia and New Zealand; two in India; two in Korea; three in Africa; three in Latin America; nine in continental Europe; and four in the United Kingdom. Creationist organizations were not entirely new to Britain. The Philosophical Society of Great Britain (now the Victoria Institute) had been formed in 1865 'to promote investigation into the relation between science and Christian faith at a time when many people believed science to be an enemy of revealed religion and irreconcilable with it', but its members have tended to favour theistic evolution rather than creationism. In 1932, the Evolution Protest Movement (EPM) was formed with the aim of publishing scientific information supporting the Bible and demonstrating that the theory of organic evolution is false. But the movement never amounted to much more than a few devoted voices crying in the wilderness. However, developments in America during the late 1960s did have some effect in Britain. During the second half of the decade, the membership of the EPM more than quadrupled (though it has never reached four figures). Then, as the result of a visit to England by the President of the ICR, Dr Henry Morris, the Newton Scientific Association (NSA) was founded in 1972. Unlike most other creationist groups, the NSA was adamant that quotations from Scripture were not to feature in its lectures or literature. It was to fight evolution with reference to science alone.

By 1979, the NSA had a membership of 160, half of whom were graduates. Its existence 'brought out' several British scientists who, until that time, had kept relatively quiet about their creationist beliefs. One of these, Professor Edgar Andrews of the University of London, became an influential writer and speaker at creationist meetings; and in 1977 he became President of the newly founded Biblical Creation Society, which was to become the most professionally organized of the British creationist groups (by 1982 it had acquired a membership of 700). Also in 1977, a newsletter called *Daylight* was started 'to give a platform to those opposing evolution, and to assist the parents and students dominated by the propaganda of the evolutionist teachers in the Catholic schools. There now exists a Catholic Creation Society, and there are various other, smaller-scale organizations producing literature on creationism. Significantly, in 1980 the Evolution Protest Movement changed its name to the Creation Science Movement. It must be stressed that none of the British creationist organizations draws more than a few hundred members to its meetings, and usually far fewer than this. Moreover, there is some overlap in the membership of the groups. In other words, although the demand for creation science undoubtedly exists, it is not numerically large.

WHAT IS SCIENTIFIC CREATIONISM?

Scientific creationism adopts two interrelated approaches to origins. First, it sets out to expose discrepancies and gaps in evolutionary theory; and second, it attempts to show that creationism provides a more satisfactory explanation of the scientific evidence. Generally speaking, it has had more success in the first of these endeavours. Scientific creationists tend to latch onto *any* dissent amongst evolutionary biologists, even when the protagonists are opposed to the Genesis account of creation. An editorial in *Biblical Creation*, while realistically aware that evolutionists were unlikely to abandon their beliefs simply because there were problems with their theory, added:

> but it is undeniable that the credibility of our religious and scientific position has been greatly strenghtened by the recent lapse in neo-Darwinian morale. And this is something we must exploit to the full. (Vol. 4, No. 12, p.35)

The headline in a recent edition of *Origins Research* reads 'Prominent British scientists abandon evolution'. The article discusses the views of Sir Fred Hoyle, Chandra Wickramasinghe, Francis Crick, and Colin Patterson, all of whom totally reject the Genesis account. Wickramasinghe was actually called to testify for the defence at the Arkansas trial, but his testimony (that the earth was 'seeded' by comets) only added to the Judge's conviction that creation science should *not* be given equal time in the schools.

Perhaps at this point we should examine more closely the positive claims of scientific creationism. It might be helpful to begin by quoting the definition used in Act 590:

> (a) 'Creation-science' means the scientific evidences for creation and inferences from those scientific evidences. Creation-science includes the scientific evidences and related inferences that indicate: (1) Sudden creation of the universe, energy, and life from nothing; (2) The insufficiency of mutation and natural selection in bringing about development of all living kinds from a single organism; (3) Changes only within fixed limits or originally created kinds of plants and animals; (4) Separate ancestry for man and apes; (5) Explanation of the earth's geology by catastrophism, including the occurrence of a worldwide flood; and (6) A relatively recent inception of the earth and living kinds. (Act 590 of the 1981 'Balanced Treatment for Creation-Science and Evolution-Science Act', *Ark. Stat. Ann* §80–1663, *et seq.*)

Of course, scientific creationists do not agree on everything. Some believe that science can prove (or has already proved) creation to be true, while others argue that although it cannot prove creationism, 'the Biblical teachings match the observed scientific data just as well or even better than evolutionary theories' (*Biblical Creation* vol. 4 no. 12, July 1982, p.35). Some argue that 'the Bible *is* a text book of Science' (Morris, 1966, p.108 ff), while others (such as the NSA) insist that the Bible must not be referred to at all in creation-science debate. Curiously enough, there is also a remarkably common belief that neither creationism nor evolutionism is scientific, but that creationism is more scientific than evolutionism (for a nice example of this see Durant, 1982, pp.17–18).

A number of different classifications have been developed for the different positions. For example, Ramm (1955) distinguished four patterns of thought concerning the origin of the universe: (1) fiat creationism; (2) progressive creationism; (3) theistic evolution; (4) naturalistic evolution. Much of the debate, he believed, had been plagued by oversimplification, as if (1) and (4) were the only alternatives. Progressive creationism (Ramm's own position) claims 'to try to avoid the arbitrariness of the transcendence of God in creation; and it has tried to avoid the uniformitarianism of theistic evolution, and preserve its sense of progress or develop- ment' (Ramm, 1955, p.76). A further set of distinctions has been made within the creationist camp between theories of Long Day-Age, Successive Creations, the Gap, and the young Earth. Some creationists believe that the world was created, if not actually in 4004 BC, then at least within the last ten thousand years. Others are not so sure about the Young Earth position, but believe that there may have been several separate creations over much longer periods of time. Much depends here on the interpretation given to the concept of 'day' in Genesis (see Zimmerman, 1959, ch. 5; White, 1978, ch. 5 and appendix; Morris, 1974, ch. 8). A related area of controversy concerns the extent to which the Bible must be taken as literally true. On the one hand, there are creationists for whom every word is to be interpreted literally. Apparent inconsis- tencies are denied with talk of miracles, or mistranslation, or else they are accepted as temporary paradoxes. Next, there are those who take most things literally, but accept poetical or even allegorical interpretations where these appear to be the writer's intention.[4] Yet others will accept a considerable amount of Biblical criticism, and may even admit that it is necessary to take account of the fact that the Bible comes from other cultures and literary traditions.[5]

Whatever their disagreement over hermeneutics, there is one point upon which all scientific creationists agree, namely that there is no scientific evidence to show that any one 'kind' of organism has evolved into another. Scientific creationists agree that there are variations *within* a gene pool, and that natural selection can take place *within* a particular 'kind', but not that it can occur *between* the kinds. Exactly what is meant by a 'kind' is never made clear. Few would define it as narrowly as a species, and for some it may even be equivalent to a phylum; but it is on this general basis that scientific creationists seek to re-interpret the evidence. Relevant fields in which they are active include not only biology and geology but also anthropology, cosmology, meteorology, philology, physics, and probability theory (see, for example, Boardman *et al*. 1973; Bowden, 1977; Clark and Bales, 1966; Culp 1975; Davidheiser, 1969; Enoch, 1967; Lammerts, 1971; Mixter, 1961; Morris, 1966; Morris, 1974; Morris and Gish, 1976; Riegé, 1971; Whitcomb and Morris, 1961; White 1978; Wilder Smith 1974; and Zimmerman, 1959).

While the creationist arguments in each of these fields are certainly contested by orthodox specialists, it would be a very great mistake to dismiss them all as the mere ravings of so many madmen. While some arguments can be fairly simply refuted (for example, those concerning the second law of thermodynamics), and some obviously have nothing to do with science (for example, Gosse's argument (1857) that God created the world 'as though' it had been in existence for thousands of years), others are not so easy to sweep aside. The literature produced by some of the leading creationists can appear highly impressive, not just to the already committed fundamentalist but also to the intelligent lay person who is prepared to listen.

An increasing number of philosophers and scientists have taken the 'threat' of scientific creationism seriously enough to offer the lay public refutations of the creationist position (see, for example, Gardner, 1957; Kitcher, 1982; Montagu (ed.) 1984; Ruse, 1982). But it can be very difficult for the non-specialist to win an argument with a knowledgeable creationist. It is not uncommon for groups that are labelled by conventional wisdom as irrational, non-rational, or just plain nutty to provide what appear to be *more* coherent and rational arguments in defence of their position than can those of us who muddle along with rather more conventional and socially protected world-views (Barker, 1984). At one stage in my research, when I had become quite well versed in the creationist literature, I tried putting their arguments to a number of my academic colleagues. I was amazed to find that on nearly every occasion we reached a point at which my friends would abandon rational or empirical argument in favour of irritated condemnation or dogmatic assertion. On one occasion a colleague ended up by exclaiming in utter exasperation, 'but they're just wrong!' The point of this anecdote is that it is perfectly possible for intelligent, well-educated people (including scientists who are not normally concerned with the theory of evolution) to find that their general knowledge is simply insufficient to enable them to refute the creationist position. By taking the creationist's part, it is possible, not only to acquire some sympathy for the frustration that they feel when they try to put across their point of view to others, but also to understand how exchanges with non-creationists may reinforce rather than weaken their view that it is they rather than the evolutionists who are on the side of science and rationality.

INTERPRETING SCIENTIFIC CREATIONISM

Although many people may accept that their religious faith is *non*-scientific, very few people will readily admit that their most valued beliefs are either *ir*rational or *un*-scientific. Science has been widely perceived to be in conflict with the accepted truths of religion since the days of Copernicus, Galileo and the Inquisition. But in modern times it has been the Darwinian theory of evolution by natural selection that has provided the principal focus for public debate about the relationship between knowledge and belief. There has been no comprehensive sociology of this debate in the present century. Of course, there is a great deal of literature informing us of the views of academics; but there is very little written about how these views are received amongst lay people (see Nelkin, 1982, however, for a promising start in this direction). The ideas of intellectuals are very easily resisted or, even more devastatingly, ignored when they do not have some kind of resonance with significant sections of public opinion.

By definition, dogmatic beliefs leave far less room for manoevre than do those of a more liberal or agnostic nature. If, as is often the case in the more fundamentalist and sectarian religions, a belief system consists of a set of clear-cut dichotomies (good–bad; true–false; God–Satan; us–them), the system retains a remarkable strength so long as all the 'bits' fit together. But if one piece is removed, the whole edifice may collapse. Thus one not infrequently hears people from fundamentalist backgrounds confessing to having *completely* lost their faith when they became convinced that the animal kingdom was produced by natural selection. As evolutionary theory became increasingly taken for granted as part of the conventional wisdom of westen society, those who rejected the theory felt the need to protect themselves and, even more importantly, their children from the rest of society. While some control over exposure to the mass media could be effected by sectarian institutions, the teaching of evolution in schools was an ever present threat to the survival of the tradition into the next generation. Scientists offered little or no hope to those who persevered with a literal interpretation of Genesis during the first half of the century, and for many Christians the options lay between accepting science *with* progressive creationism or theistic evolution, or sticking to creationism and *rejecting* science. The general feeling was that it was science *or* fundamentalist religion and that, eventually, science would win. While those who held to literalist beliefs in the United States certainly did not disappear in the 40 years following the Scopes trial, they did become increasingly withdrawn from the direction in which mainstream society was moving. What, then, were some of the factors that might have contributed towards the collapse of the distinction between science and creationism and the birth of scientific creationism?

I do not wish to suggest that creationists have made a great 'come back' into mainstream society, but I think it is possible to detect some general changes in perspective which have taken place in society as a whole, and which have given creationists the opportunity to re-assert themselves as part of a wider movement towards traditional moral and religious values. In order to do this, however, we must focus on popular rather than professional images of science.

There have been some apparently paradoxical developments in the way in which such science has been popularly perceived during the second half of this century, with elements of both acceptance and rejection clearly present for much of the time. Hopes that science was to become the God of the future began to fade around the time of the Second World War. The image of science as a universal panacea began to be affected by increasing disillusionment as it was realized that it was also associated with destruction, want and waste. Hiroshima opened many people's eyes to the potential horrors of progress in nuclear research; and by the early

1960s the devastation of the environment, pollution, and the exhaustion of natural resources had become popular subjects of discussion. Not only the obvious abuses of science but also its inherent values began to receive a bad press; its impersonal, objective, quantitative approach was seen as robbing man of his humanity, reducing the higher nature of mankind to the baser instincts of animals, and denying the beauty and the mystery of the universe. At the same time, the belief in absolute certainities was undermined by the oft-quoted, but rarely understood, Principle of Uncertainty and Theory of Relativity, thus adding to a general feeling of hopelessness and helplessness.

These attitudes towards science were part of a more general groundswell of pressure for change in America and Europe throughout the 1960s. Many young people expressed disaffection with what were often termed 'Western bourgeois values'. Towards the end of the decade, their attempts to change the social, political and/or economic structure of capitalist society had died down, and the public's attention was turned towards the hippies and the flower children. At that time the predominantly publicized theme was one of passive rejection and withdrawal from conventional society. Standards, hierarchies, and old moral codes were dismissed. People were to be equal, they were free to do anything they felt like doing. Free love, not the repressive order of the past, was the rule. Organized religion, like the older generation, was seen as hypocritical and ineffectual in anything but upholding an oppressive power structure. Admittedly, these were the views of only a tiny segment of the population; but it was a sufficiently vocal section – or at least a section that received sufficient media coverage – to produce a sharp reaction from more conservative sections of society.

At the same time, the West was feeling economically and politically threatened by the Communist and third Worlds. Americans were beginning to suspect what the British had already learned – that there was no longer any certainty that they were in control. The nuclear arms race, Russia's successes in space, Japan's economic triumph, Castro's Cuba, the humiliations of Vietnam, the Watergate affair and then the Teheran hostages – these were just some of the phenomena that implied not only that the Christian leadership of America might not be able to maintain control of the rest of the world, but also that its whole way of life might be under threat. Both at home and overseas there were strange new orders, strange new influences, strange new customs, and strange new balances of power.

In the face of such changes, there was a growing desire for order and certainty, a desire to be sure of one's grounds and to reaffirm one's roots. In some quarters, this was translated into a resurgence of traditional belief. In those instances in which this option was taken up, one (but by no means the only) explanation on offer to explain the ills of the modern world was evolutionism. At the feet of the evolutionist perspective was laid all manner of evil. Evolutionism was declared to be bad science in both the technical and the moral sense. If, the argument ran, people were taught that they were nothing but animals, one could hardly be surprised if they behaved like animals. Need one wonder, the creationists asked, that promiscuity was on the increase, and that the family was breaking up? The ideas of natural selection and the survival of the fittest had, they insisted, led to all manner of ungodly and bestial practices (Lammerts, 1971, p.229). Marx's desire to dedicate *Kapital* to Darwin (Alexander, 1972, p.80), Hitler's use of the concept of natural selection to justify the implementation of his 'final solution' (Wilder Smith, 1974, p.18ff), and the fact that many prominent post-war evolutionists were members of Humanist Associations (Morris, 1974, p.196), were all instances cited to make this point. Most seriously of all (and despite the protests of the theistic evolutionists), evolutionism was depicted as an atheistic philosophy that denied the work and even the existence of the creator (see, for example, Enoch, 1967, chs 15 and 16).

There were, of course, many other explanations which were given for the ills of modern society – evolutionism was just one – but, from around 1970, the creationists found themselves part of a far larger movement that was challenging secular, liberal society. An evangelical revival swept North America (and, to a lesser extent, Britain); house churches sprang up, and the neo-pentecostal and charismatic movements flourished. In America, televangelism enjoyed peak viewing, and the moral majority (Jerry Falwell's rallying of the conservative middle class), if not actually a majority, certainly could not be ignored. The 'New Christian Right', in its fight against liberalism and secular humanism (for it, the most heinous of all positions) was to become one of the most powerful pressure groups in the West.

But Western society *is* liberal and democratic and in general it allows for free competition in the field of religion. Even Britain, with its established Church, harbours hundreds of different religious organizations. Curiously enough, this very pluralism may encourage a healthy (some might say unhealthy) respect for science. This is because science is generally acknowledged to be the source of enormous power: science 'works'; science 'knows'. It may not be trusted to provide a metaphysic, an ethic, or a theology, but *epistemologically* science has no rival. If, in the supermarket of competing ideologies, a religion can claim the sanction of scientific approval, or – even better – of scientific proof, there are those who will assume that it must therefore be valid. Thus, it is not altogether surprising that organizations and individuals should seek scientific (or scientistic) support for their beliefs. In response to such consumer demand, the last two decades have seen the rise of a new priesthood of scientists who have offered their services in the provision of scientific justifications, not merely for creationism, but for a whole range of ideological (religious and political) positions (Barker, 1979).

Modern science has developed a multitude of specializations. Within each discipline there are many sub-disciplines which are themselves sub-divided into further specialized areas. Specialists in one area are rarely competent to judge the pronouncements of those who specialize in a different area, and beyond a certain (relatively basic) level, even the most intelligent and well educated of lay persons is reduced to a fairly simple trust (or distrust) of the expert. Arguments tend to be reduced to the form 'he's a scientist, so it must be true', or 'if he thinks *that*, he can't be a *proper* scientist'. There is, in other words, an almost religious mystique about the inner gnoses of modern science. The fact that empirical judgement has to be (at least) second-hand for all but a tiny minority means that those who want to believe have the opportunity of accepting the pronouncements of the scientist who confirms, and disbelieving the pronouncements of the scientist who denies, what they already happen to believe.

There have been some curious twists and apparent contradictions in the use to which science has been put in a religious or social (as opposed to a purely scientific or technological) context. I have suggested that although science has, on the whole, been rejected as an alternative to religion, it has been eagerly pounced upon to provide justifications for metaphysical beliefs; and, while it is sometimes claimed that science *proves* Genesis correct, there are those who will claim that it is because science cannot tell us with *certainty* whether Genesis or evolution provides the true explanation of man's origins that both should be given equal time in science classes. Thus, some creationists will claim an epistemological *relativism for science* at the same time they denounce ethical relativism in favour of *absolute moral standards*. Unless we are very clear about the degrees of confidence that we can achieve in the different areas of our knowledge, we can find ourselves, through admitting to certain uncertainties (in science), being subjected to uncertain certainties (in religion, morality and politics).

The very existence of creation science provides considerable reassurance to Biblical literalists. It provides them with the conviction that the most powerful of modern epistemologies, modern science, is on their side. Confirmed in the belief that evolution is a faith, not a fact (Clark and Bales, 1966 p.95), they can hold up their heads in a secular or liberal society, and no longer have so great a need to retreat for protection into closed enclaves populated only by fellow believers. Creationist teachers, especially biology teachers, are supported in their view that theirs is a legitimate, academic position. Children who might have been subjected to evolutionary theory at school or through the media can be given alternative textbooks or even comic-strips presenting the creationist perspective. Not only does creation science help to keep creationists and their children safe in their beliefs, but there are those who will actually convert to fundamentalist beliefs when they read or hear the word. There are even a few scientists (e.g. Culp, 1975, p.184) who claim to have converted to Christianity after becoming disillusioned with the theory of evolution on purely scientific grounds. Even if the number of such converts is tiny (Numbers, 1982, p.542), an evangelical hope is fanned by each conversion.

At the same time, many theistic evolutionists are afraid that creationists are giving Christianity a bad name by sticking rigidly to their literalist beliefs, and, thereby, risking the loss of the more important religious and ethical revelations to be found in Genesis. Recently, organizations have been founded for the specific purpose of stopping fundamentalists, on the one hand, and scientific atheists on the other, from 'rocking the boat'. Their aim is to reassure the general public that evolution and religion are perfectly compatible – indeed complementary – universes of discourse (Barker, 1979).

CONCLUSION

It seems unlikely that scientific creationism will increase its influence now that it has lost the Arkansas case. Generally speaking, the younger and the more educated tend to opt for evolution rather than creation (Princeton Religion Research Center, October 1982, p. 6), and, as I mentioned earlier, many of those in positions of influence within the institutions of education and the law are making a concerted effort to define creationism as a religion rather than a science. Those who want to keep political power do, however, need to keep a careful watch on the opinions of their electorate. It was during President Reagan's governorship of California in 1969 that the Board of Education decreed that creationism should be given equal time with evolutionism in biology classes; and in a speech during the 1980 Presidential Election Campaign, Reagan is reported as having said:

> Well it [evolution] is a theory, it is a scientific theory only, and it has in recent years been challenged in the world of science and is not yet believed in the scientific community to be as infallible as it once was believed. But if it was going to be taught in the schools, then I think that also the biblical theory of creation, which is not a theory but the biblical story of creation, should also be taught. (Ruse, 1982 p. 292)

None the less, majority wishes are not necessarily sufficient to implement changes in a democracy which, according to Western practice, implies rule by elected representatives. Those in positions of power can overrule the expressed wishes of the majority in the name of the constitution. In Judge Overton's opinion in the Arkansas trial, this is clearly declared to be not only a legitimate policy, but, indeed, a legal necessity:

> The application and content of the First Amendment principles are not determined by public opinion polls or by a majority vote. Whether the proponents of Act 590 constitute the majority or the minority is quite irrelevant under a constitutional system of government. No group, no matter how large or small, may use the organs of government, of which the public schools are the most conspicuous and influential, to foist its religious beliefs on others.

It is hard not to believe that modern science is moving towards a greater understanding of our origins. The theoretical rigour and practical impact of much modern knowledge makes it ridiculous to adopt an utterly relativistic approach to science. We can see many areas in which old ideas have been replaced by new ones so that it looks as though we are progressing towards 'the truth'. However, it should also be recognized that, when we look at the many social uses to which the concepts of science are put, there is no guarantee that there will be a steady convergence towards truth. At the popular, and perhaps not infrequently at the academic level, the creation of knowledge may be supported or rationalized by scientism rather than by empirical fact, and then we shall observe not a convergence towards one clear truth but rather a divergence of beliefs which bear more relationship to the needs, interests and circumstances of those who adopt them than they do to any objective reality in the natural world. If we are to understand what is accepted as scientifically proven truth in any particular context, and the ways in which such truth is used for the furtherance of people's ideological interests, we shall need an improved sociology of knowledge as well as a clearer understanding of the epistemological status of the differing claims. The debate between evolution and creation science provides just one area within which the phenomena of social adaptation, curiously mixed with the scientific quest, are manifested. Perhaps through the pursuit of such darknesses we shall, eventually, glimpse more light.

NOTES

I would like to thank Ronald Numbers, Michael Cavanaugh and John Durant for their helpful comments on an earlier draft of this paper. I would also like to thank the Nuffield Foundation which provided me with a grant for the research upon which this paper was drawn.

1 While there are certainly some Catholics who would insist upon a literal reading of Genesis, the teaching of evolution is not an issue for the vast majority of Britain's five million or so Catholics.

2 The full text of Judge Overton's important ruling is reprinted in A. Montagu (ed.) (1984), pp.365–97.

3 This is a quotation from the statement of belief that appears on the inside back cover of all issues of the *CRS Quarterly*.

4 For example, it has been pointed out to me by a creationist that Psalm 8:3 'when I consider the heavens, the work of thy fingers . . . ' does not imply that God has fingers.

5 Thus, when it is said that 'the sun stood still in the midst of heaven and hasted not to go down about a whole day' (Joshua 10:13), one creationist lecturer observed that although we know that the sun, as seen in relation to the world, *seems* to stand still, this is not scientific language and presumably it was the *earth* which stood still, if anything did – but we do not know (McConville, 1982).

REFERENCES

Alexander, D. (1972) *Beyond Science*, Berkhamsted, Lion Publishing.

Barker, E. (1976) 'Value Systems Generated by Biologists', *Contact*, **55**, pp.2–13

Barker, E. (1979) 'Thus Spake the Scientist: A Comparative Account of the New Priesthood and its Organisational Bases', *The Annual Review of the Social Sciences of Religion*, **3.**

Barker, E. (1984) *The Making of a Moonie*, Oxford, Blackwell.

Boardman, W.W. Jr., Koontz, R.F. and Morris, H.M. (1973) *Science and Creation* San Diego, California, Creation-Science Research Center.

Bowden, M. (1977) *Ape-Man: Fact or Fallacy? A Critical Examination of the Evidence*, Bromley, Sovereign Publications.

Brierley, P. (ed.) (1982) *U.K. Christian Handbook 1983 Edition*, London, Evangelical Alliance and Bible Society.

Cavanaugh, M. (1982) 'Science, Time Science, Pseudoscience: The One-eyed Religious Movement for Scientific Creationism', paper presented to the Society for the Scientific Study of Religion Meeting in Providence, Rhode Island, 22–4 October.

Clark, R.T. and Bales, D. (1966) *Why Scientists Accept Evolution*, Grand Rapids, Michigan, Baker Book House.

Culp, G. (1975) *Remember Thy Creator*, Grand Rapids, Michigan, Baker Book House.

Currie, R., Gilbert, A. and Horsley, L. (1977) *Churches and Churchgoers: Patterns of Church Growth in the British Isles since 1700*, Oxford, Clarendon Press.

Darwin, C. (1929) *The Origin of Species by Means of Natural Selection*, London, Watts and Co. (6th ed, 1st ed 1859).

Davidheiser, B. (1969) *Evolution and Christian Faith*, Nutley, N.J., Presbyterian and Reformed Publishing Co.

Draper, J.W. (1883) *History of the Conflict between Religion and Science*, (18th ed.) London, Kegan Paul, Trench & Co.

Durant, J.R. (1982) 'The New Creationism and the World of Science', paper presented at the Teach-In on 'Creationism in American Culture and Theology', Mimeo, Chicago, Lutheran School of Theology.

Enoch, H. (1967) *Evolution or Creation*, London, Evangelical Press.

Facey, R.A. (1981) *International Church Index (Doctrinal)*, Plymouth, PDS Printers.

Gardner, M. (1957) *Fads and Fallacies in the Name of Science*, New York, Dover Publications.

Gosse, P.H. (1857) *Omphalos: An attempt to Untie the Geological Knot*, London, John Van Voorst.

Kitcher, P. (1982) *Abusing Science: The Case against Creationism*, Cambridge, Mass., MIT Press.

Lammerts, W.E. (ed.) (1971) *Scientific Studies in Special Creation*, Selected Articles from the Creation Research Society Quarterly 1964–1968, Nutley, N J., Presbyterian and Reformed Publishing Co.

McConville, G. (1982) 'Cosmos or Chaos' talk given at British Creation Society meeting, 13 November.

Medawar, P. (1977) 'Evolution' in *The Fontana Dictionary of Modern Thought*, A. Bullock and O. Stallybrass (eds) London, Fontana.

Mixter, R.L. (ed.) (1961) *Evolution and Christian Thought*, A Symposium by Members of the American Scientific Affiliation, London, Paternoster Press.

Montagu, A. (ed.) (1984) *Science and Creationism*, Oxford and New York, Oxford University Press.

Morris, H.M. (1966) *Studies in the Bible and Science: or Christ and Creation*, Grand Rapids, Michigan, Baker Book House.

Morris, H.M. (ed.) (1974) *Scientific Creationism*, San Diego, California, Creation-Life Publishers.

Morris, H.M. and Gish, D. (eds) (1976) *The Battle for Creation: Acts/Facts/ Impacts*. San Diego, California, Creation-Life Publishers.

Nelkin, D. (1976) 'The Science-Textbook Controversies', *Scientific American*, **234**, no. 4, April.

Nelkin, D. (1982) *The Creation Controversy: Science or Scripture in the Schools*, New York, W.W. Norton.

Numbers, R.L. (1982) 'Creationism in 20th-Century America', *Science*, **218** pp.538–44.

O'Neil, R.M. (1982) 'Creationism, Curriculum and the Constitution', *Academe*, March-April.

Emerging Trends Princeton Religious Research Center, (published monthly).

Ramm, B. (1955) *The Christian View of Science and Scripture*, Exeter, Paternoster Press.

Riegle, D.D. (1971) *Creation or Evolution?* Grand Rapids, Michigan, Zondervan Books.

Ruse, M. (1982) *Darwinism Defended: A Guide to the Evolution Controversies*, Reading, Massachussetts, Addison-Wesley.

Stacey, W.A., Shupe, A., and Stacey, S. (1982) 'Religious Values and Religiosity in the Textbook Adoption Controversy in Texas, 1981', paper presented at the annual meeting of the Society for the Scientific Study of Religion, October.

Whitcomb, J. and Morris, H.M. (1961) *The Genesis Flood*, Grand Rapids, Michigan, Baker Book House.

White, A.J. (1978) *What About Origins?* Kingsteignton, Dunestone Printers.

Wilder Smith, A.E. (1974) *Man's Origin, Man's Destiny*, Neuhausen-Stuttgart, Telos-International.

Zimmerman, P.A. (ed.) (1959) *Darwin, Evolution and Creation*, Saint Louis, Missouri, Concordia.

Index